Successful event management

Successful event management

A practical handbook

second edition

Anton Shone and Bryn Parry

Australia • Canada • Mexico • Singapore • Spain • United Kingdom • United States

THOMSON

Successful Event Management

Copyright © Anton Shone and Bryn Parry 2004

The Thomson logo is a registered trademark used herein under licence.

For more information, contact Thomson Learning, High Holborn House, 50-51 Bedford Row, London WC1R 4LR or visit us on the World Wide Web at:
http://www.thomsonlearning.co.uk

British Library Cataloguing-in-Publication Data
A catalogue record for this book is available from the British Library

ISBN 1-84480-076-8

First published 2001 by Continuum
This edition 2004 by Thomson Learning
Reprinted 2004 by Thomson Learning

Typeset by Dexter Haven Associates Ltd
Printed in Croatia by Zrinski

Contents

List of figures viii
Forms for the new event manager xi
List of case studies xii
Preface to the second edition xv

1 **The events business** 1

1 **An introduction to events** 2
Introduction 2
Definitions and frameworks 3
Categories and typologies 4
Historical contexts and precedents 6
Characteristics of events 13
Summary 18
References 18

2 **The market demand for events** 19
Introduction 19
Size and scope of the events market 20
Determinants and motivations 25
The structure of demand for events 32
Summary 33
References 33

3 **The events business: supply and suppliers** 35
Introduction 35
The structure of events services: public sector 36
The structure of events services: private sector 38
Companies and their roles 40
Voluntary bodies, committees and individuals 47
Summary 47
References 48

4   Social, economic, political and developmental implications 49

Introduction 49
Social and community implications 50
Economic implications 54
Political implications 57
Developmental implications 59
Summary 62
References 62

II Managing Events 63

5   Making a start 64

Introduction 64
Getting organized 65
Event feasibility: finding and testing an idea 68
The screening process 70
Progressing the idea 76
Summary 80
References 80

6   Events planning 81

Introduction 81
The planning process 82
Objectives, environmental search and information-gathering 84
Demand and operational planning 87
Financial planning 91
Marketing planning 92
Getting it together 94
Summary 95
References 95

7   Financial management and the budget 96

Introduction 96
Objectives and financial planning 97
Creating a budget 100
The detailed budget 108
Who spends what 110
Other sources of income 112
Sponsorship and public funding 114
Summary 118
References 119

8   The event: venue-finding, logistics and ambience 120

Introduction 120
Finding the venue 121
Logistics 124

Creating the ambience 139
Summary 143
References 143

9 Marketing and public relations for events 144

Introduction 144
The target market 145
How to influence the target market 149
The marketing plan 153
Marketing for a new event 155
Marketing for repeat events and new editions 158
Summary 163
References 163

10 Managing the event as a project 164

Introduction 164
The event as a project 164
Risk management 168
Legalities and insurance 176
Systems set-up and ticketing 178
Operational activities 181
Summary 187
References 188

11 The organization manager and the team: during the event 189

Introduction 189
Organization 190
Organizational effectiveness 193
Staffing: professional or volunteer management? 196
Factors influencing the number and type of staff 199
Finding staff 204
Running the event on the day 208
Summary 213
References 213

12 Close-down, evaluation and legacies 214

Introduction 214
Close-down 215
Evaluation 220
Divestment and legacies 225
Summary 227
References 228

Glossary 229
Organizations in the events industry 233
Index 237

List of figures

Figure 1.1   A suggested categorization of special events
Figure 1.2   A typology of events
Figure 1.3   Characteristics of special events as a service
Figure 1.4   Elements in the ambience and service of an event
Figure 2.1   Assessing market scope and the economic impact of events
Figure 2.2   A combination of motives for participating in an event, such as an opera gala
Figure 2.3   Possible motives for attending events
Figure 2.4   Event component mix
Figure 2.5   Demand potentials
Figure 3.1   Infrastructure of the events business
Figure 3.2   Events organizations (private sector and others)
Figure 3.3   Matrix of sample distribution channels and activities
Figure 4.1   The implications of special events
Figure 4.2   Development of tourist destinations: some examples
Figure 4.3   Elements of tourism
Figure 4.4   Political stakeholders for events
Figure 5.1   Example of an events management committee
Figure 5.2   Development of organizational structures in events
Figure 5.3   Generating ideas
Figure 5.4   Concept screening
Figure 5.5   Example pilot questionnaire for proposed events
Figure 5.6   Events screening form
Figure 5.7   Examples of possible objectives for events
Figure 5.8   Simple pre-event planner
Figure 6.1   Planning as a management activity for an event
Figure 6.2   The planning process for events management
Figure 6.3   Information-gathering and environmental searching
Figure 6.4   Simple example of marketing lead times: Middleburg Sports Day
Figure 7.1   Examples of various event objectives
Figure 7.2   Cashflow at events
Figure 7.3   Some common budgeting mistakes
Figure 7.4   Outline budget form for quotations
Figure 7.5   Example of comparative outline budgets for a proposed company party
Figure 7.6   Break-even chart

Figure 7.7 General budget form (summary sheet)

Figure 7.8 Budget: detailed income and costs – final outcome summary

Figure 7.9 Purchase order form

Figure 7.10 Petty cash voucher

Figure 7.11 Sources of additional revenue in addition to ticket or admission prices

Figure 7.12 Types of event funding

Figure 7.13 Sources of patronage, grant funding and other income for events

Figure 8.1 Venue-finding checklist

Figure 8.2 The events management process: the organizational and logistical activities

Figure 8.3 Logistic sequence for events

Figure 8.4 Middleburg Festival equipment receival form

Figure 8.5 Alternative cafeteria flow services

Figure 8.6 Examples of some seated meal layouts (there are many others)

Figure 8.7 Issues in determining menus and refreshments

Figure 8.8 Further considerations in food and drink services

Figure 8.9 Example of a logistics production schedule

Figure 8.10 Logistics: communications contact list

Figure 8.11 Example of the component elements at a quiz dinner

Figure 8.12 The event service experience

Figure 9.1 Key questions to ask about the target market

Figure 9.2 Catchment and origin

Figure 9.3 Example of a catchment area: the Middleburg Music Festival

Figure 9.4 Influencing the market

Figure 9.5 Determinants for participation in an event (the 'buying process')

Figure 9.6 Individual's expectations of an event

Figure 9.7 Event decision-making process for a university ball

Figure 9.8 Creating the marketing plan from the event objectives

Figure 9.9 Elements of the events marketing plan

Figure 9.10 Events components and target market matrix

Figure 9.11 Examples of marketing expenditure items

Figure 9.12 Event marketing budget form

Figure 9.13 Example of a marketing schedule

Figure 10.1 Event and project activities

Figure 10.2 Work breakdown structure for a wedding marquee

Figure 10.3 Example of a Gantt chart

Figure 10.4 Various risk categories

Figure 10.5 Risk analysis quadrant

Figure 10.6 Example of a risk assessment form

Figure 10.7 Example of a risk control plan

Figure 10.8 Permits, licences and legalities

Figure 10.9 Ticket design: information to include on a ticket

Figure 10.10 Pre-operations on the day

Figure 10.11 Pre-event briefing meeting for all staff

Figure 11.1 Simplified events organization structure
Figure 11.2 Visitor services department at the Middleburg Music Festival
Figure 11.3 The culture of an event organization
Figure 11.4 Framework for an event organization's performance
Figure 11.5 Example job advert for an events co-ordinator
Figure 11.6 A committee of volunteers
Figure 11.7 Factors influencing the number of staff required
Figure 11.8 Concentration of core services and staff
Figure 11.9 Job description form
Figure 11.10 Staffing an event
Figure 11.11 Activities on the day
Figure 12.1 Final phase of event activities
Figure 12.2 Event history: contact record form
Figure 12.3 Types of information for evaluation of events
Figure 12.4 Sources of information for evaluation
Figure 12.5 Visitor satisfaction at the Middleburg Music Festival
Figure 12.6 Mystery guest report (extract)
Figure 12.7 Visitor experience chart

Forms for the new event manager

- **Starting forms**
  Pilot questionnaire for proposed events (Figure 5.5) 71
  Events screening form (Figure 5.6) 75

- **Financial forms**
  Outline budget form for quotations (Figure 7.4) 102
  General budget form (Figure 7.7) 107
  Detailed budget breakdown (Figure 7.8) 109
  Purchase order form (Figure 7.9) 111
  Petty cash voucher (Figure 7.10) 111

- **Doing the job forms**
  Venue-finding checklist (Figure 8.1) 122
  Example equipment receival form (Figure 8.4) 128
  Example logistics production schedule (Figure 8.9) 135

- **Marketing forms**
  Event marketing budget form (Figure 9.12) 157
  Example of marketing schedule (Figure 9.13) 159

- **Project management forms**
  Example of a risk assessment form (Figure 10.6) 171
  Example of a risk control plan (Figure 10.7) 172

- **Human resources form**
  Job description form (Figure 11.9) 203

- **Recording form**
  Event history contact record form (Figure 12.2) 219

List of case studies

For convenience, where costs are quoted these are given in euros. At the time of writing the exchange rate was €1.50 to £1. All case studies are real, as named. However, some more generalized examples are given to illustrate the text and to help the reader and in these cases the fictitious town of 'Middleburg' is used.

Subject	Location	Country	Year	Page
1 Olympic Games	Olympia	Greece	776BC	7
2 Roman Wedding	Rome	Italy	AD100	8
3 Coronation of Elizabeth I	London	England	1559	10
4 Paris Exposition	Paris	France	1889	12
5 European Grands Prix	European Union	—	1998	21
6 UK Wedding Market	—	UK	2000	24
7 Berlin Film Festival	Berlin	Germany	2002	28
8 North Sea Jazz Festival	The Hague	Netherlands	2002	31
9 International Festivals and Events Association	Leidschendam	Netherlands	2004	37
10 Inntel Conference Agency	Colchester	England	2000	42
11 Giuseppe Fontebasso	Turin	Italy	2004	45
12 Notting Hill Carnival	London	England	2002	52
13 French Grand Prix	Nevers	France	1997	55
14 Return of the Stone of Scone	Scone	Scotland	1996	57
15 Welsh Garden Festival	Ebbw Vale	Wales	1992	60
16 Salzburg International Festival	Salzburg	Austria	2002	67
17 University College, Cork Hockey Club	Cork	Ireland	2000	73
18 Re-opening of the Scottish Parliament	Edinburgh	Scotland	1999	85
19 Opening Night of the Millennium Dome	Greenwich	England	2000	88
20 Annual Dinner of the Ecclesbourne Valley Railway	Derby	England	2004	105
21 Sponsorship and the Tour de France	Paris	France	2003	114

22	St John of Oporto Festival	Oporto	Portugal	2003	125
23	Glastonbury Festival	Glastonbury	England	2003	139
24	Lake Vyrnwy Marathon	Lake Vyrnwy	Wales	2003	148
25	Geneva International Motor Show	Geneva	Switzerland	2000	161
26	The Moshpit at Roskilde	Roskilde	Denmark	2000	173
27	Emergency Services at Clacton Air Show	Clacton	England	2003	175
28	Insurance at the I-tech Exhibition	Maastricht	Netherlands	1995	177
29	ECOC Conference On-line Bookings	Rimini	Italy	2003	180
30	Mainz Carnival Clubs	Mainz	Germany	2003	192
31	Deventer Book Market	Deventer	Netherlands	2003	208
32	World Golf Championships	Valderrama	Spain	2000	216
33	Commonwealth Games	Manchester	England	2002	226

Preface to the second edition

This book is in two parts: the first part, chapters 1 to 4, present a picture of the events business; the second part, chapters 5 to 12, are about how to organize events. Our advice to the reader is to take this book as a complete approach: not just the text, but also the diagrams, case studies and the questions set in the case studies. This will help you learn more. For the beginner, or someone wanting 'a 30-minute guide' to organizing events, your first step is to look at the forms listed in the front of the book, to give you some idea of what you are going to need, and then start with chapters 5 and 6.

We have taken a deliberately European approach, for two reasons. First, many of the existing books about events management are either American or Australian, and tend to contain examples (especially the US texts) that may not have much relevance to the European experience. Second, and perhaps more importantly, we, as Europeans, do not explore the extent and quality of our knowledge and mutual experience sufficiently. Partly, and historically, this has been due to language barriers and to perceived cultural differences. However, in the age of the Internet and in the twenty-first century, language is an increasing irrelevance when the common language of the Net is English and, culturally, well, we are Europeans. More unites us than divides us, as most young people, having backpacked their way around the Continent, watched MTV and drunk cappuccinos in open-air cafés from Galway to Genoa, know very well. This being the case, the book contains material from all over Europe and all money is stated in Euros. As a convention, all case study material is real as named. However, some more generalized examples are given to illustrate the text and to help the reader; in these cases the fictitious town of 'Middleburg' is used. For those who live in the Dutch provincial capital of Middelburg, or any European town from Mittelburg to Middlesbrough, we hope you will excuse this small liberty and not search too hard for the Arboretum or the Venetian Bridge.

We are extremely grateful for the contributions made to this book by many people and organizations. They include James O'Neill, Chairman of the Inntel Conference Agency, and his staff at Marks Tey; Albert Kemp, Chief Executive of Insurex Expo-Sure; Hein te Riele, Director of the Deventer Tourist Service and Sally Looker, Tourism Officer of the Tendring District Council. We would also wish to express our most grateful thanks to Rudi Drost, Graham Lucas, Duncan Tyler, Crispin Farbrother, Mike Stapleton, Bays Boeijen, Ken and Christina Crossley, Eddie Shone, Jos Poth, Minesh Ghandi, Giuseppe Fontebasso, Andy Bell, Rachel Hollands, Steve Pateman, Joanne Webber, Steve Woodman, the Touristik Centrale Mainz, University College Cork, Evelien Winkel at the IFEA in Leidschendam, and to all those whole have contributed in some way, great or small.

In this second edition we have taken the opportunity to revise those sections of the book that needed bringing up to date. We have paid special attention to the case study material and have added a number of new cases, especially to chapter 7 on Financial Management, which lacked case material in the original edition. We have thoroughly overhauled chapter 10 to deal more effectively with project management, risk management and other key operational issues. We have strengthened the sections on event safety and ticketing and have brought the reference lists up to date as far as possible. We hope that these changes will ensure the book remains effective as a practical guide. This said, the book is by no means definitive and we urge the reader to bear that in mind and to use it as a starting place. Any comments which readers may wish to make will be gladly received.

Anton Shone
Conferences Direct
Derby
England

Bryn Parry
Southampton Business School
Southampton Institute
Southampton
England

www.conferencesdirect.co.uk

www.solent.ac.uk

The events business

1 An introduction to events

2 The market demand for events

3 The events business: supply and suppliers

4 Social, economic, political and developmental implications

An introduction to events

Aims

- To consider a definition of, and framework for, special events.

- To provide a categorization and typology for special events, together with an overview of the historical context.

- To identify the key characteristics of events, in order to understand the business of events management as a service activity.

Introduction

Events have long played an important role in human society. The tedium of daily life, with its constant toil and effort, was broken up by events of all kinds. In most societies, the slightest excuse could be found for a good celebration, although traditional celebrations often had strict ceremonies and rituals. In Europe, particularly before the industrial revolution, routine daily activities were regularly interspersed with festivals and carnivals. Personal events or local events to celebrate certain times of year, perhaps related to religious holy days, were also common. This role in society was, and is, of considerable importance. In the modern world some of the historic driving forces for events have changed. For example, religious reasons for having major festivals have, perhaps, become less important, but we still see carnivals, fairs and festivals in all sorts of places and at various times of year. Many of these events, although religious or traditional in origin, play a contemporary role by attracting tourists (and thus tourist income) to a particular place. Some major events, however, still revolve around periods such as Christmas or Easter in the Christian calendar, and towns and cities throughout Europe often hold major festivals based on these times. Even in those countries where religion is no longer as important as it once was, the celebration of originally religious, and other folk festivals, still takes place; so do older festivals related to the seasons, including the celebration of spring, with activities such as dancing round a maypole, decorating water wells or crowning a May Queen. Harvest time continues to provide a reason for a seasonal celebration in rural locations. At the same time, many historic, traditional or 'folk' ceremonies and rituals are, in practice, recent inventions or recreations.

We can grasp, therefore, that special events were often historically crucial to the social fabric of day-to-day life. In modern times we are often so used to special events that we do not necessarily see them in this context (e.g. Mother's Day). It is also sometimes difficult for the student of events to understand the full extent of these activities, their variety, their role and how they are run. Unlike many industries we cannot say, 'Well, this industry is worth maybe €30 billion a year,' or whatever. In fact it is almost impossible to quantify, in monetary terms, how much events are worth 'as an industry'. Such a calculation is likely to be problematic, because the range of events is staggering, from big, internationally organized sports spectaculars such as the Olympics, to the family naming ceremony of the new baby next door. All we can reasonably say, perhaps, is that we can look at any one event in isolation and see what value it generates. Indeed, certain events have the purpose of creating wealth or economic value in some way, as well as of entertaining and cementing society, but these are not the only reasons for holding events.

Definitions and frameworks

For the student of events, we have to provide some context, or framework, to begin to understand the nature of the activity and the issues about management and organization surrounding it. This being the case, and for convenience, we need to attempt both a definition and a means of classification:

Definition

> **Special events** are:
> That phenomenon arising from those non-routine occasions which have leisure, cultural, personal or organizational objectives set apart from the normal activity of daily life, whose purpose is to enlighten, celebrate, entertain or challenge the experience of a group of people.

Authors such as Goldblatt (2001) have chosen to highlight the celebratory aspect of events: 'A special event recognises a unique moment in time with ceremony and ritual to satisfy specific needs'. Although this definition clearly works for events like weddings, parades, inaugurations, and so on, it works less well for activities like engineering exhibitions, sports competitions, product launches, etc. Getz (1997), in referring to the experience that participants have, states: 'To the customer... a special event is an opportunity for a leisure, social or cultural experience outside the normal range of choices or beyond everyday experience'. This definition, too, has its advantages, but seems to exclude organizational events of various kinds.

Nevertheless, it is a place to start and from it we can begin to look at the vast range of events that take place. To do so, it helps to have some means of classification. Figure 1.1, for convenience, splits events into four broad categories based on the concept (in our definition) of events having leisure, cultural, personal or organizational objectives. It is crucial to bear in mind, when considering this categorization, that there are frequent overlaps. For example, the graduation of a student from university is both a personal event for the student and his or her family, and an organizational event for the university. A village carnival is both a cultural event, perhaps celebrating some aspect of local heritage or folklore, and a leisure event, possibly both for local people and for tourists. Therefore, overlaps should be seen as inevitable rather than exceptional, and any attempt to categorize an event, even by analysing its objectives, its organizers or its origins, will have to take account of this, even if we can agree that this event does fall into such and such a category.

Categories and typologies

In the following section we will begin to consider how this proposed categorization might be developed to take in the great variety of events. It is a useful starting point, and one we can adopt to help us look at the context and precedents for modern events, and as a means of understanding their breadth and variety.

In looking at the various kinds of special event, whether these are leisure based, personal, cultural or organizational, it is possible to identify a number of characteristics that they have in common to them, thus helping us understand what special events are and how they work, as well as differentiating them from other activities.

Our definition of events could be given a shorthand version: 'Those non-routine occasions set apart from the normal activity of daily life of a group of people' does not necessarily give a feel for the specialized nature of the activity. We can say 'specialized' because of the uniqueness of events, but also because such events may often be celebratory or even ceremonial in some way. This is an aspect, that other authors, including Goldblatt, have highlighted. Clearly this approach can be applied to activities such as weddings, product launches, prize-givings, etc. On the other hand, it may be less suited to events such as exhibitions, sport days, or annual conferences, although it can be argued that even an exhibition of paintings or a sales conference may have an element of ceremony

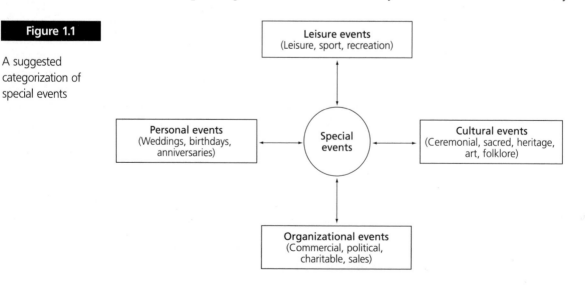

Figure 1.1

A suggested categorization of special events

about it, since someone has to open it; but in so far as exhibitions, conferences and so on are non-routine, the definition is usable. For the purpose of illustrating the four categories, and to demonstrate historical progression, this chapter explores four case studies: for leisure events, the ancient Olympic Games; for personal events, a Roman wedding; for cultural events, the coronation of Elizabeth I of England (which, for those interested in the overlaps, could also be said to be political and therefore organizational); and for organizational events themselves, the Paris Exposition of 1889.

Special events vary tremendously in size and complexity, from the simple and small, such as the village fête, to the huge, complex and international, such as the Olympic Games. To understand the relative levels of complexity involved we can attempt to provide a typology. It is necessary to consider events as having both organizational complexity and uncertainty. Complexity is fairly easy to understand, whereas uncertainty, as a concept, is a little more problematical. By uncertainty we mean initial doubt about such issues as the cost, the time schedule and the technical requirements. Thus, it can be understood that, at the beginning, the uncertainty about the cost, the timing and the technical needs of organizing the Olympic Games far exceeds the uncertainty of, say, a training conference or a small wedding reception. In order to quantify the complexity, in the typology in Figure 1.2, varying levels of organizational complexity have been used, ranging from individual to multinational. Using this typology it is possible to propose a classification of various events, in order to understand the comparative demands that such events might place on organizers or events managers.

Even where an event is relatively simple, the number of people attending may make it very complex indeed. There is a world of difference between a

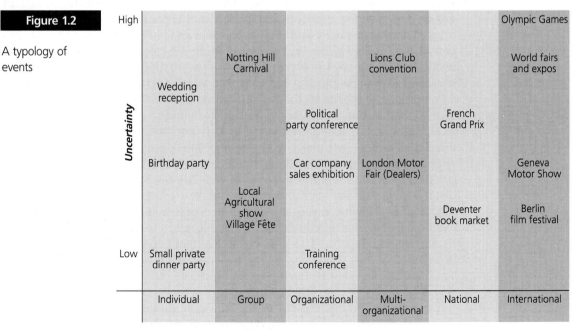

Figure 1.2

A typology of events

Source: Authors, adapted from Slack et al., 2001.

birthday party for six people and a birthday party for 60, even though the format, structure and basic idea may be the same. The typology must be seen with this limitation in mind. Indeed, it is this concept of size which often means the difference between an amateur organizer, or a family member running an event, on the one hand, or having to employ an event manager, go to a hotel, or find specialist advice on the other. Size or number of attendees is something that easily catches people out. We can all organize a dinner party for eight or ten people, even a buffet for maybe 20 or 30, but after that the sheer effort involved would overwhelm us: not enough space, not enough equipment, not enough people to help and so on. The events management business, whether it is about the annual dinner of the local town council or the European Figure Skating Championships, is often, in the contemporary world, about the need for trained staff, specialist companies and professional expertise.

Historical contexts and precedents

Events management can be thought of as an art, rather than a science. Historically, the organization of small local events was relatively uncomplicated and needed no extensive managerial expertise. The organization of a wedding, for example, could be done, most often, by the bride's mother with help from the two families involved and the vicar, priest, religious or other official representative. (In past times, especially up until the Victorian period, 'expert' advice often came in the form of a Dancing Master, employed to give the wedding festivities some formality of style. There were also quite specific local rituals to be observed, which acted as 'checklists' for the activities.) Some weddings are still done this way, and are within the ability of non-specialist people to organize and run: the bride and groom deal with the ceremony, the bride's mother orders the cake and a buffet from a local baker, family and friends do some or all of it; the reception is held in one of the family homes or a church hall, flowers come from gardens or are obtained from a nearby flower shop, and so on. All these tasks were, and can still be, coped with in an intimate and sociable way without need of great cost or fuss.

While special events, by their nature, were (and are) not routine, pressure for formal organizational or technological skill was not so great in the past for these local, family or small-scale activities. This is not to say that large-scale events management is a particularly recent development, only that the modern world, with its many complexities, often requires specialists to do what, in gentler times, could be done by thoughtful amateurs or ordinary people. We should not mistake history, however. The scale and complexity of, say, the Greek or Roman gladiatorial games (which comprised vast numbers of activities, set-piece contests and even theatrically mounted sea battles – the Romans were sufficiently advanced that they could flood their arenas) – would certainly have had what today would be considered as a professional events management organization to run them. This can also be seen in our first case study, of the ancient Olympic Games, which helps to illustrate our first category of leisure events.

Looking back in history we can see, however, that events have always had a significant role to play in society, either to break up the dull, grinding routine of daily life (toiling in the fields, perhaps) or to emphasize some important activity or person (such as the arrival of a new abbot at the local monastery). We can trace all sorts of special events far back in time, even if they are the result of some recent 're-invention'. For as long as mankind has lived in family groups there will have been celebrations of weddings, births, religious rites, and so on. In following up the categorization suggested earlier, of events being: leisure, personal, cultural or organizational in origin, we can therefore seek various historical examples or precedents. This said, we must be careful not to believe that earlier times or other societies have the same cultural attitudes as we have today.

Case Study 1 *Leisure/sporting events: the Olympic Games*

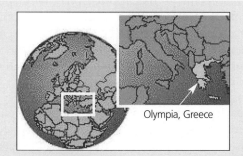

Olympia, Greece

Factbox

- Ancient Olympic Games first held in 776BC, last held in 393.
- Restarted in modern times in 1896.
- Held every four years.
- Ancient games were part of the religious festival of Zeus, the chief Greek god.
- Modern games are a major economic activity.

The modern Olympic Games are loosely based on the games of the ancient Greeks. Those games, first held in 776BC at Olympia, in Greece, had the purpose of celebrating the festival of Zeus, the most important Greek god. They were organized by the temple priests and their helpers, and carried on for years at four-yearly intervals, even though Greece was normally at war (quite usual in those times).

One of the most important aspects of the games was the truce that existed to allow them to take place and to enable the participants, mostly the nobility and professional athletes, together with pilgrims (who were travelling to the temple of Zeus at Olympia), to get to the games safely.

The ancient games at first had only one component, the 'stade', a footrace. Later they included not only the stade (about 150 metres, hence the word 'stadium'), but also the pentathlon (the discuss, the jump, the javelin, another race and wrestling), together with a chariot race, a horse race and the pankration – a very violent form of wrestling. All of these were performed naked, in the Greek style, although, as the games also celebrated military prowess, the final foot race was performed in full armour.

The games lasted for five days and included various religious ceremonies, the main religious aspect being the worship of Zeus, although the women had their own games in honour of the goddess Hera (married women were not permitted at the men's games, even to watch). The games were organized by the religious authorities of Olympia and involved professional trainers and referees for the events as well as judges (Swadding, 1999; Wels, 1995).

There were also social events and, rather like the modern games, a parade of champions on the final day. The ancient games continued, in all, for about 1,200 years and were closed down by the Roman Emperor Theodosius II in 393 (the temple at Olympia was destroyed later, about 426). The modern games began again at Athens in 1896, followed by Paris in 1900, and then more or less every four years to the present day.

▶

◀

Based on this case:

Investigate the modern Olympic Games.

1. Where were the most recent games held?
2. How many people attended them?
3. How many people participated?
4. How were the games organized and what support services were involved?
5. How many people did the games employ during the peak period?
6. To what use were the games' buildings put after the games had finished?
7. How much do the modern games differ from the ancient ones?

Related website for those interested in the Olympics: www.olympic.org

The second category of special events, in our approach, is that of personal events. This includes all the kinds of occasions that a family or friends might be involved in. Many modern aspects of family life can be seen to revolve around important occasions: birthdays, namings, weddings and anniversaries all fall into this category, as do many other personal events and celebrations (a dinner party is a special event in our definition). Of all these, weddings can be one of the most complicated to organize, involving friends and family and a whole range of related service activities, from catering to entertainment, as well as the formal aspect of the marriage ceremony itself. This is not to say that all weddings are a 'big performance', some are small, friendly and relaxed, and just as good for it – size is no measure of the success of an event. Almost all cultures known to history have some form of partnership ceremony, and in looking for a historical precedent for personal events, the Romans can provide an example.

Case Study 2 *Personal events: a Roman wedding*

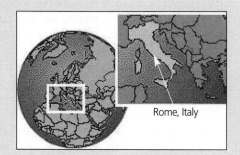

Rome, Italy

Factbox

● The Roman empire covered a huge area of Western Europe, from Britain to north Africa.
● Rome was pagan until the AD300s, when it began to become Christian in religion.
● Roman weddings had many similarities to modern ceremonies, but also a number of differences.

As with modern weddings, Roman weddings were organized by the families of the bride and groom. A ring was often given as an engagement present, although no ring was involved in the ceremony itself until changes in the ritual after the second century AD (Kamm, 1995). The bride wore a special bridal gown, generally with a flame-coloured veil and garlands of flowers. The wedding would be arranged with the respective families each dealing with various aspects. A legal contract was signed by the two fathers on the day of the wedding. The joining of hands at the ceremony was ensured, not by a priest, but by a married woman, known as a 'pronuba'.

At the ceremony, prayers would be said to the family gods and especially to the goddess Juno, with a sacrifice offered to the god Jupiter. This might involve the killing of a donkey, as donkeys

▶

were thought to have considerable sexual prowess, so that the sacrifice was thought to ensure a suitably exciting wedding night.

Following the ceremony the party would make their way to the bride's parents house, where there would be a major feast in the Roman style, of some excess, and a great deal of food and wine would be consumed. Once the feast was over, there would be a torchlight procession from the bride's parent's house to the bridegroom's house. It would generally be led by torch carriers, often children, and accompanied by flute players and the families, with friends, relatives and other locals joining in. There was a great deal of loud and happy singing during the procession and the cheerful shouting of obscene poetry and jokes, known as 'Fescennine Verses'. This was the Roman equivalent of writing obscene messages on the couple's car with foam, and often referred to how good the donkey was in bed.

On arrival at the bridegroom's house the bride would anoint the doorposts with oil as a sign of dedication to the gods, and the bridegroom would carry the bride over the threshold. At this point we will leave them to it.

Based on this case:

Perhaps from your own experience of going to a wedding:

1. How did it differ from the Roman one?

2. Who organized what?

3. Suppose you have a wedding to organize with 100 guests, how long does it realistically take to get things done?

4. Also, begin to look for possible similarities between the special events in these case studies – what are their common characteristics?

Related website for those interested in Roman history: www.roman-empire.net

Special events cover all kinds of human activity, not only sporting and family activities, but also cultural and commercial or organizational activities. Culture, with its associated ceremony and traditions, has a role in all kinds of social activity, and for all kinds of people, organizations and institutions, but has been especially important for governments and leaders, such as royalty. In cultural events ceremony becomes very evident, often as a way of emphasizing the significance of the event itself or of the person at the centre for the ceremony, the intended effect being to secure support, or to allow as many people as possible to recognize the key individual. For example, the news media often show heads of state (kings, queens, presidents) inspecting a 'guard of honour' when arriving at the airport of a country they are visiting: they listen to the national anthem and then walk past the guard of honour. The original purpose of this ceremony was not for the head of state to see the guards, but for the guards to see the head of state, so that the guards would recognize the person they were to protect.

In the Middle Ages, events and ceremonies played a major role ensuring that a dull daily existence was enlivened and that people were entertained, or at least impressed. There was no TV, video, movies or Net for entertainment, as all these are less than 100 years old. It was, for example, accepted wisdom in the England in the Tudor period (about 1500–1600) that 'In pompous ceremonies a secret of government doth much consist' (Plowden, 1982). Government, in this case the king or queen, was expected to make a good show, or put on a good display for the people, and the people expected to see royalty in all its glory; it was intended to ensure, to a certain extent, respect and allegiance.

Case Study 3 *Cultural events: the coronation of Elizabeth I*

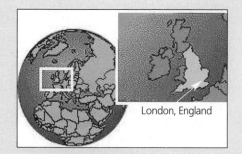

London, England

Factbox

- Coronation of Queen Elizabeth I of England
- Took place over four days in January 1559
- Run by the Lord Chamberlain
- The event comprised:
  A river procession on the Thames
  A foot procession through the city
  The coronation ceremony and a banquet.

At a time when the country had a huge foreign debt and the treasury was empty, with a new queen not known for spending money, the coronation of Elizabeth I had a huge amount spent on it, to put on a good show. This was felt to be important in order to generate loyalty and allegiance to the new Queen and to ensure stability of support for the monarchy and the government (which at that time were the same thing).

The ceremonial lasted several days. It began with the Queen travelling along the River Thames to take possession of the Tower of London, escorted by her guard (the 'gentlemen pensioners'), the royal court, the Lord Mayor of London and many others, including several bands of musicians, in a fleet of barges, boats and other water craft (Plowden, 1982). This river journey took up most of the first official day of the event, after which the Queen stayed at the Tower (then a royal palace, as well as the most important fortress of the country), while other preparations were made.

Two days later a huge procession took place, on horse and on foot, from the Tower of London to the City of Westminster (London consists of two cities, London and Westminster) and to Whitehall Palace. This took the entire afternoon to travel through the medieval city, so that as many people as possible could see the new Queen. Unlike modern processions, the medieval one stopped frequently for the Queen to look at displays and tableaux, to talk to all kinds of people from the great to the poor and to receive gifts and listen to loyal speeches. The coronation itself followed on Sunday 15 January 1559, in Westminster Abbey, where English kings and queens have been crowned for centuries. There then followed a great banquet, which ended at one o'clock in the morning.

A celebration of this size would be a challenge to even a modern events manager; at Elizabeth's coronation it was the responsibility of the Lord Chamberlain and the Treasurer of the Household. The court of a medieval monarch was not only involved in the occasional coronation, but existed in a more or less constant state of pomp and ceremony – so much so that its organization reflected this. The Lord Chamberlain's department was responsible for entertainment of all kinds and had a special office called the 'Office of the Revels', which arranged anything from plays to pageants and consisted of a relatively large number of specialized staff, by the standards of the period (Plowden, 1982).

Based on this case:

Think of a recent ceremonial event you have seen, perhaps a royal or government event, a church event, or some ceremony that takes place locally in your town or city, perhaps involving the mayor.

1. What was this event about and what was special about it?

▶

2. Was there much ceremonial, perhaps a procession, music, ceremonial dress or some kind of tradition being enacted?

3. Does the ceremony still have a modern use?

4. What is that use?

5. If it is a traditional event, does it now have some other useful purpose, such as attracting tourists or emphasizing the long history that it relates to?

Related website for those interested in Queen Elizabeth I: www.luminarium.org/renlit/eliza.htm

One of the things which these historic examples show is that there have long been specialists of various kinds to organize events (the temple priests for the Greek Games, the Lord Chamberlain's department for Queen Elizabeth). Some events, such as the coronation of a king or queen, have been, and still are, highly complex. Very often, where great ceremony was needed for state events, the military could also be called on to help organize them, and army officers were often seconded to do just that, as is still the case with much modern state ceremonial: parades, state visits, pageants and festivals.

Although the organization of historic ceremonial events might be seen as a matter of the injection of military organizational skills, very often this prowess was no such thing. In fact, great historical ceremonial disasters were quite common. The modern events manager has no monopoly on things going 'pear shaped'. Many coronations and other great events were, in parts, famously shambolic. Even where these involved a non-military event, such as the great royal fireworks held in 1749 to celebrate the peace of Aix-la-Chapelle, for King George II, there was no guarantee of success, in spite of the fact that these were organized by George Frederick Handel, the famous composer, and set to his music. The fireworks were to be held in a specially built pavilion in Green Park, London. Handel was designated 'Comptroller of the Fireworks'. This was such a major event that a full dress rehearsal was held, which went perfectly. However, on the night itself Handel had an argument with Servandoni, the pavilion designer, at which swords were drawn, and during the middle of the performance, with 100 musicians playing and a crowd of over 12,000 people watching, half the pavilion burned down.

The modern world is no different. Faster maybe; more complex perhaps; but no less susceptible to things going wrong, falling down, being rained on or flooded out; the guest speaker getting stuck in the traffic; acts of God, both tragic or comic; the groom still drunk after the stag night, the buffet being dropped on the kitchen floor and the bride falling over the cake at the reception. In some ways, events management is a rather thankless task, one of those roles where everyone notices when something goes wrong, but few people notice the tremendous effort involved in getting even a simple event right. Indeed, some of the things that go wrong at an event may be beyond the organizer's ability to prevent: the weather, the traffic, power failures and so on.

Nevertheless, events can be considerable triumphs of organization and leave lasting legacies. The fourth in our categories is the organizational event; this may be anything from a political party conference to a motor show. There are any number of suitable examples. Some of the world trade fairs have left interesting legacies. As trade and commerce developed following the industrial revolution, many countries sought to celebrate and display their industrial achievements. This led to a number of industrial and commercial exhibitions in many major cities. Such exhibitions had often developed out of local trade fairs in towns and cities around mediaeval Europe. Fairs had been held for many centuries as a way to show off all kinds of products, goods and other wares. One of the first great international industrial fairs was the Great Exhibition in London of 1851 (there had been earlier ones, such as that in Paris of 1849), which was held in a specially built hall, the Crystal Palace, that housed some 13,000 exhibitors from all over the world.

These fairs have taken place at irregular intervals in many major cities ever since. Recent fairs or 'Expos' have taken place in New York, Montreal, Seville and, in 2000, Hanover. In the Victorian period many cities held fairs; not only London, but also Amsterdam (in 1883 with the International Colonial Exposition and several later fairs), and especially Paris, which held a series of fairs from 1855 to 1900 (and two since, in 1925 and 1937). One such event, which has left a very obvious legacy, was the Paris Exposition of 1889.

Case Study 4 *Organizational events: the Paris Exposition*

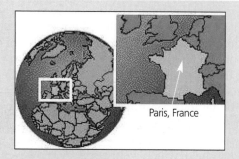

Paris, France

The fair was opened on 6 May 1889, a wonderful spring day, by the French president, Sadi Carnot, who rode in a horse-drawn procession from the Elysée Palace. The procession, led by a detachment of mounted cuirassiers, made its way along the Champs Elysées and the Avenue Montaigne amongst joyful crowds, and entered the exhibition area passing under the arches of the Eiffel Tower, arriving at the Central Dome at 2.00 pm. A short ceremony took place at which the Exposition was formally presented to President Carnot: 'This splendid result exceeds all hopes…' Indeed it did. The exposition was huge. It covered the whole of the Champ de Mars and the Esplanade des Invalides, and stretched along the Quai d'Orsay and the Trocadero Gardens to the Eiffel Tower, some 228 acres (95 hectares), including a huge Ferris wheel. There were almost 62,000 exhibitors from all over the world and by the time an exhausted President Carnot had left at 5.30pm, almost half a million people had streamed in through the 22 entrances to the exhibition, which then lasted 176 days. Some 32 million people visited the fair and amongst the exhibits was the world's first ever motor car, a Benz (Harris, 1975).

Factbox

● The Paris Exposition of 1889
● Intended to display France's industrial power
● Resulted in a major building programme in the exposition area, including the construction of the Eiffel Tower
● 32 million people visited the fair

The 1889 Paris Exposition was the idea of the French Prime Minister of the time, Jules Ferry. He wished to see an exhibition that would demonstrate France's industrial might, its commercial activity and engineering skill. The result was the largest, most varied and successful world fair ever held until that time.

The lasting legacy of the exposition is the Eiffel Tower. When the event was being planned, a member of the French cabinet, Edouard Lockroy, had suggested a thousand-foot tower to highlight its importance. The idea of a tower built of iron and steel was not new, as one had been suggested by the Cornish engineer, Richard Trevithick, in 1833, and another by Clarke and Reeves, two American engineers, for the Philadelphia Exposition of 1876. But it was Gustave Eiffel who supervised the building of the Paris tower. It was begun on 26 January 1887, and opened at ten minutes to twelve on 15 May 1889, to Eiffel's considerable relief, and has been the symbol of Paris ever since – though for the first 20 or 30 years it was rather disliked by some.

Based on this case:

Think of a recent event engineering project you have seen launched in public.

1. What was its purpose?
2. How was it organized?
3. In the long term, was there some benefit from having it, even if it was knocked down later?
4. Does this apply to other kinds of events?
5. How could a town or city benefit from holding an event?
6. Could that event be used to help renovate a rundown area?
7. Who would pay for the event?

Related website for those interested in the Eiffel Tower: www.tour-eiffel.fr/teiffel/uk/

Characteristics of events

In our definition of special events, we noted key characteristics of events as 'non-routine' and 'unique'. However, events have many other characteristics in common with all types of services, and in particular with hospitality and leisure services of many kinds.

These characteristics can be grouped together as being: uniqueness; perishability; labour-intensiveness; fixed timescales; intangibility; personal interaction; ambience; and ritual or ceremony.

Figure 1.3

Characteristics of special events as a service

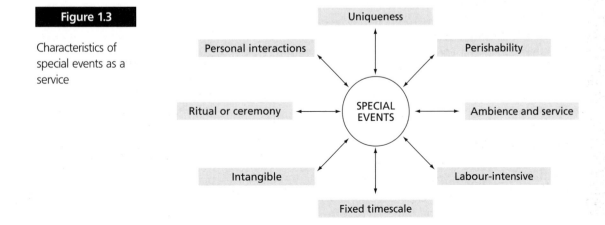

Uniqueness

The key element of all special events is their uniqueness: each one will be different. This is not to say that the same kind of event cannot be repeated many times, but that the participants, the surroundings, the audience, or any number of other variables will make the event unique. Even where we have looked at special events that are very frequent, such as weddings, all are different because different people are involved, the choice of location, the invited guests, the timing, and so on. The same is true of events that may have followed the same format for years and years. The ancient Olympic Games took place at four-year intervals for nearly 1,200 years, or put more simply, 300 repeat editions. But each was unique, because each had different athletes, different organizers and a different audience. The format also changed slowly over time. At the beginning, it was a religious festival for the Greek god Zeus, and only a 150-metre footrace, the 'stade', was run. At the end, there was no major religious aspect, but the athletics had become the main activity, with 12 or so different sports in the games.

The uniqueness of special events is therefore the key to them. We are not doing something that is routine, nor are we producing the same item of work repetitively. Nevertheless, it is important to recognize that certain types of event do recur; they may recur in the same kind of format (such as weddings – each wedding is different but the format or structure is similar), or they may recur on the basis of time interval (such as an annual conference – again the format or structure is the same, but the participants and the subject will be different). Uniqueness alone, however, does not make a special event. Events have a number of characteristics and their uniqueness is closely related to aspects of perishability and intangibility.

Perishability of events

Almost by definition, if we regard events as 'unique', then the event is tremendously perishable; it cannot be repeated in exactly the same way. Two wedding anniversaries at the same location, with the same number of people, will not be the same. Even where a reasonable level of standardization is possible, like with activities such as training seminars, each will be different and will be very time dependent. They exist briefly and cannot be repeated in precisely the same way. Perishability also relates to the use of facilities for events. Let us suppose we have a banqueting room. It may be used to its peak capacity only on Saturdays, for weddings, so the rest of the week its revenue-generating potential may not be exploited. If the room is empty for even one day of the week, the revenue-generating potential of that day is lost for ever – it is perishable. The room can be used on a different day, but the day it is empty cannot be replayed and used for an event.

One of the key issues, therefore, in the events manager's role, is the extent to which facilities and services can be used effectively, given the uniqueness or irregularity (perhaps better to say infrequency) of use. In consequence, events can be expensive to provide. Many items will have to be produced on a one-off basis and cannot be used again. For example, a large banner saying 'Happy Wedding Anniversary Anna and Frederick' would be a unique item and thus (relatively) expensive to provide. On the other hand, a banner saying 'Happy Anniversary' may have a number of potential uses and can be stored.

The issue of perishability also means that events venue managers may have to use a variety of techniques, such as differential pricing, to try to encourage activities in quiet periods when a facility or service on offer might not sell. Perhaps a mobile disco can be obtained at a discount for an event on, say, a Tuesday, rather than at a peak period of the week or year, like a Friday or Saturday night or New Year's Eve. This too illustrates the perishability issue; if the disco is not booked one night of the week it will have lost that night's revenue forever.

Intangibility

When you go out to buy a chocolate bar or a pair of socks, you are buying something tangible – you can see it and touch it. With events, however, the activity is more or less intangible. If you go to a wedding, you will experience the activities, join in, enjoy and remember it, but there are only a few tangible things that you might have got from it – perhaps a piece of wedding cake and some photographs, or a video you took of the happy couple and the rest of the guests. This intangibility is entirely normal for service activities: when people stay in hotel bedrooms they often take home the complimentary soaps and shampoos from the bathroom, or matchbooks from the bar. These are efforts to make the experience of the event more tangible; a memento that the experience happened and to show friends and family. It is important for event organizers to bear this in mind, and that even the smallest tangible item will help to sustain people's idea of how good an event has been. A programme, a guest list, postcards, small wrapped and named chocolates, even slightly more ambitious give-aways such as badged glasses or colour brochures help in the process of making the intangible more tangible.

Ritual and ceremony

For authors such as Goldblatt, this is the key issue about special events, the major characteristic that makes them special. In our historical examples it was very evident that ritual and ceremony often played an important part. In practice, many modern ceremonial activities are 'fossilized' or reinvented versions of old traditions. The original tradition might have had some key role in the ceremony, now lost, but the ritual of doing it (like the inspection of guards of honour) still continues. Often the ritual ceremony is there because it does, in fact, emphasize the continuity of the tradition, even though the reason for the tradition has gone. In Ripon, England, a horn is blown at dusk to signify the setting of the night-watch. Now it is just a small event for tourists, but in olden days this had real purpose: the town was in open countryside and could be invaded or attacked by brigands or barbarians, and the sounding of the horn was to set the guard on the town walls and to ensure that the night watchmen, known as 'wakemen', came on duty. Even this was not thought enough, and Ripon being a cathedral city, God was appealed to: 'If God keep not ye citie, ye wakemen waketh in vain'. Put in modern English, if God didn't look after the town, the watchmen were wasting their time. Thus, for hundreds of years, this short ceremony has taken place in Ripon and continues every nightfall even now. The watch is still called to the walls, although the walls are long gone and the last watchman long dead.

Modern events may not, in any way, rely on old tradition and established ceremony. If you think of a contemporary ceremony, such as the awarding of the Berlin

Golden Bears, these are essentially prizes given for good film-making, and the whole ceremony was specially made up. This is true of all kinds of events; in fact, it is often the case that a town or city wishing to attract tourists might do so by creating a brand new special event, containing a wholly new ceremony, something for the visitors to watch. This can be done for all kinds of special events, and the creation of new ceremonies and 'new' traditions is very common, although it can be argued that for a special event to have a 'traditional' element in it, that element should have some basis – however tenuous – in historical reality.

Ambience and service

Of all the characteristics of events, ambience is one of the most important to the outcome. An event with the right ambience can be a huge success. An event with the wrong ambience can be a huge failure. At a personal event, such as a birthday party, the ambience may be simply created by the people who are there, without the need for anything else – good company amongst friends can make an excellent event (see Figure 1.4).

Some events, however, may need a little help to go well. At a birthday party, there might be the need for decorations, music and games, as well as food and drink. But it is very important to realize that the presence of these elements does not guarantee that things will go well: there can be a wonderful environment, expensive themed decor, large amounts of excellent food and drink and the event can still be a flop. One of the roles of an events manager is to try and ensure the event succeeds by careful attention to detail and by trying to encourage the desired outcome. Nevertheless, people cannot be compelled to enjoy themselves. If they've had a bad day, or feel grumpy, your wonderfully well-organized event might get them in a better mood, or… it might not.

Personal contact and interaction

In manufacturing situations, customers have no contact with the staff producing the goods, only with, perhaps, the sales team. In service situations, customers have frequent contact with staff, and this often determines the quality or otherwise of the experience. People attending events are frequently themselves part of the process. For example, the crowd at a sports tournament is not only watching the event but is helping to create the atmosphere; it is interacting with itself, with participants and staff and is part of the whole experience. Much the same is true of the guests at a Christmas party: it is the guests themselves interacting with

Figure 1.4

Elements in the ambience and service of an event

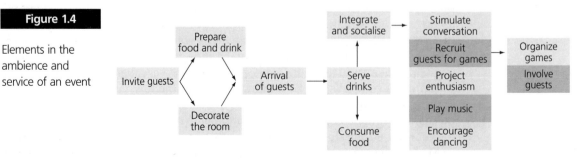

Source: adapted from Berkley, 1996.

each other, with the hosts and perhaps with entertainers, that creates the atmosphere and contributes to how enjoyable the event is. A room decorated for a party may look nice, but will not come to life until it is full of guests. Therefore, in considering how to make an event successful, event managers must be fully aware that this is largely dependent on the actions and reactions of people attending. It is perfectly possible to have the same event twice in a row, such as a pageant or procession, and one may be a complete success and the other a complete failure, due to audience reactions, interactions or backgrounds. An awareness of the attendees is vital on the part of event planners.

Labour-intensiveness

The more complex and the more unique an event is, the more likely it is to be more labour-intensive, both in terms of organization and of operation. The organizational issue relates to the need for relatively complicated planning to enable the service delivery to be efficient, or put more simply, for the event to be a good one (this is why some events may be outsourced to event management companies, caterers or other types of event suppliers). The uniqueness of this type of service implies a high level of communication between the organizer and the event manager. Such a high level of communication and planning will take time and effort, even where the event may be repeating a well-known formula, or operating within a common framework such as a conference. The operational element may also require high levels of staffing in order to deliver the event properly. A banquet for 300 people will require not only food service staff, but bar and drinks staff, kitchen staff, management and perhaps support staff, such as cloakroom attendants, cleaners and staff to set up and break down the room. Staffing needs are also likely to peak at certain times. In the case of the banquet, peak staffing will take place at service time, but a long sequence of preparation and closedown has also to be taken into account.

No two events are likely to require the same number of staff, except in so far as events that have an element of routine, such as banquets and conferences, will require a known number of staff. Managers can forecast staffing needs for these types of events from experience, depending on the number of guests, the types of service, the experience and quality of the staff, the time required to complete the service and even the layout of the building. Staffing ratios will be dealt with later in more detail (see chapter 8 under Catering). The labour-intensiveness of special events is rather less predictable, as it depends entirely on the type of event in addition to all the above conditions. An event such as an athletic competition will require a completely different staffing structure to support it (including competitors, judges, timekeepers, etc.) than a company annual outing to a theme park. An event manager will have to forecast staffing needs directly from the requirements of running the event, based on what the organizer specifies as the event's objectives and needs, and on the experience and forecasts of departmental leaders.

Fixed timescale

Events, rather like building projects, run to a fixed timescale, unlike routine activities which can carry on indefinitely. The timescale could be very short, such as for the opening ceremony for a new road, or very long, as with the Paris

Exposition noted earlier, where the planning phase took about three years. Even these are not extremes. Many special events are actually composed of a sequence of short bursts of activity, with pauses or breaks in between. Constant ceremony, lasting many hours, might become dull and tiring. The example of the coronation of Elizabeth I shows that while the event lasted several days, it was composed of several shorter activities of varying lengths, with breaks, depending on what was going on and why. For those planning special events, this issue of timing must be kept in mind; for an event to be successful and striking, it will need to hold people's attention and interest them, and it is better that this is broken up into sections than it takes place all at once, without a respite. This is not to say that the fixed timescale cannot be varied. Some events, such as a birthday party, may carry on longer than intended because 'it just happened', other events may even be extended in a planned way, for some special reason, e.g. to recover the costs.

Summary

Special events have always had a major role to play in human society. In many respects, modern events are not much different from those of ancient times, especially in helping to enliven daily life. In understanding this, we can also see that society has developed and changed. Increasing public knowledge, and technology, often mean higher expectations of modern events. Whatever role events play in the social context, the management of them can be seen as a service activity. This context helps us understand how events work, what their major elements are and how we can classify them.

References

Berkley, B.J. (1996) 'Designing Services with Function Analysis', *Hospitality Research Journal*, 20, no 1, pp.73–100.

Getz, D. (1997) *Event Management and Event Tourism*, New York, Cognizant, p.4.

Goldblatt, J.J. (2001) *Special Events: The Art & Science of Modern Event Management*, Chichester, Wiley, pp.1–10.

Harris, J. (1975) *The Tallest Tower*, Washington, Regnery Gateway, pp.3–13, 108–18.

Kamm, A. (1995) *The Romans: An Introduction*, London, Routledge, p.88.

Plowden, A. (1982) *Elizabethan England*, London, Readers Digest, pp.10–55.

Slack, N., Chambers, S., Harrison, A. and Harland, C. (2001) *Operations Management*, London, Pitman, 3rd edn, pp.585–95.

Staines, J. and Buckley, J. (1998) *Classical Music*, London, Rough Guides, pp.174–81.

Swadding, J. (1999) *The Ancient Olympic Games*, London, British Museum, pp.53–93.

Wels, S. (1995) *The Olympic Spirit*, San Francisco, HarperCollins, pp.20–34.

2 The market demand for events

Aims

- To examine the scope and scale of the events business.

- To consider the determinants of demand for events.

- To illustrate the structure of demand for events.

Introduction

It is very common for individuals and organizations to wish to quantify things – we like to be able to say that a particular industry or its market is a particular size. There are several reasons why statistical measurement of events activity might be considered useful. First, data is required from which we can evaluate the significance of events to a particular location, whether that is a town, city, or some other geographical region. In this respect data helps quantify the role that events play in the economy and in society. Second, data is essential to the planning of facilities and services. This has been shown in the construction of special sporting facilities, for example, but also for the development of tourism and other community facilities. Third, data is particularly needed by those organizations (stakeholders) in the events business, by government departments, and by individual event organizers for the marketing and promotion of events, the prediction of demand and statistical comparisons.

There is a feeling that an expansion of events activity is taking place, and this is reflected in the increasingly rapid development of specialist events management companies and related service providers. There may be a number of reasons for this. In Europe, increased wealth (and the associated benefits of disposable and discretionary income) and many years of peace in the industrialized countries have strengthened the inclination to travel, to experience new ideas and to enjoy recreational activities. This, coupled with an active awareness of traditions, has seen an increase (in some cases a re-invention), of many kinds of events, especially in the cultural field (such as opera at Glyndebourne and film at Deauville). While this is true culturally, it is also true of the commercial, sporting and personal fields, for much the same reasons. As demand has grown, so too have the mechanisms to supply services to satisfy it, hence the reason for major international organizations and companies taking an interest in event activities. (Cause and effect can be argued here: is the increase in the number of organizations providing events services entirely due to demand, or has the potential demand been suppressed because of lack of available services?). Nevertheless, many of these general demand factors are not apparent to the organizers of individual events, who are probably more interested in the individual motives of participants and visitors, to ensure their event is a success.

Whereas demand for a routinely manufactured product is known and largely predictable, demand for events is less easy to predict. This is partly an issue of participants' motives to attend an event, but also because demand might be suppressed by factors not immediately obvious to organizers (such as lack of disposable income for the target market group at a particular time of year). This leads to some unpredictability. Latent demand may also be significant. For example, the demand expansion for Eurostar services through the Channel Tunnel significantly exceeded the expected demand, because it tapped latent (hidden) demand: there were always going to be people who wanted to travel between Britain and mainland Europe with ease, in speed and in moderate comfort, without having to bother with a ferry crossing. This latent demand turned out to be very large indeed. Similar demand aspects may be at work in the events business – who knows how successful an event might be if demand is hidden or latent?

Size and scope of the events market

The events market is so diverse and fragmented that it is problematic to say what the business is worth as a whole. In fact, to attempt to quantify it might be a fruitless exercise. Although such a quantification might be seen as a challenge by some academics and researchers, the nature of the business and the limitations of data availability have to be appreciated. Imagine trying to accumulate data for attendance at carnivals in every European town and city.

The student of events management would therefore be best advised to steer clear of this problem; indeed, even the serious researcher should not regard an assessment of the total value of the market to be a particularly viable exercise given the lack of suitable frameworks. (Although, as better quantitative information becomes available, this position may change.) How, then, can we seek to address the issue of the scope and scale of the events business? This can be done to some extent by breaking the business down into small components. We can then say that a certain part of the business is worth a given amount of money, has a certain number of participants or has a particular impact. We could take a geographical region and ask, 'Can we quantify this type of event in this area?' In some cases this is possible. For example, the total wedding business in a country such as the UK is thought to be worth some €2.6 billion. This is based on the known number of weddings (which are recorded officially) and an estimate of the average cost of having a wedding. A similar kind of exercise could probably be done on a European scale, thus giving us a notional figure for the European wedding market. For a few categories of events, estimates have been made on a European scale. These estimates range from those which have been done in reasonable depth, such as the economic impact studies of the European Grands

Prix (see case study 5), by Lilley and de Franco (1999), to the study by Nils Klevjer Aas (1998) of European Film Festivals, which is an example of the approach taken to assessing a type of event, in a European context, where information is limited and incomplete, but the best that can be made in the circumstances.

In building up a picture of event activity we are, in effect, 'building a wall'. At present all we have is a few bricks, from widely different sources, and not much by way of foundations. As the events industry is not typically seen as a homogeneous whole, there has been no drive to seek common statistical information, either by the industry or by other users of statistical data, such as governments and academics. In the range of events activity, the nature of personal events, voluntary events and similar activities mean that almost no data is collected for many kinds of events, except by occasional sampling, or perhaps by the event organizers for their own use or for a few household surveys. Even where events are organizational or commercial in nature, the extent of data collection is very limited indeed and often particular to that event alone. There is no common format even for the collection of attendance data, nor, in the foreseeable future, is there likely to be (although some countries, such as Germany, do require certain types of attendance and other data to be collected for tourist related festival activities). This means that data collection relies predominantly on a few sources and most often on casual estimates. The accuracy of much event reporting tends to be limited, for a whole range of reasons, not least that accurate data is often collected only for admission-paid events, and even then the likelihood of publication is small, since many organizations record data mainly for their own internal use, if they record it at all.

Case Study 5 *The size and scope of events: the European Grands Prix*

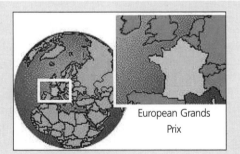

European Grands Prix

The study of European Grands Prix by Lilley and DeFranco, possibly a model of good practice, looked at the economic impact of the 11 annual Grands Prix held in the European Union (this included the Monaco Grand Prix, as its economic impact was felt almost wholly within the EU). Although this was a study of a fairly uniform type of event, it offers a framework for analysing other events.

The methodology used by Lilley and DeFranco could also be adopted for other major event categories, since the purposes of the study were to:

Factbox

- European Grands Prix.
- Eleven events a year.
- Average admissions per event 150,000 people.
- More than 2 million spectators for all events.
- Around €500 million spent by spectators.
- Major local and regional economic impacts.

- Measure the size of the total attendance at each event.
- Measure the size of the non-local attendance.
- Determine how much money was spent by non-local attendance in the local area.

▶

Data was collected directly from the racetrack's own attendance information, used in conjunction with a number of interrelated surveys dealing with where the attendance came from and what was spent on tickets. In addition, phone interviews of sample groups of the local hotel, restaurant, retail and other service industries were undertaken to assess the impact of race visitors on them. This large-scale data collection effort was then analysed to produce the survey results, both in terms of the 11 individual races and the total impact.

This approach clearly highlights the potential of major studies to enlighten us about the nature of events. However, it is intensive, costly and time-consuming (the study took three years to complete). In normal circumstances our knowledge of the events business is limited by the meagre data available and by methodological limitations (professional studies being rare). In general terms there is a need for a level of uniformity and comparability in the collation of basic statistics of events, and a need for a start to be made on a framework. This is, initially, a task for academics and industry professional bodies (of which there are few). Consequently it may be some time before even the most sketchy outline of the full scale and scope of the events business is built up.

Based on this case:

Identify an event or festival in your region and investigate what information the organizers collect about the participants, visitors, income and size of the event.

1. Is this information kept internally or is it disseminated publicly, and if so, how?

2. What key elements of information might help us build up a picture of the events business and how might this data be collected?

3. What are the current problems and limitations of data collection?

4. For any given activity or group of activities, what sources of information might be available, and how might we classify such sources?

Related website for those interested in this study: www.fia.com/etudes/f1_impact/sommaire.html

Looking at the problem positively, we can focus on individual events. A practitioner, researcher or student could make a fairly accurate analysis of the size and scope of an event, given time, effort and the co-operation of the organizers. More importantly, in terms of the market demand, once this focus on an event has been made, the market for the event can be analysed too – we can say what kind of people are likely to attend, or have attended in the past; something of their likely media habits and their motives for going to the event; and what benefits they get from attending or participating. These issues do help our understanding. Richards (1992) made good use of this approach in discussing how events and festivals can be planned and marketed and how market information should be recorded. He identifies five basic areas for continuous monitoring:

- Visitor numbers
- Visitor spend
- Visitor activity and participation
- Advertising effectiveness
- Visitor satisfaction.

On this basis, any assessment of the scope and scale of the events business could achieve its ends by looking at the component parts of the business. At an industry level, a note of caution is necessary: we have financial assessments of only a few parts of the total market. The vast majority of elements of the events business have no available estimates of demand, income, expenditure or impact. Indeed, many types of events may never have realistic estimates, especially smaller voluntary events. If we, in our categorization of special events, have included

Figure 2.1

Assessing market scope and the economic impacts of events

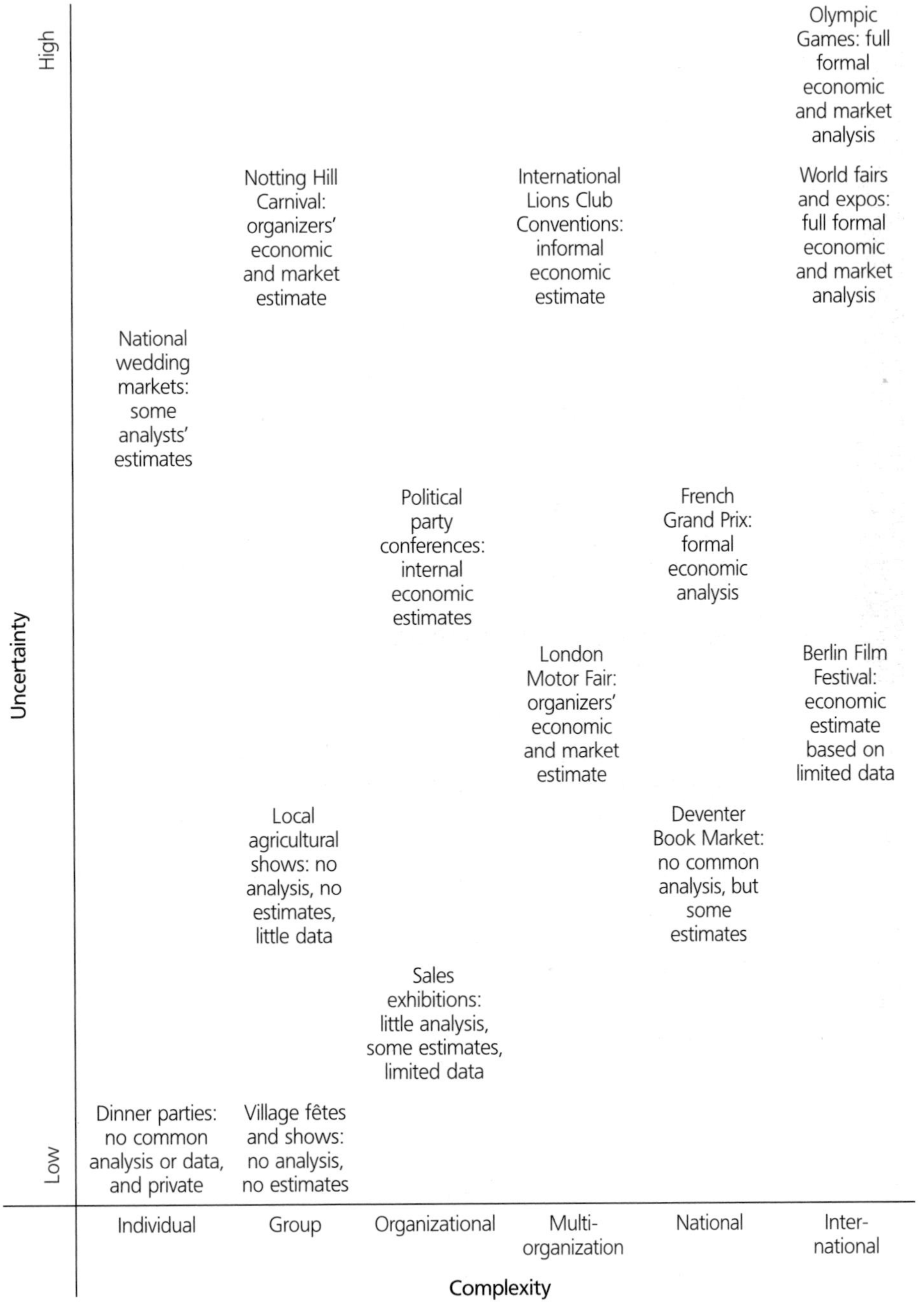

Source: authors, adapted from Slack et al., 2001.

personal events as a key category, there is no way in which the amount of money that is spent on private informal gatherings, such as birthday parties, is ever going to be much more than reasonable estimates, nor for the sake of privacy should this be otherwise. The need for usable statistical data is a key one, however. This being so, event organizers and events management companies need to record more comprehensively the key indicators and publish them in the public domain, in order to raise the profile of the industry, assist the planning of facilities, services and training and help focus marketing and promotional efforts.

For an indication of the possibilities of estimating the market for the events business, consider the adaptation of the earlier typology of events in Figure 2.1; from this, readers may wish to insert their own event, or another event known to them, to see how the typology can be applied. Rather like the first periodic table in chemistry, the typology is incomplete, but a means by which we can insert and apply other examples. The vast range of events not listed far exceeds the small number of events that are given, as examples of their class. However, there is nothing to prevent an assessment of one event being made in terms of its worth, or of its market. There are even a number of classes of events that could have their worth, market size and market components realistically estimated. This approach, of taking one element (and recognizing it as part of a much greater whole), may be a more useful means of gaining an impression of the scope of the events business.

Case Study 6 *Estimating market size and scope of events: the UK wedding market*

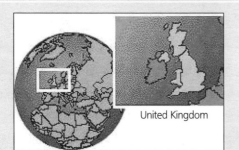

United Kingdom

Factbox

- UK Wedding Market.
- 325,000 events a year.
- Average €8,000 per event.
- Estimated €2.6 billion market.
- Largest components are catering, the reception venue and the honeymoon.

The wedding market is one of a large number of discrete sectors of the events business, and is also one of the few for which there is some assessment of its size and extent. Many component parts of the events business cannot be quantified because of their *ad hoc* nature (for example charity events, school sports days, private dinner parties, etc.), and even where there may be potential to collate data about a particular sector of the market it may be difficult to disaggregate the size and extent of the business from other activities.

Both Mintel and Keynote (market research companies) undertake reports on the UK wedding market, as well as a large range of other industry and sector reports on anything from the size of the hotel market to the size of the lingerie market. In attempting to quantify the size and extent of the UK wedding market, Mintel observes that there is considerable regional, cultural and socioeconomic variation in what a wedding costs. Therefore, even though the national average cost of getting married is thought to be of the order of €8,000, this can vary from €5,000 to €20,000, depending on

▶

location and extent of the celebrations, and comprises a long list of items: engagement and wedding rings; engagement party, stag night, hen night, evening wedding party, music, band; wedding dress, shoes, accessories and bridesmaids' outfits, groom's outfit, going away outfit; bride's bouquet, other flowers, posies and corsages; cars or carriages; registry, church or other venue fees; invitations and other stationery; photographs, video; reception venue or marquee; catering and drinks, wedding cake; first night hotel, honeymoon; various other expenses.

In terms of market demand, the UK wedding market has been gradually declining, with a fall in total number of events from about 400,000 a year in 1981, to 327,000 in 1997, although the average cost of an event has been rising. Some expenditure, such as that on wedding gowns, has doubled in the ten years between 1989 and 1999 and continues to increase, to the extent that the average cost of a gown by 2002 was thought to be almost €1,400. The decline, however, in overall demand suggests a change in the social determinants for getting married, in so far as marriage is becoming less popular, and that not only are UK couples getting married later in life, but many are happy not to be married at all. This reflects a change in the family and social structures of the UK, and in the underlying social determinant for being married. In comparison to many other types of event, the determinants for getting married are primarily social, although there are a range of secondary motives such as the ability to have family and friends attend a major life event, and the opportunity, in the case of some types of wedding, to display wealth or status. This change has been somewhat reflected in alterations to English marriage law, whereby couples can now get married in a large number of licensed venues ranging from hotels to castles, whereas prior to 1996 the ceremony itself could only be carried out in a church or registry office. This change has also had some curious side-effects on elements of the wedding market and costs, not only in the changing pattern of ceremonial venues, but also in the perception of suitable clothing for weddings, which has tended to become less formal and more flamboyant.

Based on this case:

If you have attended a wedding recently:

1. What type of event was it – formal or informal?

2. How many people attended and what was their background: were they family, friends, acquaintances, neighbours, work colleagues – who was involved and why?

3. Was there anything unusual about the event – such as special costumes or a historic venue?

4. Is the market for weddings in your location changing?

5. If so, why?

6. Are these changes due to social factors, and if so, what are they?

7. How is data collected for this type of event, and how do researchers and analysts use the information to produce reports and estimates of size and scope?

Related website for those interested in consumer research reports: http://www.keynote.co.uk

Source: Keynote, 2000.

Determinants and motivations

The events business cannot be seen in marketing terms as a homogeneous whole. The wide variety of events, the fragmentation of the business and the wide range of differences in determinants and motivations, make an assessment of the forces driving the total market for events rather a challenge. Until a more complete framework for the categorization of events exists, it is only possible to look at individual sectors or individual events to assess market demand and the determinants of demand. Historically, the demand for events can be seen to have been determined largely by social factors. These included the need for social integration, interaction between individuals and communities, mutual support, bonding and the reinforcement of social norms and structures. In addition there were issues of status, the need for public celebration and the development of religious, civic, trade and community rituals and ceremonies.

In the modern world these determinants also exist, and events continue to be driven by social and psychographic factors. Human society, whilst it may have developed technologically, still has the need for integration, interaction and community. In addition to these key social needs, events are also driven by economic, organizational, political, status, philanthropic and charitable needs. The development of events management companies and a larger and more cohesive service infrastructure for events is itself indicative of change in the forces that underpin demand for events activities. In examining the determinants for events we can conclude that the creation of events is also driven by economic factors, an increasing standard of living, changing demographics and the improving education of the population. Within the European Union a high level of industrial development and general wealth ensure relatively high levels of disposable income, which is increasingly used towards hospitality, tourism and recreational activities, such as visiting or participating in events. Much the same is true of the commercial sphere of activity (contrary to some views of the effect of technology on commercial enterprises), and the demand for commercial events, such as conferences, exhibitions, product launches and so on, continues to increase.

In attempting to analyse the key drivers of demand for the events business we can perhaps conclude that for any given event there is range of motives or determinants and these motives can be said to be both primary and secondary. For example, the primary motive for putting on a dinner party may be to entertain one's friends, but there may be secondary motives such to increase one's status by showing off a new house where the dinner party is to be held.

The primary motive for holding an athletics competition may be to provide an opportunity for local athletes to measure their abilities against others; the

Figure 2.2

A combination of motives for participating in an event, such as an opera gala

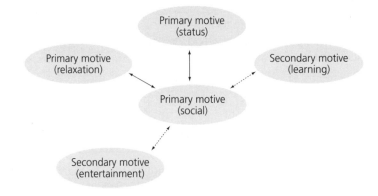

Source: adapted from Teare et al., 1994.

secondary motives may be to provide a social integrating mechanism for people with the same interests, and also, perhaps, to raise money to support an athletics club. We can see from these examples that there is unlikely to be one single motive for most types of event.

There is a tendency to see the motivation for attending and participating in special events in terms of personal motivation; indeed Getz (1997) takes this general approach in considering the satisfying of various personal needs as a mechanism for getting people to events. Motives for participation in events might be physical, social or personal, but might also be organizational, and this should not be overlooked. In terms of the primary and secondary motives described above, the satisfaction of needs can vary considerably from event to event. The primary need for attending a dinner party might well be the mainte-nance of friendships, whereas the secondary motive might be to explore the possibility of getting off with the host. The primary need for attending a motor show might have nothing to do with personal needs, but everything to do with the fact that the organization you work for has sent you for organizational reasons. In this respect, the classic and often over-quoted theories of motivation, such as those by Maslow, do not provide us with a real picture of why people go to events. Equally, in understanding why people attend or participate in events, a marketing approach that seeks only to satisfy one single need might not be enough to get people to the event, without there being some additional benefit or package of benefits.

Participation in events may be a result of a wide range of potential motives, not just social ones. Personal expectations, tourism, support for other participants in the activity, or the propensity to attend events as a form of relaxation or enter-tainment, may be reasons. In the case of those events for which an admission charge is made, the ability and willingness to pay the price is an issue, and secondary cost implications may also impact on personal events. In the case of the dinner party, whether one's friends attend is not simply a matter of the wish to interact with each other but it is also a question of their ability to do so, in terms of transport to get there, travel costs, distance, time and effort, or whether

Figure 2.3		
Possible motives for attending events	**Examples of Social Motives** Social Interaction with others Creation of community spirit Status or recognition of achievement Philanthropy or charitable contributions	**Examples of Organizational Motives** The need to make sales The need to have an organizational presence Status or recognition Sponsorship or community support
	Examples of Physiological Motives Relaxation or recognition with others Sexual enjoyment with others Exercise or physical challenge To eat, drink or be entertained	**Examples of Personal Motives** Seeking new experiences Learning and education Creativity and exploration Fulfilment of ambitions

Source: adapted from McDonnell et al., 1999.

some other personal priority (like the need to look after the kids) exists at the same time as the proposed date for the party.

This does not mean to say that knowing the motives for attendance will necessarily help organizers in trying to discover out how many people will actually attend an event. We might find that there is no useful market information whatsoever for an event we are planning, no studies, no collated data. This should not stop us searching for clues. What might be the total market size? What proportion of that total market is in our catchment area? Are there any clues from previous or similar events? Suppose our proposed event is industrial heritage based, for whom might industrial heritage be of interest? How big is the market for it and what might the catchment be? Without research data on market size, we might look initially for other evidence, such as the circulation numbers of popular magazines on the subject (these can be obtained from magazine marketing circulation information, sometimes printed in the magazine itself), although this approach is still little more than guesswork. The same might be true of small events. Our 'first ever' village fête might only have a total potential market of the village population, say a village of 500 people, and not all of these will be there. In short, attendance estimates are just that – estimates. However, the process can, and should, be helped by a little market research: take a sample of the target market and ask them if they are going to attend, but beware – there is a difference between interest and action!

Case Study 7 *Motives for attending events: the Berlin and other European film festivals*

Berlin, Germany

Factbox

- Berlin Film Festival.
- Sells 35,000 tickets for a 12-day event.
- Screens 240 films.
- Attracts major film stars.
- Attended by 12,000 journalists and film-makers.
- Helps to promote Berlin as an international city.

The 50th Berlin Film Festival took place between 9 and 20 February 2000 in a number of venues and cinemas throughout Berlin, many of which, including the Berlinale Palast, the Cinemax and the Sony complex, were newly opened, as part of the large-scale redevelopment of the city that took place during the 1990s, especially around the Potsdamer Platz, where much of the festival activity goes on. The festival is a major international cultural event for Berlin and attracts not only the moviegoing public, but also large numbers of celebrities and journalists.

A number of major film festivals have developed over the past 80 years in Europe. 1932 saw the first Esposizione d'Arte Cinematografica in Venice. Held on the terrace of the Hotel Excelsior alongside the Venice 18th International Art Exhibition, as a way of boosting tourism, it attracted some 25,000 people. Later, in 1935, it became an annual event. In the 1930s, Italy and Germany were linked in a political axis and the decision to split the Venice Golden Lion film

▶

prize for 1939, between these two countries caused anger in France – which felt that its own film, *La Grande Illusion*, had lost out to political intrigue. Later that year, France responded by establishing the Festival International du Film in Cannes, although politics made a more dramatic intervention when the newcomer lasted just one day – the day of the outbreak of World War Two.

In 1946, the Association Française d'Action Artistique organized the first full Cannes Film Festival. Then, the festival was a tourist and social event, focused on the few hundred participants who attend a series of parties at hotels along the Croisette and in nearby villas, but as film festivals matured, the commercial aspects began to become more explicit. In 1960, the informal Cannes Film Market, which had grown up alongside the Cannes Film Festival, became an official event; with ten participants (film producers, buyers, etc.) and one screen. By 2002 this part of the event alone attracted 7,368 participants, across 29 cinemas.

The Berlin International Film Festival (the Berlinale) was established in 1951, at the Titania-Palast cinema, as part of an initiative to recapture the city's former cultural significance. By 1955, the International Association of Producers, which formally recognizes film festivals, had officially elevated the Berlinale to a status paralleling that of the festivals in Cannes and Venice. In 1978, the Berlinale moved from summer to winter, enabling the expansion of its Film Fair, which became the European Film Market. In 1970 at the Berlinale, a screening of the film *O.K.* (dealing with a war in Vietnam) caused the jury's resignation and the competition to be halted, prompting the establishment of the International Forum of New Cinema. In 1977, the Berlinale transferred film history retrospectives to the Deutsche Kinemathek and inaugurated the Informationsschau section; the latter evolved into the Panorama. The following year, organizers add the Kinderfilmfest of children's cinema and in 2002, the Perspektive Deutsches Kino section. The 50th Berlinale attracted 390,000 professional and non-professional participants and 3,420 media representatives, from 70 countries, reported the event.

Festivals had to find ways to differentiate themselves, or to respond to changes in festivalgoer expectations. So, in 1947, the International Festival of Documentary Films was held at the Playhouse Cinema, Edinburgh, and in its over 50 years existence it has evolved into the Edinburgh International Film Festival. In 1976, the first Festival Du Cinema Americain was held in Deauville, Normandy, developing into a competition-based film festival. The Berlin Festival is a means of launching new films, made not only in Europe but also abroad, including the USA. The event is competitive in so far as a jury awards a range of prizes for film-making activities, which are known as Golden Bears (the bear is the symbol and mascot of Berlin). During the 12 days of the year 2000 festival, some 240 films were shown, not only feature films, but also documentaries and shorts. They included some well-known international films and many lesser known ones. Some attracted major audiences not only for the film itself, but also to see some of the stars who attend the festival, particularly where the launch of a new film is taking place. These major films and the presence of their stars can cause frantic scenes, with the presence of international celebrities attracting the intense attention of fans and journalists.

The Festival not only deals with the mainstream of film-making; there are fringe activities including the 'Panorama' section, which gives advance previews of the next season's films; the Kinderfilmfest (children's film festival); the International Forum of Young Cinema and, separately, the European Film Market, for producers, distributors and other film professionals. Such a major event also attracts political interest, including, in 2000, a visit by the German Chancellor Gerhardt Schroeder, who mingled with the stars at the awards ceremony.

◄

Based on this case:

What kind of people would visit the film festival? Hughes (2000) regards motivations for attending the arts as wide ranging.

1. If visitors were classified into various categories of, say, film-goers; film-makers; the local public; film stars; film stars' fans; politicians, etc., what would be their respective motives for going to the festival, both in terms of their primary and secondary motives?

2. How should organizers seek to address the motivations of each category of visitor?

3. Identify a film festival in your region – how many people go to it?
4. What might be the total market size?
5. How does the distinction between the core festival, 'official' peripheral sections and non-official activities impact on the festival itself?
6. What bearing might the festival's event dates and location have on your answers?

For those interested in the Berlin and European Film Festivals: www.filmfestivals.com

Source: Downey M. and Schutze S. 2000. Revised from published sources 2004.

The range of motives can also impact on the attendance for those types of events, such as large-scale festivals, where more than one activity is taking place. In this respect it is highly likely that more than one market segment will be present with more than one motive for being there, an issue that Hall (1997) addressed in his generic product/market model, adapted in Figure 2.4.

Figure 2.4

Event component mix

THE EVENT 'UMBRELLA'

Example: The North Sea Jazz Festival

Event emphasis

The core event | The fringe event

Example: Music Festival | Free ancillary activities

Specialization within the market for the event

Core events activities | Fringe events activities

Example: Bands Solos Big Masterclass Concerts | Bands Kids Open Air Sales

Individual components or specialized activities at the event

Example: 70 bands 50 soloists etc. | 30 bands 1 clown 48 sales stalls etc.

Individual target market groups attending an element of the event

❶ ❷ ❸ ❹ ❺ ❻ | ❷ ❹ ❺ ❼

Example: Various age/interest (market) groups | Different groups attend fringe

Source: adapted from Hall., 1997.

In the case of the model, it has been supposed that the event is composed of a number of activities, some of which are core activities and some of which might have 'grown up around it'. This is often true of many kinds of events: conferences, for example, may have associated exhibitions; carnivals may be composed of a large number of different activities linked by the carnival theme (see also case study 30, the Mainz Carnival). Although an event may be a single activity (such as an anniversary dinner) with one homogeneous group of people attending (one market segment), certain types of events comprise a range of activities, and these are attended by different groups or segments, possibly with different motives for being there.

Case Study 8 *The event 'Umbrella': North Sea Jazz Festival: the Hague*

The Hague,
Netherlands

Factbox

- North Sea Jazz Festival.
- Total participants and visitors: 150,000.
- Number of musicians: 1,200.
- Three-day festival in July.
- No formal economic analysis found.
- Predominant market: jazz fans age 35–55.

There are a very large number of cultural and arts festivals held every year throughout Europe, ranging from folk festivals to poetry festivals, from highland dancing to classical music. Jazz is a major music medium, and there are perhaps some 300 major and minor jazz festivals and events across Europe each year. These are held in all kinds of places, from major cities to small villages, and attract both Jazz fans and the general public. There are well known jazz festivals in Glasgow, Scotland; Cork, Ireland; San Sebastian, Spain; Aanekoski, Finland, to name only a few. One of the major European jazz festivals, however, is that held at the Hague in the Netherlands: the North Sea Jazz Festival.

The Festival attracts, directly, some 70,000 people. The three-day event is held in July at several venues in the Hague including the Congress Centre. The programme of jazz bands, groups and musicians is one of the major cultural events in the European calendar, and includes not only the main festival programme itself but also activities for children, supporting sales activities and exhibitions and an additional free programme for the public in the city centre, called Jazz Heats the Hague (www.northseajazz.nl). This part of the festival is held in the evenings from 7.00 pm until midnight, in the form of summer open-air concerts in the city. This open-air programme attracts a further 75,000 people, and adds much to the general atmosphere of celebration and relaxation. It also serves to bring jazz to a wider audience than jazz fans.

In total, the festival, in its 27th year in 2002, reached almost 150,000 and was declared the 'Best Jazz Festival of Europe' by *Jazz Times* magazine. The programme, over its three days of events, concerts and open-air entertainment, is provided by almost 1,200 musicians. The target market for the event comprises people from all age groups, with the key age groups of jazz fans being 35 and 55, but it also includes families, tourists, and people living in the Hague itself, from office workers to government ministers. Many of the visitors stay in the city's hotels and guest houses, for which this is a peak period.

◀

Based on this case:

1. What might be the primary and secondary motives for a jazz fan attending this event or a family attending one of the summer evening open-air concerts?
2. What are the marketing benefits, to the main festival at the Congress Centre, of having three days of free evening open-air concerts in the city, for the public?
3. Do these extra events, for example, help create demand for the main event?
4. What kinds of businesses in and around the Hague benefit from the festival?

Related website for those interested in the North Sea Jazz Festival: www.northseajazz.nl

The structure of demand for events

In general, for the events organizer, an interest in the potential sources of demand is key to providing a successful event, because without this knowledge it will be impossible to provide what the target market expects (Swarbrooke, 2002). Indeed, the target market for the event, even if properly promoted, might or might not materialize. This is because, for a number of events, we are doing something new, and therefore the estimate of the potential market is just that – an estimate. On the other hand, there are events where the market is known and fixed, personal events being one example. Equally, there are events that, whilst retaining their uniqueness, recur at intervals, such as annually or biannually, and in this case the market is relatively well known from previous experience. If 5,000 people came to a town's firework fiesta last year, and have done so for the past five years, then, assuming all other factors remain more or less the same, there can be a reasonable degree of certainty that 5,000 people will come this year. Here, though, is a limitation to the marketing theory that people will come and buy your product or attend your special event provided you have done everything right – it might, for instance, rain on your firework fiesta. To take up a point made in chapter 1, events are perishable. A one-day event might well suffer from an unexpected external factor, the weather (as with the British Grand Prix at Silverstone in 2000, when rain made access by car to the car parks, which had become muddy fields, impossible; since Silverstone had no public transport facilities worth mentioning, the event attendance was very nearly ruined), the traffic or a clash with another event; all factors beyond the control of the organizers.

In consequence, there may be all kinds of reasons why an event might not attract the numbers its organizers expect. People might not wish to come to the event at

Figure 2.5
Demand potentials

Current demand – that which our event satisfies at the moment

Future demand – that which our event could satisfy over a normal growth period

Latent demand – that which is sleeping until you provide an event for it

Suppressed demand – that which exists for our event, but cannot get to it due to being suppressed by price, time, availability, lack of disposable income or other reasons

all. On the other hand, the assessment of the market for an event could be based simply on known 'current' demand. This kind of demand may only be part of the event's potential. In terms of new events we may be tapping demand that has been latent or suppressed in some way. There are, in the sense of demand potentials, four kinds of demand: current, future, latent, suppressed (see Figure 2.5).

Suppose a town has a range of cultural and sporting events in its calendar. These events take place every year and will often attract different target market groups: those who attend the regional soccer tournament might not be the same people as those who attend the annual early music festival. The market for events is therefore diverse and changing. Some events will also be more popular than others, some will be new that year, some may not, for a range of reasons (from costs to popularity, or shortage of volunteer expertise), run again next year. So the issue about running an event is not simply about the current market, it is also about whether the expertise, inclination, funding and support exists for an event to be planned and run. In the case of the North Sea Jazz Festival, the event began in 1975 with a small number of visitors, a few venues and fewer than 300 musicians. The level of demand was relatively small, but in each successive year the event has grown, and the level of demand to visit and participate in the event (150,000 visitors and 1,200 musicians) could not have been foreseen 25 years ago. At that time, demand for a jazz festival in this location was latent. Rather like building Eurotunnel between Britain and France, the effect was to create a new market and then expand on it. Equally, it is perfectly possible that there might be further potential and unexploited demand for the jazz festival, which is not being tapped for a variety of reasons. This is true of many types of event.

Summary

In examining the scope and determinants of demand for events, we have concluded that due to the unusual and fragmentary nature of the events 'industry' (which includes anything from private dinner parties to the Olympic Games), an overall assessment of the market size of the business is a difficult process. It is preferable to look at individual events, or groups of the same kinds of events, to assess their scope, impacts and extent; and although it is possible to make some estimates for certain sectors of the events business, this is not sufficient to provide a picture of the whole. People attend special events for a whole range of reasons; these may be social, organizational, physical or personal. In general, however, events are largely social occasions, and it is in this light that they should be seen.

References

Aas, N.K. (1998) 'Flickering Shadow: The European Film Festival Phenomenon', Strasbourg, European Audiovisual Observatory, http://www.obs.coe.int/online.publication/expert/00001262.htm (5 January 2004).

Downey, M. and Schutze, S. (2000) 'The Future is now', Paris, Filmfestivals, http://www.filmfestivals.com/berlin_2000/news/news_future.htm (5 January 2004).

Getz, D. (1997) *Event Management and Event Tourism*, New York, Van Nostrand Reinhold, pp.1–23.

Hall, C.M. (1997) *Hallmark Tourist Events: Impacts, Management and Planning*, London, Belhaven, pp.137–48.

Hughes, H. (2000) *Arts, Entertainment and Tourism,* Oxford, Butterworth Heinemann, pp.17–19.

Lickorish, L.J. and Jenkins, C.L. (1997) *An Introduction to Tourism,* Oxford, Butterworth Heinemann, pp.134–68.

Lilley, W. and DeFranco, G. (1999) *The Economic Impacts of European Grands Prix*, Brussels, EU Sports Workshop, http://www.fia.com/etudes/f1_impact/sommaire.html (25 June 2000).

Keynote (2000) *Bridalwear: Market Report,* Hampton, Keynote Ltd, http://www.keynote.co.uk/kn2k1/GlobalFrame.htm (15 November 2002).

McDonnell, I., Bowdin G., Allen, J. and O'Toole, W. (1999) *Festival and Special Event Management,* Brisbane, Jacaranda Wiley, p.115.

Mintel (1997) *Leisure Intelligence Report: Wedding Venues,* London, Mintel Marketing Intelligence, pp.8–11.

Richards, B. (1992) *How to Market Tourist Attractions, Festivals and Special Events*, Harlow, Longman, pp.26–32.

Slack, N., Harrison, A., Harland, C. and Chambers, S. (2001) *Operations Management,* London, Pitman, 3rd edn, pp.585–95.

Swarbrooke, J. (2002) *The Development and Management of Visitor Attractions*, Oxford, Butterworth Heinemann, pp.58–84.

Teare, R., Mazanec, J.A. et al. (1994) *Marketing in Hospitality and Tourism,* London, Cassell, pp.44–63.

3 The events business: supply and suppliers

Aims

- To consider the fragmentary nature of the events business.

- To provide an overview of events services.

- To examine the role of public sector, private sector and voluntary bodies.

Introduction

The reader will have observed that we have, so far, tended not to refer to the events business as 'an industry'. This is mainly because of the fragmented nature of the activities that make up the huge breadth and range of this business. There is comparatively little explicit structure to it, unlike many industries which perceive themselves as a cohesive whole, for example, banking or retail. There is no one single major supply element to events, although there are some representative bodies, and some understanding that events are a major economic activity, however difficult to quantify.

In contrast to many industries, the events business is not wholly driven by the need to make money. Indeed, the business has a very large element of personal, voluntary, charitable and philanthropic activity. The broad range of events allows all kinds of organizations and individuals to participate in an enjoyable way for the mutual benefit of all concerned. The social benefits of this approach are very considerable, not only in terms of social integration and the contribution that people can make to their community, but also in terms of friendship and good neighbourliness.

This is not to say that a large commercial sector does not exist; it has developed rapidly during the last 15 years and will continue to do so. The market for events has expanded to the point where the need for a much better professional infrastructure is evident. The increasing number of events management companies and professional events organizers is an indication of this demand. Events management did not, however, suddenly appear out of nowhere. These businesses have long existed as part of the tourism and hospitality industries, but events management as a stand-alone segment is now commonplace.

The structure of events services: public sector

As the events business has developed, the levels of specialization and technical requirements have increased, due to greater expectations on the part of organizers and participants, and this has led to a rapid development in event-related services and support organizations. While it is still the case that a small personal event, such as an anniversary, may be a comparatively simple affair, with little need of organizational or technical support, larger activities, VIP events, launches and corporate hospitality activities often require a great deal of support from conception onwards (Hall, 1997). This support may be via commercial organizations (the private sector) or via the public sector.

The extent of these support services may be rather startling to the uninitiated, but think of all the activities that are involved in a carnival, and the potential for complexity in the support of the larger events business may become more evident. In fact, many of the support activities that we think of as being 'the events business' are really only the private sector element; the public sector tends to be insufficiently considered, but is equally important.

A developing public sector infrastructure exists, which takes in:

- European Union and national government departments responsible for tourism (or sport, depending on the type of event): for example, the Tourism Division of the UK Department of Culture, Media and Sport; the Secretaria de Estado de commercio, turismo y de la pyme (the Spanish Government Department of Commerce, Tourism and Small Business) and similar government departments throughout Europe.

- National (and regional) tourist organizations (NTOs) responsible for developing and marketing tourism activities: for example, the British Tourist

Figure 3.1	
Infrastructure of the events business	

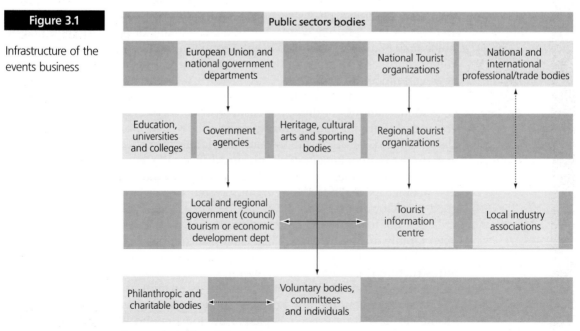

Source: adapted from Tribe, 1999.

Authority (BTA); the Netherlands Board of Tourism (NBT) and similar national authorities, who collate information on tourist-related events and promote and support some of them.

- National trade associations and industry professional bodies: for example, the UK Association of Events Managers, the European Federation of Conference Towns, the International Festivals and Events Association (Europe).
- Regional or local tourist offices and visitor and convention Bureaus. For example, the Birmingham Visitor and Convention Bureau, the Scottish Tourist Board, or the Dutch VVV (Vereniging voor Vreemdelingenverkeer), tourist information offices in towns and cities.
- Educational institutions, including colleges and universities teaching events management.

In many cases, especially with professional bodies, and with events education, these are at a fairly early stage of development, largely because of the current development stage of the events business. However, as the business matures, it is likely that public sector organizations will begin to play a greater role (especially where there is a public agenda for social inclusion or tourism development activities), and clearly, at the moment, some types of organizations are better developed in some countries than others. Bowdin et al. (2001) notes that the range of associations within the events business is actually quite large, but rather unconsolidated in comparison to other industries.

Case Study 9 *Example of public sector organizations: International Festivals and Events Association (IFEA)*

Leidschendam,
Netherlands

Factbox

- International Festival and Events Association
- A trade body.
- Promotes co-operation between event producers and suppliers, and especially sponsors.
- Works with other public sector bodies e.g. governments and other associations.
- Provides an educational and research programme.

There are a large number of public sector organizations involved in events management and the related activities of tourism and leisure. These range from national government departments covering tourism, to small voluntary committees set up to provide a particular event. The International Festivals and Events Association is a well-established trade body whose primary objective is to promote co-operation between event producers and suppliers. It particularly promotes communication between managers, organizers and event producers on the one hand and sponsors and fund-raisers on the other.

The Association has been in existence since 1992 and is based at the Netherlands Board of Tourism at Leidschendam. It has sought to promote its services between organizers and producers, sponsors and fund-raisers, and in this respect provides extensive publicity as part of the promotional effort, including a quarterly magazine, *Festivals Europe*, which has a readership of approximately 10,000 worldwide. IFEA is essentially a European-based association with almost 2,500 members, many of whom organize and produce popular and well-known festivals throughout Europe, such as Aarhus Festuge, Edinburgh International Festival, Cheltenham Arts Festival, Limerick Food Festival, Rotterdam Festival and the Haydn Festival at Eisenstadt.

IFEA is also involved in education and research, and provides a degree-level programme in conjunction with Purdue University to enable students to become Certified Festival Executives (CFE). In addition IFEA co-operates with the Centre for Tourism at Sheffield Hallam University to provide research support for the activities of the Association. In this respect, although IFEA is in origin a trade promotional body and a lobbying group, it is moving towards the activities of a professional body with its educational and research aspirations.

IFEA objectives are to promote co-operation between managers, organizers, producers, public relations managers, fund-raisers and sponsors of festivals and events. It also provides publicity for members' festivals and exchanges information and advice to members (as such, it acts as a distribution channel). The IFEA is run by a secretariat and an executive board made up of nine members. In addition, it also provides working groups on membership development and research.

Based on this case:

Identify a number of public sector bodies involved in events management.

1. What do they do, and why?
2. Which government departments might have an interest in events, and why?
3. Compared to other industries, why are professional associations relatively weak and underdeveloped in the events business, and how might those that exist strengthen their development?

Related website for those interested in the IFEA: www.ifeaeurope.com

Source: Anton Shone, with thanks to IFEA.

In addition to public sector organizations (and the private or commercial sector), it must not be overlooked that many events are organized by voluntary bodies, such as committees, or individuals (either amateur or professional events organizers). Voluntary bodies can organize a whole event based on voluntary help, or a mixture of voluntary help, support from local authorities and other organizations, or with partial use of commercial organizations in some roles. Essentially, personal events such as dinner parties follow this 'voluntary' framework – you do it yourself or receive help from friends and family to do it and perhaps you buy in food from a caterer. The other type of organization is the voluntary organization supported by the public sector, as noted earlier – a town carnival might be organized by a voluntary committee, but it also might be helped by the local council's events or tourism department (or a combination of these). Special events organizations should not, then, be seen simply as the province of profit-making companies or individuals – these are only part of the whole.

The structure of events services: private sector

The events business is not solely concerned with the provision of activities, entertainment, refreshment and equipment; it encompasses a wide range of interlinked activities. Although the most basic type of event may require only those things, the larger and more elaborate an event becomes, the greater the need for increased technical and logistical support of one kind or another. With an increasing complexity of needs and demands, the standard of organization required for large-scale events is very high and a whole series of specialist activities has grown up to service these needs. Although many of the organizations in production, distribution, venue and ancillary services might be thought of as private sector, this is not entirely the case, as the quadrant diagram (Figure 3.2) shows.

These organizations, typically, either package services and provide the whole thing or provide one element of the service needed by an event organizer or organizing committee, who may wish to do the rest for themselves. The type of organizations capable of providing complete packages for events are normally:

- Event management companies
- Production companies
- Event catering companies
- Party planners and professional events organizers
- Exhibition and theatrical contractors
- Technical service and multimedia companies.

A wide range of companies provide other services which can be hired in, contracted or purchased (depending on the service). These cover directly related services such as the provision of hospitality, or indirect services that exist not only to provide something for the events business, but also perform to a function for the local community. For example, transport and guiding services, whose role is to get participants and audiences from the point of arrival to, and sometimes around, a venue; Then there are various other services such as retailing, medical support, administration, secretarial and travel (Kotas and Jayawardena, 1994). It can be seen

Figure 3.2	
Events organizations (private sector and others)	

Production	Distribution
Event management companies Event catering companies Party planners Production companies Exhibition and theatrical contractors & designers Technical services Professional events organizers Multimedia support companies Voluntary bodies, committees and individuals Education and training	Individual events and venues Event and conference agencies Trade media Hotel booking agencies Incentive travel agencies Visitor and convention bureau Exhibition organizers Ticketing agencies Trade exhibitions National and local tourist bodies
Venues	**Ancillary Services**
Event room / hall / grounds hire Catering and kitchen facilities Accommodation Food and drink suppliers Business support services Medical and créche services Information and customer services Technical support Waste disposal and grounds clearance Toilets, washrooms and public facilities Parking Security Set designers	Accommodation providers Photographers and video makers Transport and guiding services, ground handlers Transition services Music and entertainment providers Travel companies Costume hire services Marquee hire services Printers Floral contractors Database support services Fireworks display operators Professional and trade bodies National and local government services

from this approach that a matrix of distribution activities already exists in the events business. There is a range of distribution channels, like those of most industries. For example, when buying a holiday, the purchaser may go to a travel agent, who might provide a whole package holiday (in the same way that an event management company can provide a whole event package). Alternatively, the purchaser might put together a holiday from various component parts, such as a flight and a hotel, having chosen the destinations using information from a tourist office (equally, a client wanting an event could do it themselves by assembling the various parts, a venue, a caterer, an entertainer, and so on). The distribution channels are therefore the mechanism by which venues, markets and events activities are put together. The choice of channel depends on the experiences and expectations of the buyer, and by the influences, such as through marketing, that the various companies or other sellers can exert.

The use of these various organizations is a matter not only of budget, but also of the experience (or lack of it) on the part of buyers, of the standard to be achieved at a given event, of the time available to make arrangements and of the requirements of the organization making the booking and completing the planning process. Needs, and therefore the approach, vary.

Companies and their roles

Event Management Companies

Event Management Companies (EMCs) are a quite recent innovation (but there are historical precedents) and have often grown out of related service or hospitality providers, which have specialized in providing of the complete event.

Figure 3.3

Matrix of sample distribution channels and activities

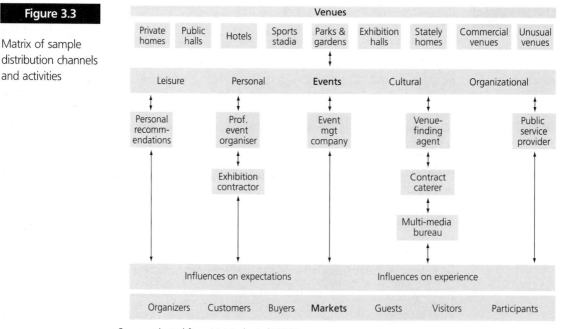

Source: adapted from McIntosh et al., 2000.

Events, as we have noted, may range from product launches and dinner dances to themed gala evenings or charity sports competitions. EMCs tend to be involved where the organizers have a requirement for major or VIP events, or corporate hospitality or where, for example, a product launch demands specialist design and innovation. The benefit of having an EMC is the range of expertise, ideas and experience they can draw on. Taking the case of a gala evening, such as a themed dinner, the events management company will be capable of providing the expertise for almost any theme the organizer may choose. This will include the planning, menu and theme design, in terms of identifying a suitable menu to go with the theme, as well as full catering support in food production and service at the event. Development of the theme would include specialist sets, props and, if necessary, costumes for participants or guests, and all the range of support requirements from special effects and lighting, to music (live or recorded) and entertainment.

The creation of special events of this type is highly complex and, above all, requires extremely careful planning and costing. The choice of the theme itself should be a matter of careful discussion between the event management company and the buyer or client. A great deal depends on the objectives, the venue, the nature of the facilities (such as kitchens and even wash-up areas), the size of the venue, its design features, and elements such as the availability of licensing, parking, loading, power and access. However, all these things are within the expertise of an EMC to arrange and sort out, so that a client does not have to do the hard work of organizing an event themselves, but simply employs the EMC, gives them a brief and lets them get on with it.

Production Companies

Organizers are often confronted by unique problems when seeking to create an event of a professional standard. This is particularly the case for high profile events. The ability to develop such events may be beyond the knowledge of the average organizer, delegated to do the job within a committee or other organization. Nevertheless, high profile events, VIP ceremonies, roadshows, major competitions or product launches all require specialist technical facilities and knowledge. Increasingly, events of this kind are put into the hands of production companies. These companies are able to package together the wide range of technical support that high profile activities often require. This technical support might range from set design to the training of presenters.

A production company will probably be able to undertake most, or all, of the following activities: 1) Project management, in the case of large-scale projects where the whole event is delegated by the organizer to the production company as a contractor (especially those events that might also involve building or construction, either of the permanent or temporary kind); 2) Design, including set and backdrop design, staging, lighting and all the range of audio-visual support needed for high quality presentations; 3) Venue management, where an organization may, for example, wish to take over a unique venue, such as a castle or stately home, to use for its event and which therefore requires expertise to be brought in that the venue itself might not normally possess (outsourcing); 4) Participant or audience handling, which ranges from the simplest issues of ticketing and security to the full provision of VIP seat booking or allocation of accommodation or pavilion space; 5) Technical support, ranging from simple provision or hiring in of equipment to the full preparation of computer graphics, slide or video production and related facilities; 6) Training of presenters and speakers, often including not only the basic training but also scriptwriting and video production.

Naturally, the packaging of the whole production process does not come cheaply, but production companies have a level of expertise that most organizers simply do not possess, so that whilst it might be possible for a organizer to put together a highly complex upmarket event, the organizer would have to be both well trained and extremely experienced to do so. Given that few organizations, especially volunteer ones, possess experienced organizers, it is often necessary to bring in production companies for high profile events.

Case Study 10 *Example of private sector organizations: the Inntel Agency*

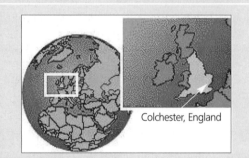

Colchester, England

Factbox

- Inntel, Colchester, Essex, England.
- Specialist conference, hotel and events agency.
- 64 staff in four key operating departments.
- Family-run business established in 1984.
- Turnover in excess of €32 million.
- One of the UK's largest agencies of its type.

There are a large number of private sector organizations (companies, etc.) involved in commercial activities in the events management business. Some of them have a single line of activity, some are multi-activity. Inntel is a well-established company providing various linked services in conferencing and event management, based in Colchester in the south-east of England. Established in 1984, it now employs some 64 staff who cover a number of key departments.

Inntel began life as a hotel booking agency, dealing with hotel reservations for companies and other organizations within the UK. It has gradually expanded to take in conference activities, especially conference venue-finding, and finally events management activities. It therefore maintains a multi-role portfolio of business and has a national profile as an agency in this field. Inntel consists of four primary operating departments:

Conference placement

This is the main element of Inntel's conference business. Clients who are looking for a suitable venue for their event can do so themselves, which can be time consuming, or they can place their enquiry with an agency such as Inntel, which will lessen their effort and possibly benefit them by obtaining more competitive rates for venue. The agency will take details of the prospective requirements of the client and will then identify a number of suitable venues to enable the client to choose from. This process may involve further assistance by the agency such as the provision of brochures or the organization of site visits. The agency will then receive a commission from the selected venue. The benefits to the hotel of agency business is that of adding a distribution channel, particularly one targeted at corporate or group business. The benefits to

▶

the client are ease of finding suitable venues, especially those that the agency would regard as reliable.

Hotel reservations

Much the same process is involved for hotel reservations as for conference placement (Horner, 1995). Enquiries come into the agency from individuals or organizations (which may or may not be conference related) and the agency identifies suitable accommodation; and an element of skill is needed in matching the client with a choice of suitable venues. Because of the large amount of business that Inntel handles, it is capable of obtaining discounted rates from accommodation providers such as the major hotel companies, which act as an incentive for clients to use the agency. In a similar way to the conference placement activity, agencies receive commission from the hotel where the booking has been made.

Event management

Increasingly, as organizations have begun to concentrate on their core activities, they no longer have the staff to do their own event organizing and have therefore needed an event organizer or agency. The task of putting together often complex conference and event activities is taken on by the agency, which has the necessary expertise and time to achieve a better result. Sometimes this can be via a professional event organizer, or often the agency can provide the total package or venue-finding and event organization. This role is undertaken by Inntel through its Event Management Division, which covers not only the prior arrangements and general at-conference organization, but also deals with the in-event activities (such as registration) and post-event activities (such as feedback and reporting).

Contract management

This is probably the least understood role of agencies. We have just noted that many organizations simply do not have the staff, or inclination, to become involved in venue-finding or event organization, (it could be inferred that this simply means small organizations, but often it is quite the opposite). A number of extremely large public companies and national organizations prefer to contract out their conference activities to an agency. This enables organizations to concentrate on their own main activity, but also to draw on the agency's expertise whenever conferences or events are required. Where this is the case, a contract is developed between the organization and the agency. Once set up, the agency will become a 'nominated supplier' for that organization. It is incorrect to believe this implies that all events for the contracted organization go through the agency directly. Very few contract arrangements mean the agency becomes a 'mandatory' supplier; most are non-mandatory and the agency may have to physically make its presence felt in various divisions of a company to get the business. This is often done by site visits, familiarization presentations, or, for example, setting up the agency's stand in the foyer of the contracting organization's office or offices. Basically, to get the business, the agency has to go to the company and sell itself to individuals in the company who buy conferences and events.

Based on this case:

1. What are the advantages and disadvantages of an events organizer using an agency?

2. As an event organizer, what choices do you have to organize your event – who else could you go to besides either doing it yourself or getting an agency to do it?

3. Do agencies make their turnover just in commission from venues, or do they obtain it in fees and other revenues from their professional activities?

Related website for those interested in Inntel: www.inntel.co.uk

Source: Anton Shone, with grateful thanks to James O'Neill of Inntel.

Events Catering Companies

The most important input to the events business is probably the need for catering. This covers all aspects of refreshment for participants, audiences, crew and staff. Catering can be provided in three main ways: It is undertaken either in-house (i.e. by an organizer or venue), or by contractors permanently employed at the venue, or, alternatively, on an *ad hoc* basis at the venue. A venue might not be able to provide specialist catering for an event. For example, for a church fair, the church hall might have a kitchen but no caterer to run it. A larger venue may be needed nearby, or a marquee may have to be erected. For these situations the catering arrangements will have to be determined well in advance.

Catering operators range in size and in the types of service they provide. EMCs were earlier mentioned as sometimes having developed from catering operators. The larger contract catering companies also run the in-house services of a number of venues and *ad hoc* provision for conferences, exhibition and other events including corporate hospitality. Independent caterers also have a share of the *ad hoc* conference business. In addition, in the price-restricted part of the market, such as for charitable events, there are small independent caterers who provide basic, but sound, catering in the form of buffets. This type of catering for small events may be unserviced, that is to say the food/drink is delivered with disposable plates, etc., and the organizer simply lays it out for participants or guests to eat. Bakeries often provide this kind of unserviced buffet, simply delivered and paid for on the spot and perfectly adequate for the job. A similar service is sometimes provided by supermarket companies.

Many major hospitality or catering companies have divisions dealing with events catering, sometimes – perhaps wrongly – known as 'Outside Catering'. Events catering companies range in size from small family businesses, which look after things such as local weddings or village fêtes, up to major international caterers which hold contracts for significant large-scale events such as international air shows and sports tournaments, major 'society' weddings, VIP dinners, corporate hospitality and so on. Consider the complexity and size of the catering provision for the Wimbledon Lawn Tennis Tournament, the Paris Air Show or the Olympics, and it can be seen that this is a very large business indeed.

An organizer may choose any one of the above 'packaging' organizations depending on the requirements of each particular event: what are the event's objectives? Who are the participants? How large will the event be? How complicated will the catering provision need to be? In some cases, it might even be conceivable that all three types of company are needed together, but this is not very common.

Party Planners and Professional Events Organizers

Although major companies, like those above, are increasingly common in the events business, so too are a wide range of smaller organizations and individuals willing to provide events-related services. The most common of these are probably party planners and professional events organizers. The first tend to offer a range of services particularly for the personal events market, the second, for the corporate market. This would include the organization of parties, celebrations, weddings, anniversaries and many of similar events. While many people are happy to organize their own events on this small and more intimate scale, not all have the time or wish to expend the effort on doing so, and are happier to pay a professional to come along and deal with all the nitty-gritty detail of planning, organizing, operating and managing an event so that everything goes smoothly. Professional party planners or event organizers are obviously more used to doing this than is the average person, who might only have to put on a biggish event occasionally, and might otherwise have to rely on friends and family to help.

Case Study 11 *Events management as a career: Giuseppe Fontebasso*

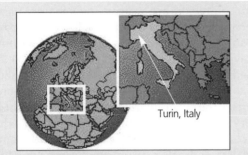

Turin, Italy

Factbox

- Giuseppe Fontebasso.
- Lives and works in Turin, Italy.
- Has a degree in hotel management.
- First major event was the Turin Motor Show.
- Age 35.
- Runs events activities with his partner.

Events management has only comparatively recently been seen as a potential career. Many of the people involved in events management have developed their jobs through related activities such as corporate hospitality and entertainment, travel agency and tour operation, theatre and media. There are a large number of quite small event management operators, individuals and partners. However, a number of major companies have taken an increasing interest in events management, especially those histori-cally involved in the activity, or through acquisition of similar companies. Outdoor catering companies are one example, where there has always been a major market for outdoor catering, for instance at sporting events and competitions; these

companies have then expanded into the events market as it has matured.

Giuseppe Fontebasso's career in events man-agement developed from his parents' restaurant business in Turin, where he grew up. He took a degree in hotel management in Switzerland, and helped cover his fees by working in vacations in the family business and also in related banqueting and corporate hospitality activities. On graduating, his first major events experience was at the Turin Motor Show, an important annual event for motor manufacturers and dealers.

Giuseppe also spent a year in the UK with a contract catering company, Ring and Brymer. During this time he participated in a number of large-scale events, such the Farnborough Air Show, Wimbledon Tennis Championship, and various golf events at St Andrews, Turnberry and Wentworth, through which he was able to develop his management and interpersonal skills, and increase his knowledge of events planning and production techniques. The year also included a range of private functions and smaller events, providing parties and corporate hospitality all over the UK. Following this experi-ence and using his existing qualifications and knowledge of the hospitality industry, Giuseppe then returned to Italy to set up his own small events management company with his partner.

Based on this case:

Using the national and trade press, identify a range of possible jobs which might lead to a career in events management.

▶

1. Which are the main companies in your area involved in this activity?

2. What qualifications, skills and experience might you need?

3. What might be the advantages and disadvantages of a career in events?

Related website for those interested in events management as a career: www.worldofevents.net

Exhibition and Theatrical Contractors

Exhibition (and some theatrical) contractors are a surprisingly mature part of the industry and have existed for many years. Their function is to provide exhibition (or backdrop) services of one kind or another ranging from design and management for large exhibition-type events to the provision of relatively simple one-off stands. Some venues in the field are able to provide in-house services, but may rely on exhibition contractors to create and supply complete shell schemes for exhibitions. Given that some parts of the events market (manufacturing companies, for example) have a long history of organizing combined launch and exhibition events, a number of exhibition contractors also have expertise in events production. However, some specialize and act as suppliers of systems, either for hire or for purchase. Typically, contractors will provide the shells in a venue and individual exhibitors will fill a shell with their own material, displays and staff for the duration of the exhibition or show. The contractor will then come in and break down the shells and clear the area.

Technical Services and Multimedia Support

In addition to catering, technical services may be bought in. Not all venues have the technical support or equipment to cope with the full range of services sometimes demanded by organizers. Indeed, the small hotel, marquee or village hall used by parts of the market may have no facilities at all beyond the space and the furniture. Equipment and technical support can be hired in from a range of companies, some of whom simply provide equipment, some of whom provide equipment, training and technical support. Basic presentation equipment can be hired in, ranging from overhead projectors to slide projectors and video players. The higher levels of technology can also be hired in to provide complete presentations on anything from multimedia to video walls. Print shops are capable of copying both black and white and colour material for guest packs, tickets, handouts and support material such as badges or place cards. Video production companies are also common and are used for videoing the proceedings themselves, and often having their own recording, sound editing and production facilities. The range of technical facilities provided by the companies in this field is extremely wide and reflects the importance that organizers, particularly of high profile and VIP events, attach to the need for technical facilities, whether these are a simple overhead projector, computer-video or liquid crystal display (LCD) projection, prompting systems (autocues), or any other of a wide range of systems to support a stage presentation, ceremony or commentary.

Voluntary bodies, committees and individuals

Event management is one of those activities in which there is a large and active voluntary input. Many events, ranging from charity functions to village sports days, from birthday parties to local traditions, are undertaken by volunteers. This might be the family or friends for a birthday or wedding, a volunteer group for a sports day or a fête. It might be a small committee set up for the purpose of running the event – anything from an annual rose-growing competition to the recreation of a historic battle in full costume.

This type of organization is often significantly overlooked in studies of events activity, as there is a (perhaps natural) tendency to look at larger-scale professional events as the model for events management. To take such a restricted view would be wrong, and would ignore the long social history of events, festivals and traditional folklore activities. A typical voluntary committee might be made up of six or so people interested in putting on a particular event. This group might be already elected to perform some task, in, say, running a voluntary society, as a hobby or recreational interest, or might be formed specially to do the job. The effectiveness of voluntary bodies is often very high, due to the commitment, work and effort that the volunteers are willing to put into the activity, and also because of the lengths to which they might go to obtain resources, help, facilities and services for their event.

It is also the case that, for larger or more important events, these might be planned and managed through co-operation between volunteers and professionals. An event might be volunteer managed, through an executive committee, but employ a professional events organizer to plan and run the event. On the other hand a professionally managed event might not only employ volunteers as staff, but might co-ordinate the activities of a range of voluntary bodies to produce the event (such as at a carnival, where the organizers might be the city council tourism department, co-ordinating the efforts of everyone from the city band to the local majorettes).

Summary

The increasing complexity of events management has seen the development of companies with specialist roles in management, production and hospitality. Some of these companies, such as exhibition contractors, have been around for many years; some, such as production companies and events management companies are relatively recent. The public sector infrastructure of the events business is also becoming more evident, with an expansion of interest from tourist authorities and the government, and an increasing number of trade and professional bodies. The breadth of the events business is such that there is also a very considerable voluntary sector, organizing anything from small personal events to local shows and sporting competitions. The size of this voluntary sector is difficult to judge, but it is as much a key component of events activities as are the developing private and public sector structures.

References

Bowdin, G., McDonnell, I., Allen, J. and O'Toole, W. (2001) *Events Management*, Oxford, Butterworth Heinemann, pp.12–14.

Davidson, R. (1995) *Business Travel,* London, Longman, pp.32–38.

Goldblatt, J.J. (2001) *Special Events: The Art and Science of Modern Event Management*, Chichester, Wiley, pp.15–30.

Hall, C.M. (1997) *Hallmark Tourist Events: Impacts, Management and Planning*, London, Belhaven, pp.100–117.

Horner, P. (1995) *Travel Agency Practice*, Harlow, Longman, pp.223–4, 242–8.

Kotas, R. and Jayawardena, C. (1994) *Profitable Food and Beverage Management,* London, Hodder and Stoughton, pp.192–235.

McIntosh, R.W., Goeldner, C.R. and Ritchie, J.R.B. (2000) *Tourism: Principles, Practices & Philosophies,* New York, Wiley, 7th edn, p.133.

Richards, B. (1992) *How to Market Tourist Attractions, Festivals and Special Events*, Harlow, Longman, pp.10–110.

Tribe, J. (1999) *The Economics of Leisure and Tourism*, Oxford, Butterworth Heinemann, 2nd edn, pp.2–32.

Social, economic, political and developmental implications

Introduction

It would be very easy for us to see special events purely in a social context. In the past, many events were largely personal and private affairs and the implications of having a special event in a community were largely social. An event such as a village wedding was both a cause for celebration and a means by which the whole village could interact together. Indeed, events of this type often involved the whole community in some way, in addition to the immediate families of the couple to be married. There were often local rituals to be undertaken; these varied from place to place and were part of the social fabric and history of the area. Such rituals, now often long forgotten, served to reinforce community ties and to make events different in many small ways from those of their neighbours. Local village events, for example, were sometimes much rowdier and more spontaneous than today (e.g. May Day), but many of these local traditions faded away during the Victorian period as the nature of society changed, to be replaced by a rather more constrained way of doing things. The reason for this loss was the rather fossilized nature of Victorian society and a tendency in our modern society to regard spontaneity as odd or out of place, as we have forgotten many of the traditions and differences that characterized our communities until the 1840s.

However, the social context is only one element of events and there are often other implications (Figure 4.1). We can look back and understand that events such as the Roman gladiatorial games, or public festivals such as the 'Saturnalia', had both religious and political implications. In the modern world, similar parallels can be drawn from festivals such as the Welsh National Eisteddfods, which have social and community impact, as well as political and economic ones.

Contemporary events are frequently seen in terms of the community, and events managers often go to some lengths to involve the local community. Social integration is not the only outcome of many modern events, because as the size and complexity of events has increased (especially of organizational and sporting events), so have the potential impacts on the economic and political life of the area, or community, whether that is a town, city or region. For example, tourist towns and resorts have long understood the benefits of running special events during the tourist season, perhaps to bring more people to the town (and thus encourage further spending in local shops and businesses) or to extend the season in some way. The Blackpool illuminations, that great triumph of light and colour, with its miles of lights, displays, tableaux and illuminated trams, was intended to extend the tourist season. In this it has very much succeeded, and the event attracts a huge number of people from all over the North of England and Scotland every year, giving the resort's economy a very significant boost.

Some types of events, especially sporting events, play a political role, in addition to the social and economic roles. The Olympics are a prime example of this. There is considerable international competition to stage the games, on the one hand because of their perceived economic benefits, but on the other because there are also positive political impacts, such as improving the international image of a country or, in the case of some types of event, as a means of gaining other political benefits such as kudos or public exposure. For this reason politicians often attach themselves to activities such as the Oscars or the Brit Awards, as they gain from the reflected glory of the celebrities attending such events.

Social and community implications

Human society is complex and interactive, and all human societies celebrate, whether they are modern and technological or old and traditional. The means of celebration are very diverse. Sometimes special events are spontaneous – your

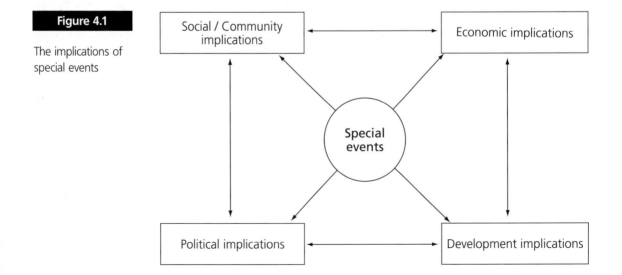

Figure 4.1

The implications of special events

friends at work find out it's your birthday, and almost straight away they've got you a card, found a cake (even if it's just a muffin with a candle), and opened a bottle of wine (which, being alcohol, was banned from the premises by the tedious management, but hidden by the wise staff). These events serve to strengthen social bonds as well as to spread enjoyment around. Many events are less spontaneous and more carefully planned, but those events whose progress is frequently planned down to the last detail, such as weddings, have intense social implications (Goldblatt, 2001). They have an impact on participants, emotional and intellectual outlook, in terms of pleasure, social interaction, stimulation of the mind and the senses – ranging from the consumption of food and drink, to enjoying the atmosphere (or not enjoying it, since not everyone likes every event), participating in activities such as games or dancing, or doing unusual or sometimes outrageous things.

There are a number of more general social implications of having a special event. In community terms, many events, particularly personal ones and events run by the community itself, have the benefit of improving social ties, and are an opportunity for the community to demonstrate that it can pull together for the greater good. These can be anything from local arts festivals to the Eurovision Song Contest. Even a tree planting day or street party can provide such opportunities. The role of events in encouraging social interaction and the celebration of happy occasions is probably more important in a society which, as a result of modern media, modern work methods and the relative decline of the 'traditional' family structure, feels a greater need to maintain social contact. Without the social contact that events often give, the feeling of social isolation in a society where even work can be conducted in a solitary way, such as from a computer in the home office, can be very great. Human beings are social animals (an issue typically overlooked in the hype that often goes with new technological innovations), and the growth of the events business may in part be due to the need to increase opportunities for social and physical interaction in the community, at a time when less interaction is possible in the work or home environment than at any time in the past. In such a case, organizations (particularly those that rely on technology) may have to give more serious thought as to how to help their employees interact and develop the social skills and interests that are the key to maintaining a cohesive intersocial structure.

Social impacts can also be seen in a wider context, perhaps as a potential mechanism for strengthening weak community structures in a particular location. The Notting Hill Carnival in London was one of the major driving forces behind improvements in relations between local communities with different ethnic backgrounds, and ultimately helped to drive forward many community social and political initiatives. But care must be taken not to see special events as some kind of panacea for local social or economic problems. There are no panaceas, only a range of tools which, if handled correctly, and if well received on the part of local people, might work positively for the benefit of all. You cannot impose a special event and say: 'There you are, enjoy that.'

Case Study 12 *Community implications of events: Notting Hill Carnival*

Notting Hill, London

Factbox

- Notting Hill Carnival, London.
- Annual celebration with parades and music.
- Comprising five disciplines: Mas' (Masquerade), Calypso, Pan (steel bands), static sound systems and Soca (a blend of soul and calypso).
- Attracted some 1.3 million people over two days in 2002; the August event is at the heart of six weeks of related events.

In 1958, a series of racist attacks in Nottingham is thought to have triggered other incidents around Britain and to have prompted the Notting Hill riots in London. The following year, Claudia Jones (the Trinidad-born editor of the *West Indian Gazette*) is credited with organizing a Caribbean carnival at St Pancras Town Hall, as a response to the riots and the BBC broadcast the event on its 'Six Five Special' television programme. In the mid-1960s Rhuane Laslett, apparently unaware of the annual Caribbean carnival – now held in Seymour Hall and the Lyceum – organized an outdoor carnival procession as part of the Notting Hill Summer Festival. This small procession, starting from Acklam Road (with costumes borrowed from Madam Tussauds) attracted about 1000 people and is generally seen as the start of the modern Notting Hill Carnival.

The event has gradually expanded and is now seen as one of Europe's largest open-air carnivals, although attendance has varied from 1.4 million in 2002 down to 600,000 in 2003, when the number of people attending was less than the 900,000 who attended the Zurich Love Parade (www.streetparade.ch). It is such a firm fixture on the calendar that it took a central role in Queen Elizabeth's Golden Jubilee parade during 2002. Still focused around Portobello Green, it features live music and bands drawn from cultures all over the world; the August public holiday parades are the main focus of a series of events stretching over six weeks.

The carnival takes place over the last Sunday and Monday in August, and parades, processions and music attract a throng of visitors and celebrants. It is no surprise that during its existence the celebrations have been the cause both of community cohesion and community disharmony. The sheer volume of visitors can place great strain on the fabric and infrastructure of the very community that they have come to be part of. Attempts to fund-raise to cover some operating costs have frequently been through sponsorship, which came to provide over half of the income of the Carnival Trust (NHCT), so much so that this prompted a backlash, and a curb on large-scale advertising by sponsors was announced for 2002.

The carnival has developed from a relatively small, community-based event to a major feature of London's summer calendar. During its existence, it has been the focus of community will, community cohesion, community celebration and, occasionally, community issues and community anger. Now much respected, the carnival has had its ups and downs. Large numbers of people interacting together are largely peaceful, but occasionally there have been violent incidents, sometimes not helped, in the past, by ineffective policing. In 1976, a riot at the Notting Hill Festival is said to have left some 400 constables injured. Images of the police defending themselves with dustbin lids and milk crates prompted an increased police presence and changed tactics at future carnivals. By 2001, policing the almost entirely peaceful Notting Hill Carnival involved about 10,000 officers deployed over the two days, alongside 600 carnival stewards. Nowadays, the

▶

carnival attracts more than a million people, many of whom are tourists coming to experience the spectacle. This puts some strain on the local infrastructure, such as public transport, toilets and emergency services, but the local authorities have become more practised in the event, and public services are better geared for it than in its early days.

A turbulent period for the management and governance of the Carnival Trust ended in 2002, when Chris Mullard became chairman. The Carnival Funders Group (CFG) comprising the Arts Council of England, Association of London Government, Greater London Authority, London Arts and the Royal Borough of Kensington and Chelsea kept a close view on these organizational changes. Mullard argued that the priorities were:

1. That the carnival should transcend groups and individuals

2. To demonstrate the carnival was good for London and that London was good for the carnival

3. To provide a vision of a multicultural and diverse London.

Some view changes such as regulating the sound systems, which close down at 7pm, and the secondment of a police sergeant to the Trust, as evidence of increasing professionalism; others see them as further evidence of the event moving away from the community and becoming just another 'corporate event'.

Based on this case:

Examine a community-based event in your local area.

1. What benefits does the event bring, in social and economic terms?

2. What evidence is there of community cohesion or community disharmony about the event?

3. How effective is the balance between community involvement and the input of professional agencies?

4. How is the event likely to expand over the coming years ?

Related website for those interested in the Notting Hill Carnival: http://www.lnhc.org.uk; also www.rbkc.gov.uk/nottinghill

Source: authors, 2004.

Events can be seen both in terms of performing a social role and, for certain types of events, acting as a stimulus for other social activities, such as tourism. For a town or city wishing to become a tourist destination, elements such as attractions, accommodation, transport, infrastructure and facilities must be present. In looking back at the historical development of some major destinations, it an be seen that all these are present, although the destination may not have had anything to offer in the beginning apart from a natural attraction (such as a beach or a rural landscape). This has been the case for resort towns such as Brighton, England, Howth, Ireland or Scheveningen, the Netherlands. In addition to the attractions of the seaside or countryside, some towns have relied for their tourist development on the architectural attraction of a great building,

Figure 4.2			
Development of tourist destinations: some examples	**Location**	**Origin of tourist interest**	**Type of attraction**
	Brighton, England:	Sea bathing. Prince Regent's Mistress.	Natural/man-made attraction
	Salzburg, Austria:	Historic medieval city.	Man-made attraction
	Scheveningen, Holland:	Sea Bathing, Proximity to The Hague.	Natural attraction
	Interlaken, Switzerland:	Lake views and scenery.	Natural attraction
	Galway, Ireland:	Galway Arts Festival, Galway Races.	Event attraction
	Gleneagles, Scotland:	Golf and golf tournaments.	Event attraction

such as a castle or stately home, or on an event such as a market, fair or religious festival. Some destinations developed simply because royalty or the upper classes visited them, such as Brighton, where the Prince Regent kept his mistress.

A destination was often intended to build on existing elements such as a pleasant location, warm climate or tourist attraction in or near the town (Shaw and Williams, 1997); the availability of local accommodation, places of refreshment (restaurants and cafes) and good transport networks (by road or rail) also helped. In many tourist resorts there was no major physical attraction, such as a national museum or theme park, but often the tourist season could be driven entirely by special events, anything from a carnival to a jazz festival or seaside air show (see Figure 4.3).

In looking at the social implications of events, we have seen that the main impacts are for events to create better social interaction, help develop community cohesion, increase cultural and social understanding, and improve the community's identity and confidence in itself. These are very important gains for many communities. We must, though, sound a note of caution, particularly for large scale, mega-events. As with some of the issues of sustainable tourism, depositing a major international event on a small undeveloped community could do some damage to that community, perhaps resulting even in the destruction of its identity, particularly if the activity is badly handled, organized without thought for the outcomes, or without regard to the carrying capacity of the location (i.e. how many people the location can cope with). Nevertheless, the vast majority of events have tremendous positive outcomes: they serve to celebrate and to entertain, to strengthen and improve social bonds, and they increase community involvement and confidence. Most events can be seen in this light.

Economic implications

The impacts on a local community of a major event, be it a sporting event, or a large cultural event such as a festival, can be looked at in terms of cost-benefit analysis or through economic multiplier analysis (Braun and Rungeling, 1992; Tribe, 1999). An event itself may not, for example, provide huge direct employment, but the indirect effects on local businesses, local services and local infrastructure and environment could be extremely significant. A number of festivals have had this type of analysis carried out, such as the Edinburgh Festival, where about 85 per cent of income came from tourists, making the

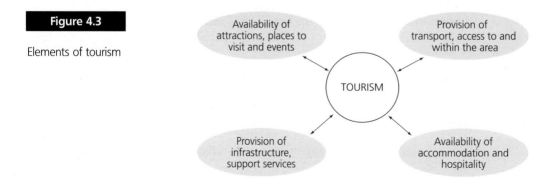

Figure 4.3

Elements of tourism

Availability of attractions, places to visit and events

Provision of transport, access to and within the area

TOURISM

Provision of infrastructure, support services

Availability of accommodation and hospitality

impact rather greater than if the money had simply been 'recycled' by local people (i.e. spending money on a festival, art activity or event, rather then on some other local activity such as day-to-day shopping) (Hughes, 2000). The indirect effects of incoming spending of this kind may include the support of activities such as retailing (visitors buying anything from magazines to clothing) and catering (visitors using restaurants, coffee shops and pubs), to less obvious visitor support of services such as transport, taxis, printers, technical equipment, local musicians and entertainers, marquee contractors, photographers and many other types of supplies and suppliers. Some towns, cities and resorts have seen events as their economic salvation when other forms of tourism, such as business, or heritage tourism, might not be appropriate to their area. It is also thought that events that have many participants, as opposed many spectators, have a greater economic impact on a destination. Thus it might be quite reasonable to say that a fairly low-key event, such as a three-day international conference of dentists, might have more economic impact than, say, a premier league soccer match, because even though the soccer was higher profile, its spectators are more transient. A number of event-stimulated developments have been undertaken on this economic basis, such as the construction of Symphony Hall in Birmingham or the Exhibition and Congress Centre in Maastricht.

Case Study 13 *Economic implications of events: the French Grand Prix, Nevers*

Nevers, France

Factbox

- The French Grand Prix, Nevers.
- 185,000 spectators and participants.
- Contribution to regional economy: €50 million.
- An average spend of €273 per person.
- The circuit employs an extra 8,000 paid staff during race week.

The French Grand Prix held at the Circuit De Nevers Magny-Cours is a major international sporting event with significant economic impacts for the central France region. It is one of the most popular international events of the year, attracting some 185,000 people (1997 figures) and putting it in the top rank of French events. For comparison, the UK Grand Prix at Silverstone attracted some 170,000 people.

A study, carried out by Lilley and DeFranco, which looked at European Grands Prix, concluded that the event at Nevers resulted in very significant impacts indeed. The visitors to the event came not only from France, but also from other parts of the EU and further afield. This resulted in some very high average spending patterns, as many visitors not only attended the race days but also stayed overnight in local hotels, or at nearby campsites, spent money in local bars and restaurants, used local transport services including taxis and coaches, and spent money in shops and retail outlets in the surrounding area as well as at the facilities at the Circuit De Nevers Magny-Cours itself. In 1997 the contribution to the local economy amounted to some €50 million. This can be broken down into several elements: money spent at the circuit; at food and drink outlets; at retail outlets; at hotels and

▶

other accommodation; on local transport and related services.

On average, a visitor to the Grand Prix spent about €273 per person. The data was identified from a range of sources, including ticket sales. The businesses that benefited from the 185,000 visitors included restaurants and bars; accommodation providers; newsagents; petrol stations; pharmacies; photo shops; gift shops; booking and travel agents. Although it is less the case at Nevers (because of its location) some European Grands Prix also provide major business for local night-clubs and discos, and local specialist retailers (e.g. clothes and designer shops), as well as food shops and supermarkets.

Based on this case:

1. Can you identify both the direct economic benefits and the indirect benefits?

2. What are they, and why are they important?

3. Can the local economy be sustained without them?

4. Can any local economy survive without special events?

5. What are the alternatives?

6. Why are some locations better suited to events as an economic activity than others?

7. Does an event of this type displace income from other activities (e.g. might local hotels be full anyway, and might this existing business be displaced, and if so, will it return)?

Related website for those interested in the economic impact of the event: www.fia.com/etudes/f1_impact/sommaire

Source: Lilley and DeFranco, 1999.

This is not to say that the running of a major special event is the correct solution to the economic problems of any town, city or resort. If a public body, such as a city council, invests in an event, or in the physical event facilities (as with the Sheffield International Student Games) it must perhaps forego investing in something else, say an industrial or retail development. There is an opportunity cost, and even a danger that, as in the case of the Sheffield Games, the event might itself run at a loss. In considering the possibilities for the economic regeneration of an area, the running of a major event is only one option, not a panacea, and may be a significant cost or burden on the sponsoring organization, such as a city council. For this reason, special events are often used as part of some wider initiative, so that an element of synergy can be gained from the event in conjunction with, say, building a new arena. Equally, it might be recognized that the objectives of a particular event are to provide short-term, not long-term, gain. This objective alone might be worthy enough.

In the context of a community, the running of a major event is often perceived as having a positive social and economic impact, in much the same way that the construction of a factory or tourist attraction would. This economic impact is not very well documented, but some studies, especially of sporting events, such as games and grands prix, give various clues as to the benefits of events. In the case of some events, the operation and running of them is seen as a matter of civic business, that is to say, the event may be organized or even sponsored by the city or town council and based, at least in part on the economic and social benefits that it brings to the community, in terms of increased numbers of visitors or an increased visitor spend. Given the size and extent of some events, the economic and social benefits may be very great (Law, 1993).

Political implications

In past times, it might be thought that the political implications of events were relatively modest. However, this is clearly not so. For example, the political nature of the Roman gladiatorial games was well understood, and the ability of the Roman emperor or members of the Roman upper classes to put on a major spectacle contributed much to their status. Similarly, in mediaeval times much political status was attached to royal events such as jousts and tournaments. Therefore, certain types of events do have political impacts, even if that impact is only to provide a mechanism to indicate some form of political status. The opening of the town's festival, or a civic reception to celebrate some new feat of progress, are opportunities for the mayor and council to be seen in public, officiating at the ceremony with appropriate purpose and dignity. The political implications are simply that the town's dignitaries are expected to be seen doing what the townspeople elect and pay them to do. In this respect many modern events fulfil the same purpose, and politicians gain the benefit of being associated with useful civic activities and positive special events.

The genteel pride with which civic dignitaries were regarded is sometimes neglected today, but towns and cities often organized events or constructed things that demonstrated their commitment to the good of the general population and to technical or civic progress. This might be anything from the construction of a new hospital to the maintenance of some curious quirk of local tradition (such as 'cheese rolling', performed in Brookworth, England). Old photographs of ceremonies and celebrations often focus on this aspect of civic pride, something that, in our modern age, can be overlooked in an effort to seem 'modern', but which was, in past times, crucial to the ritual and traditional nature of events and added to the political status of these dignitaries involved.

Today, it is major events which tend to attract the attention of politicians (and media). Hall (1997) comments on the very political nature of events such as the Olympics and events designed to influence public opinion about a particular politician or ideology.

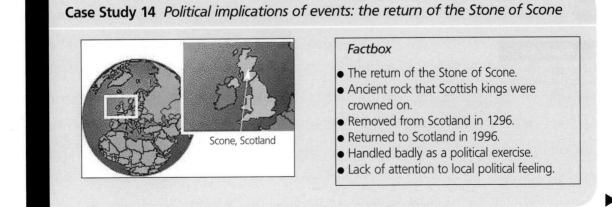

Case Study 14 *Political implications of events: the return of the Stone of Scone*

Scone, Scotland

Factbox

- The return of the Stone of Scone.
- Ancient rock that Scottish kings were crowned on.
- Removed from Scotland in 1296.
- Returned to Scotland in 1996.
- Handled badly as a political exercise.
- Lack of attention to local political feeling.

It should not be supposed that just because an event can be staged, it will be a success. This is not so. Such an outcome is amply illustrated by the 'ceremony' that accompanied the return of the Stone of Scone from London to Edinburgh in 1996. The stone, also known as the 'Stone of Destiny', is reputed to be the stone upon which the ancient Scottish kings were crowned. It was removed from Scotland in 1296, by the expansionist and acquisitive King Edward I of England, about the same time as he removed the alleged Crown of King Arthur from the Welsh. The Stone was kept for 700 years under the coronation chair in Westminster Abbey.

In 1996 the deeply unpopular Conservative government in London sought to make political capital by returning the stone to Edinburgh. In this way, it was reasoned (wrongly) that the Conservatives might gain some votes in the elections due to take place thereafter, from this 'gesture of magnanimity'. It has been argued that they would have been better to put it in a box and send it quietly to Edinburgh on the first train out of London Kings Cross railway station. However, it was felt that there would be a political benefit in returning it with some ceremony. Therefore the Stone was sent to Edinburgh with a military escort in what 'came across as an unsuccessful publicity stunt' (Godfrey-Faussett, 1999) in which much of the London-based media, including the BBC, were involved.

The Stone was carried north on (of all things) a khaki-green military Land Rover. It was escorted to the border at Coldstream (the site of its removal 700 years before), and handed over to the Scots on the Scottish side of the border bridge, where it was received by pipers and the Royal Scottish Archers (Queen Elizabeth's ceremonial Scottish bodyguard).

This contrived effort met with considerable public indifference. It was seen as a political 'lollipop'. Although the Scots were happy to have the Stone back, and it now rests in Edinburgh Castle with the Honours of Scotland (the Scottish crown jewels), the manner of its return did not achieve the political gains the Conservatives wished, and resulted in much embarrassment for them.

Based on this case:

1. Why might a politically inspired special event not work?

2. Could this event have been planned in a more sensitive way towards the Scots, and if so, how?

3. Would this have meant the elimination of the obvious political stimulus for the event?

4. What kind of event might have gained some positive outcome?

5. Could an event with no political overtones actually gain a positive result for the politicians involved?

Related websites for those interested in the Stone of Scone: www.cnn.com/WORLD/9611/15/stone.of.scone/ or www.scone-palace.net

Source: authors.

Figure 4.4

Political stakeholders for events

High-profile public events are attractive as mechanisms for producing social and economic benefits of the type noted earlier, and can focus and stimulate political will to promote and run them. Many events can be extremely positive in creating useful outcomes for the nation, region or area concerned. Nevertheless, political interest (see Figure 4.4) in an event may not be related to the good of the community or the local population, and there may be a hidden political agenda behind the event (as in the case of the Stone of Scone). Indeed, there are also examples of dictators and corrupt politicians using events to distract attention from some political problem, or as a mechanism to improve their image (the Berlin Olympic Games of 1936, in which the Nazi party attempted to get political kudos out of the event, are a classic example of this). It is therefore important to understand that some types of events may well have a political element, and the student and practitioner of event management needs to be able to recognize when that political element may or may not be positive.

Having sounded this note of caution, the most common political outcomes of events are positive and useful. A major event held in a town or city might not only help provide social and economic benefits such as community cohesion, jobs and income to local people, but it might significantly alter the image of the place in the long term. This can be a useful outcome especially for those locations that might have endured a long period of economic decline or social drift, for which a major special event could not only rekindle community involvement and civic pride, but also transform visitor perceptions of the place from negative to positive. The series of garden festivals held in various towns and cities in the UK during the 1990s performed just this task. A similar role is performed by the creation of a city as a European City of Culture, as in the case of Glasgow in 1990, whose image was transformed by this method, and other cities since.

Developmental implications

By their nature, the vast majority of special events are fleeting, with little or no developmental impact. It is necessary only to consider the large number of, say, weddings, that take place, to recognize the limitations of most kinds of event in terms of developmental and environmental impact – there is no impact, apart from having to sweep up the confetti. This is true of most events. Even some larger-scale events, such as a horse-racing day, might have little long-term impact except to provide some manure for the roses. It is therefore important not to get carried away on the bandwagon of environmental impacts, sustainability and disturbance. To do so would demonstrate a poor understanding of the real nature of most events as modest, passing affairs.

A few events, however, have some developmental impact, usually because this is a specific aim of their creation. Developmental events may be used as one tool in a toolbox of potential mechanisms for redevelopment, image-building and regeneration, as a means of producing some positive outcome. This outcome might be to support tourism or to improve the environment of a given location. There could be other ways of achieving this. It might be easier and more cost-effective to construct a new business park, hospital or conference centre, rather than to invest time and money in a developmental event in order to get some longer-term outcome from it. Indeed, the developmental impact of events will mainly relate to some physical construction or re-use needed to put the event on, rather than to the running of the event itself. It depends entirely on the purpose of the event. Within these caveats, some events have been well known for their impacts, most notably the garden festivals mentioned above. These were intended as a mechanism to regenerate run-down areas, and have been a modest success in achieving this aim, but not as great a success as might have been possible, because in some cases the post-event planning mechanism was a shambles, and the job was left partly unfinished.

Case Study 15 *Developmental implications of events: Welsh Garden Festival*

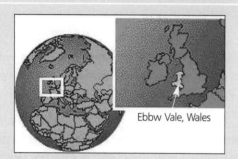

Ebbw Vale, Wales

Factbox

- Garden Festival, Wales, at Ebbw Vale, 1992.
- Purpose: Redevelopment of a derelict steel-works.
- Two years to prepare, open for six months.
- The long-term outcome was the provision of a large business park providing employment and a better local environment for residents and visitors.

During the late 1980s, the UK government was wrestling with the problem of land reclamation in a number of run-down industrial areas, locations where the former industrial base had collapsed as a result of economic and industrial change. Such change had left large areas with derelict land, for which there was no immediate hope of re-use without substantial work and investment. Typically, these areas also had severe image problems and included parts of the north of England and Scotland (Liverpool, Stoke-on-Trent, Glasgow and Gateshead near

Newcastle), as well as Ebbw Vale in southwest Wales (the last in the sequence of festivals).

The mechanism chosen for the regeneration was the Garden Festival. These festivals had three primary aims: first, to reclaim the land from its derelict and unusable state; second, to improve the image of the area, by making the chosen location over to gardens and parkland; third, to encourage inward investment in new businesses, to create employment and a better local economy. A large number of areas were submitted for consideration, most of which, like Liverpool, were in very urban locations. Ebbw Vale was somewhat different, in that it was a very derelict and damaged former industrial site (steelworks and coal mines), in what was otherwise a relatively rural location, near the Brecon Beacon mountains, at the heads of valleys near Merthyr Tydfil. The organization of the Festival Company comprised local councillors, members of the Welsh Development Agency and the Wales Tourist Board (Meudell, Mullins and Scott, 1993), who can also be considered as the political stakeholders (see Figure 4.4).

The Festival ran for six months between May and October 1992, after some two years preparation work planning and reclaiming the site, planting it as gardens, parkland and countryside. Over a million people visited the festival, which required some 800 staff at its peak, and was intended to provide an excellent family day out. The key issue from the developmental point of view, was, however, the legacy of the festival, in terms of its original aims.

▶

Clearly, the objective of land reclamation had been achieved: the area of the festival had been transformed from its almost unusable state to a condition where it was pleasant and suitable for further re-use once the Festival had finished. Second, it helped the image of Ebbw Vale considerably, as people visited the festival grounds who would otherwise never have gone to such a run-down area. These visitors included not only families but also politicians, civic officials and business people. The change of image helped stimulate the third and final aim, that of economic regeneration and achieving inward investment (i.e. attracting new businesses and thus providing jobs). The festival grounds became a 36-acre business park in the Blaenau Gwent development area, with some of the reclaimed land remaining in use for a shopping village and the Victoria Festival Park (Ebbw Vale), a country park with nature trails, a lake, gardens and woodlands, and a number of the features that were originally in the garden festival itself, including sculptures, a wetland centre, a tropical plant house and an oriental pavilion. The park has its own visitor centre and restaurant, and remains popular with tourists and visitors to the area. The outcome has been both economic regeneration and (on a smaller scale in terms of the festival park) the provision of an improved local environment capable of attracting visitors and visitor spend.

Based on this case:

1. How and why does the developmental impact of the Welsh Garden Festival differ from the vast majority of special events?

2. Are hallmark special events of this type the only mechanism for stimulating tourism?

3. Are such events necessary, or are there other methods of improving the environment in run-down or derelict areas?

4. In order for special events to have this kind of positive impact on the environment, what legacy is needed in terms of infrastructure, transport and communications?

Associated website for the Festival Park: www.blaenau-gwent.gov.uk/about_us/gard-fest.htm

Source: authors, updated 2002.

The developmental and environmental impact of events does vary. The Garden Festivals were intended to have both an image-building and environmental impact, while other events have had image building and reconstruction impacts. The Festival of Britain in 1951 left a legacy of the Royal Festival Hall and the Hayward Gallery on London's South Bank. The Sheffield Student Games in 1991 resulted in the development of a range of sporting facilities, including the Ponds Forge Pool, the Don Valley Athletic Stadium and the Sheffield Arena. The redevelopment of Sheffield was also supported by investment in a tram system and in the private sector construction of the Meadowhall Shopping Centre, as well as more recent associated work in terms of a multiplex cinema and other businesses along the route of the tramway between Meadowhall and the Arena. The curiosity of the Sheffield development was that the Student Games made a loss in direct financial terms (and left a €64 million debt), but their longer-term impact in helping to turn round Sheffield's once grim image and in helping stimulate other developments has been substantial. Yet this scale of development is unusual: most special events have no such impacts, and do not need to, as these are not part of their objectives.

Summary

The extent to which special events impact our lives may surprise the uninitiated. Daily life is improved in many ways. If this were not so, events would have had little or no impact on the cohesion of human society. In fact, events have a major impact and have been a feature of society from its earliest beginnings. Events serve to strengthen social bonds, to bring enjoyment and celebration to individuals, families, communities and society as a whole. There are also economic and political benefits, including the provision of direct and indirect employment, the enhancement of facilities and the improvement of local services, which are often stimulated by events. While some large-scale or developmental events may give us pause for thought about their wider impacts, especially culturally or politically, the vast majority of events serve to improve and enhance our society, at a time of significant social change.

Events can also be seen in the context of promoting and sustaining tourism. Not all tourist destinations have physical attractions; consequently, some destinations rely on a continuing programme of events during the tourist season to sustain them. This ensures both the provision of short-term events-related jobs and, crucially, helps to secure permanent jobs, which a small town might not otherwise be able to retain without the continuing stream of events visitors and tourists. In this respect, the involvement of locals, for example, in running their own small sales-stands at fairs and shows, in catering, and in casual employment in key activities, helps to keep tourist spending in the local economy (much more directly than it would if tourists simply spent their money at national chain retailers in the town). The focus on community involvement in events is therefore important, and methods of engaging the community need to be carefully considered, especially by event tourism providers.

References

Braun, B.M. and Rungeling, B. (1992) 'The relative economic impact of convention and tourist visitors on a regional economy', *International Journal of Hospitality Management*, vol. 11, November, pp.65–71.

Godfrey-Faussett, C. (1999) *Edinburgh*, London, Cadogan, p.83.

Goldblatt, J.J. (2001) *Special Events: The Art and Science of Modern Event Management*, Chichester, Wiley, pp.1–5.

Hall, C.M. (1997) *Hallmark Tourist Events: Impact, Management and Planning*, London, Belhaven, pp.84–99.

Law, C.M. (1993) *Urban Tourism*, London, Mansell, p.39.

Lilley, W. and DeFranco, G. (1999) 'The Economic Impacts of European Grands Prix', Brussels, EU Sports Workshop, http://www.fia.com/etudes/f1_impact/sommaire.html (6 January 2004).

Hughes, H. (2000) *Arts, Entertainment and Tourism*, Oxford, Butterworth Heinemann, pp.172–79.

Meudell, K., Mullins, L. and Scott, H. (1993) 'Developing Culture in Short Life Organisations', in *International Journal of Contemporary Hospitality Management*, vol. 5, no 4, pp.15–19.

Owusu, K. and Ross, J. (1988) *Behind the Masquerade: The Story of the Notting Hill Carnival*, London, Arts Media Group, pp.86–90.

Shaw, G. and Williams, A. (1997) *The Rise and Fall of British Coastal Resorts*, London, Mansell, pp.65–9.

Tribe, J. (1999) *The Economics of Leisure and Tourism*, Oxford, Butterworth Heinemann, pp.186–7.

Managing events

5 Making a start

6 Events planning

7 Financial management and the budget

8 The event: venue-finding, logistics and ambience

9 Marketing and public relations for events

10 Managing the event as a project

11 The organization manager and the team: during the event

12 Close-down, evaluation and legacies

5 Making a start

Aims

- To introduce some of the ways you can get organized.

- To consider the process for screening event ideas.

- To discuss the potential objectives of running events

Introduction

This chapter is the first in the sequence of chapters dealing with how to run an event. We have tried to present this as a series of steps. In practice, though, as the event begins to come together, many of the parts of the process will overlap, so if you are using this book for the first time you might want to follow the order of the chapters, or you might simply want to dip in and look at the elements you need.

For most events, time, money, people and effort could be in short supply and the end result needs to be the best possible blend of resources available. It is necessary, at the beginning, to recognize that existing organizational structures (such as a company management hierarchy), that serve an organization very well ordinarily, might not be suitable for the non-routine activity of organizing and running a special event (Badmin et al., 1992). At a professional level, and for those organizations and individuals involved in the production of events, there is a need to use techniques that will ensure an effective, enjoyable and safe outcome, and this will require a more organized and structured approach than the cheerful informality of a family party.

Getting started has two aspects: finding people to do the job, which might be yourself and some friends, or a committee of some kind; and sorting out, or screening, the idea. The idea might be ready made – you might have been set a task: 'Your job is to organize this year's flower show' or the task might not yet be known, except that it has to solve some problem or other: 'We need to raise some money to paint the village hall'. So the first few steps in getting started are deciding who will do the job, and what the idea is and whether it is feasible.

Getting organized

The initial stage of getting an event started depends on what kind of activity is going on, or, put more precisely, what the objectives are (and whether there are primary and secondary objectives). The event can be personal, leisure, cultural or organizational. It may be organized by volunteers or by professionals. Some events are organized by a single dedicated individual with comparatively little support and encouragement, others are organized by committees or large groups of enthusiastic people. Getting started partly depends on what we know about the event and who will be doing it. In some cases we know what the event will be, but not who will do it; in others we might have people who can organize it, but we don't know what sort of event can be offered. For convenience, and because we have to start somewhere, let's start with who is going to do it.

If you are reading this book, it might be you. You may not be doing it alone, but have other people to help, or you might be part of an organizing committee looking for ideas, or your job might be to organize the organizers. Mostly, a group of people will be involved. Sometimes the group may already exist; a committee that runs a club of some kind, perhaps a sports club, social club or hobby club, will also run the event. This has the benefit of using an existing committee, whose committee members know each other and know their respective strengths and weaknesses. For a special event, the committee might want to add one or two extra members or advisers from people who have arranged similar events before, or might want to form a smaller sub-committee to deal with the event, rather than the 'parent' committee doing it. A useful size for a committee is thought to be about six key people; but group size does vary, although the larger the group the more difficult it may be to achieve an integrated approach (Forsyth, 1999). Even with a small group there may be problems of cohesion, or difficulties in getting people to work together, so that careful leadership might be essential to the group's progress.

Equally, a new organizing committee may be required. Forming this group from scratch may not be easy, because of the range of expertise that may be needed (and not necessarily available). Richards (1992) and Hall (1997) make a number of important points about finding suitable candidates: our initial instinct may be that we can get our friends to be on the committee, but they may not have the right kind of skills needed, or have the time or inclination. The search for people will need to consider:

- How much time will organizing the event need from each person – can they spare this time to do the job properly?

- Have they any background of doing it before – have they done anything similar, have they a reputation for good work in an activity we might need, e.g. as a good organizer or good at finding resources?

- Do they have good working relationships with other people – will they pull their weight and do they get on well with others?

- If they have some particular weakness in organization, has another member of the committee got that as a strength, so that the committee has a balance of expertise?

Most of all, the composition of the committee needs to be such that it is able to deal with the key jobs, whether these are organizing, marketing, finance, finding resources, recording, or just plain 'being enthusiastic and keeping things going'. In essence, the organization structure, whether it is a committee, a working party, an advisory group or a co-ordinating team, will need to be able to achieve the requirements of the job. It must be noted that, especially for volunteer groups, the pool of expertise may be limited and that this can act as a constraint on how fast things can be done, how well they might be done and how good the outcome will be.

The organization of events can also vary according to how an event has grown. What was originally a one-off volunteer-organized event may have grown to the point where it is annual and organized by professionals. As events grow and their organization possibly changes, there may also be changes in the culture of the organizing body for example, from informal to formal, or from amateur to professional. Sometimes this kind of change may lead to conflict about how the event is to be run. This also implies that there is a continuum of organizational types, perhaps dependent (although not entirely so) on the growth stage of the event.

Figure 5.1

Example of an events management committee

1 Chair / President

2 Operations Officers

1 Finance Officer

1 Marketing Officer

1 Health, Safety and Legalities Officer

In addition, various other people might be invited to attend some of the meetings, depending on the type of event and the agenda of the meeting:

Representatives from the venue / licence holders / sponsors / police / first aid / fire service local council / local associations related to, or attending, the event / bank manager / Chamber of Commerce member / insurance adviser / professional specialists etc.

Figure 5.2

Development of organizational structures in events

Origin of the event idea

↓

Creation of an informal organization or committee

↓

Emergence of a leadership structure, perhaps with some professional help

↓

Establishment of a formal organization

↓

Professionalization

Source: adapted from Hall, 1997.

As a starting point, we will assume an early stage of development of the event, and that there is a largely volunteer committee doing the work. (As Hall notes, some events organizations do not get beyond the volunteer approach, nor do they need to). However, once the organizing committee has met and people have got to know each other a little, perhaps informally as well as formally, the first issue is what the event is going to be. As noted earlier, we might already, but perhaps we don't know, and have no ideas, so what happens next?

Case Study 16 *Changing organization at the Salzburg Festival*

Salzburg, Austria

Factbox

- Salzburg International Festival, Austria.
- Established in 1920.
- In 2002, 231,000 visitors attended the 185 events comprising the festival and spent €21.8 million.
- 4,876 journalists, from 30 countries, were there.
- 75 per cent of visitors are from outside Austria.

After several years' work, Max Reinhardt, with several friends and colleagues, succeeded in establishing a music festival in the Cathedral Square, Salzburg, Austria, during 1920. Although a lack of finance caused a break in 1924, the festival grew, under Reinhardt's volunteer directorship, into an international event, expanding into several venues and beyond music into drama. Quickly moving onto the international stage, the festival began radio broadcasts within five years (radio being relatively new at that time). The festival has continued to the present day, despite various

political difficulties in the 80 years of its existence. Today a public square in Salzburg is named after Max Reinhardt.

Politics has sometimes impacted on the festival's evolution. Despite its early success, and its ability to attract foreign visitors, various political actions affected the Festival in its early years, while it was still run, largely informally, by Max Reinhardt. In 1933, the then German Nazi regime imposed a 1,000-mark visa on visits to Austria, which cut the number of German visitors from over 15,000 to just over 800. In 1938 Austria was annexed by Germany and the Nazis took over, but not all Austrians supported this. The film *The Sound of Music* contains not only the famous scene of the Austrian Captain von Trapp tearing down the Nazi flag from outside his home, but also covers the escape of his family, including scenes from the Salzburg Festival itself, some of which were filmed in the Mirabell Castle and other parts of the city. Germany and Austria made war on much of Europe in 1939 and were defeated. After the war, in 1945, the radio broadcast of the Festival is credited as being the first common act in Austria by the occupying powers (Britain, America, France and Russia).

In 1950, the Salzburg Festival Foundation was set up, which put the event onto a formal and professional basis with a board of directors, and in 1952 the festival became a founding member of the European Festivals Association. The festival benefits from the efforts of a broad base of supporters, ranging from high-profile managers to experienced arts patrons, who, since 1961,

▶

have operated under the umbrella of The Association of Friends of the Salzburg Festival. In 1983, performances were relayed live for the first time to visitors in the Cathedral Square. During the 1990s, organizers began long-term co-operation with sponsors such as Nestlé, ABB and Allianz, and a reorganization of the festival's board and activities, introducing such innovations as subscription tickets for young people and 'Curtain Up' access to rehearsals, took place.

The expanding 'festival district' now encompasses permanent venues, e.g. the Festival Halls; historic properties, such as the Felsenreitschule or Summer Riding School; open air and temporarily covered spaces, including the Cathedral Square and the courtyard of the Residence. This evolution in its organization demonstrates both the financial scope of large festivals and the civic pride that they can build upon. The festival, during its long existence, has contributed significantly to the revitalization of Salzburg as a cultural centre (together with the city's association with Mozart), and to the imaginative use of many of its fine historic buildings for public activities.

Based on this case:

1. Has the organizational development of the Salzburg Festival followed that shown in Figure 5.2?

2. Is professionalization an inevitable consequence of the organizational progress of all events?

3. Can you identify an event in your area that continues to be organized by volunteers even after many years of existence?

4. What benefits has the festival brought to Salzburg, and for whom?

5. What problems might be associated with the success of a festival and how might they be addressed?

6. What impacts might political changes have on festival activity and can festivals have political effects? (See also the Notting Hill Carnival.)

For those interested in the Salzburg Festival: www.salzburgfestival.at; European Festivals Association: www.euro-festival.net

Source: authors.

Event feasibility: finding and testing an idea

The feasibility of an event might not have been considered because it seemed 'such a good idea'. But without doubt, most event planning would benefit from a brainstorming phase when various ideas are thrown in and tossed around to 'see which is the best'. Unfortunately, this often involves little more than the organizing committee having a couple of beers and saying, 'Yeah, we've got it, it's going to be fantastic'. To a detached observer, this conclusion will probably result in the response: 'Is it?'

In practice, there is a need for a systematic approach, as with much of events management. Being systematic helps us in situations where we have limited expertise, and when the time period in which events have to be scheduled may be quite short, and have to rely on volunteer labour or community support to achieve our aims. In regard to feasibility, major events might well get into intensive methods of assessment, such as cost-benefit analysis or investment appraisal. For the more common type of event, perhaps of the kind put on by a town or village or by a voluntary organization, a relatively straightforward series of tests could be applied, in the form of 'screening'. From this first phase, more detailed planning can follow.

There are three screens or filters that we can put suggestions through. These are the marketing screen, the operations screen and the financial screen. All are intended to sort out less viable ideas and help to identify the idea(s) that will work the best when tested against the objectives or criteria set. It is important to recognize, however, because of the varied nature of special events, there may not be one 'perfect fit'. The end of the screening process may still result in several acceptable ideas – or in none. The organizers will finally have to make a choice about what to do. In addition to these processes, once an event has been agreed on, the first of many planning activities must begin. This first activity is about the 'lead time' for the event, or, put more simply, whether there is enough time to get it booked and organized. (In much the same way, key dates apply to organizing conferences or exhibitions; Seekings, 1999.) In most cases the answer will be yes, it can be done in the timescale, but careful planning and forethought about the critical timing issues will focus attention on whether the event really is achievable in the time available. Many events go badly because of lack of time to organize them properly, and many project management texts argue that a poor level of planning during the early stages, due to a shortage of time, creates problems that will surface later.

We should bear in mind that all special events require a feasibility process, although some events happen simply because they have to. Typically, it is unlikely that personal events require a feasibility: you obviously don't feasibility-test a dinner party, but you do think about what is needed to get it right. With personal events, the 'feasibility' is not a formal process, but is much more likely to be an informal, even unconscious, decision about what will happen. There may be constraints, such as the availability of money or where to have it, but these may affect just the size or magnificence of the event rather than if it goes ahead or not. In this case the event is predetermined, and the real issue is how to make it happen.

On the other hand, many events do not develop by such a simple process, especially given the vast range of special events that take place. Let us consider the three screens, or filters, that we should put potential events through. These are the marketing screen, the operations screen and the financial screen. Suppose the scouts need to raise money for a new roof for the Scout Hall: there may be many possible events that could be put on to raise the money, but there has to be some way by which a selection is made. Perhaps a list of ideas of what the scouts could do, is put together:

- A car wash day
- A theatrical play
- A sponsored swim
- A sale of pledges (a pledge is a gift contributed, then auctioned)
- A table-top, jumble or car boot sale.

The criteria for what to do might include: what type of event has been successful in the past; what can be organized, given the resources of the scout-pack; what might earn the most money, and so on. These are relatively simple considerations, but they still represent a very basic kind of feasibility.

For larger-scale, public and organizational events in particular, there may well be an issue of how to choose from a range of possible activities for, say, fund-raising, or for a product launch, and how to screen the choices to identify the one most likely to be effective, Camacho (in Richards, 1992) noted: 'However good an idea may seem to be, if it cannot win sufficient support, and if it is unlikely to attract the public of a locality...the best thing to do is to drop it'.

The screening process

The process of screening is very important. Not only does the event have to be possible to carry out, it must also attract sufficient support to be successful. Let us consider this process in more detail.

The first stage of the screening is to come up with the initial concept or set of ideas that would be tested (see Figure 5.3). In some cases, a better range of ideas might be obtained by skipping through this general process and simply brainstorming a long list of (possibly) raucous, heroic, obvious, typical or ludicrous events and then dealing with the list in a serious way through a series of criteria to evaluate what really is feasible. There are several possible ways of doing this, by using evaluation criteria (such as cost-benefit analysis, Tribe, 1999) or concept screening (see Figure 5.4).

Figure 5.3	**General process**	**How the scouts might do it**
Generating ideas		

General process

Idea or objective
↓
General nature of the event
↓
Purpose of the event
↓
How should it operate?
↓
What benefits are there to participants?
↓
Concept(s)

How the scouts might do it

To raise funds for scouts
↓
Needs to be a public event
↓
Needs to raise money for the roof
↓
Should operate as simply as possible
↓
The locals should get something out of it
↓
Various ideas
↓
Car wash   Play   Swim   Pledges   Jumble sale

Figure 5.4	**General Process**	**The scouts**
Concept screening		

General Process

Many concepts or ideas
↓
First screen: marketing
↓
Second screen: operations
↓
Third screen: financial
↓
Remaining concept(s) and choices

The scouts

Car wash   Play   Swim   Pledges   Jumble sale
↓
Too many sponsored events locally, locals not very interested, so screen out swim and pledges
↓
Play needs very complicated organizing and a long time to arrange, so not ideal
↓
Jumble sale didn't make much money last year
↓
Remaining concept: car wash morning

The marketing screen

Having identified a number of ideas or concepts for a possible event, there has to be a process whereby the organizers or clients can sort out what concepts will be most suited to the target market. This implies a good knowledge of the target market: the type of people, their demographic or social profile, age group, familiar activities, past experience of events, size of the target group, and so on. This can be approached in two ways. Either the results of the initial brainstorming or listing session can be checked roughly against the opinions of the organizing committee (who, after all, will have to be committed to an idea in order to make sure it has a chance of success), or some pilot research can be done to see what the potential market makes of the list of potential events. This may be essential, as there is the possibility that the organizing committee may not be representative of the target market (e.g. in terms of age group, life experiences, gender, etc). Detailed research about the event finally chosen could be carried out in the planning phase, but an initial pilot questionnaire could explore first reactions to the range of ideas (Goldblatt, 1997) (Figure 5.5).

The essential factor that the marketing screen is intended to deal with is whether the various ideas or concepts will work in the target market. In addition,

Figure 5.5

Example pilot questionnaire for proposed events

SURVEY OF MIDDLEBURG RESIDENTS AND VISITORS

The Middleburg Garden Club is proposing to raise money to revitalize the Arboretum and Venetian Bridge. We would like to put on a suitable event in the Arboretum walled garden in July and would be most grateful if you would return this questionnaire, either in the post to the secretary (address on reverse), or put it into the special post box set up in the town library foyer.

Please pick two choices – 1 for your first choice, 2 for your second choice

Suggested events:

Garden Club show of prize-winner blooms ☐

Evening fireworks extravaganza ☐

Summer dance and buffet ☐

A production of Shakespeare's *A Midsummer Night's Dream* ☐

Treasure hunt through the park, finishing at the Knobbers Rest bar ☐

Concert in conjunction with the Middleburg Concert Orchestra ☐

Have you got another idea?..

Preferred timing, please tick one box on each line:

☐ Monday ☐ Tuesday ☐ Wednesday ☐ Thursday ☐ Friday ☐ Saturday ☐ Sunday
☐ Morning ☐ Afternoon ☐ Evening

Many thanks for your kind help. We look forward to welcoming you at the event, which will be advertised soon.

Name: ....

Address:...

it will be necessary to consider whether the ideas are sufficiently different from (or even similar to) successful competing events. Special event organizers are often very poor at pulling in information about other events that may be taking place at the same time and targeted at the same market as their own concept. This may result in clashes of dates, or two different organizing groups putting on almost the same type of event. The issue of 'environmental search' (or 'environmental scanning', as given by Costa and Teare, 1996) is a way of doing this. Identification of competing events can be difficult, but should at least involve compiling a list of dates when similar events take place in the area, obtainable from tourist information, from local What's On publications, magazines or trade press, together with a knowledge of activities in the calendar, or by checking local newspapers for the same period in the previous year, and getting people in the organizing committee to ask their friends and other contacts if anyone is aware of similar events. This should produce a list of what else is going on, which will help serve a number of purposes:

- It will identify dates to avoid
- It will give a feel for what goes on and what the local market likes
- It may give additional ideas or identify gaps in the market that are not being filled.

In this way it will be possible to create a shortlist of events that will satisfy the overall objectives of the organizing committee or clients (if this is a commercial or paid event), but will also suit the available target market and run at an appropriate time, not competing with other activities. This done, there is the final question of whether the list of 'possibles' fits in with the organizational type. There is not much point in putting on a 'Tarts and Vicars' theme for the Sisters of the Immaculate Conception annual fund-raising tea. The marketing screen is intended to identify what will work in a given market; what else might be going on by way of competition; what an organization would see as appropriate; and most of all, what demand there should be from the target market. Having done this, the organizer can move on to the operations screen.

The operations screen

So far, from a list of ideas or concepts screened against the marketing criteria for an event, there will probably still be a large number remaining that might work. However, the event manager also needs to consider what is achievable. All events have various resource needs, based on how adventurous, ambitious or limited the ideas are, what expertise and staffing is available, what locations or venues are available with capacity at the required dates, what timescale and what technology or other equipment will be needed. Due consideration needs to be given to legalities – are licences needed? (See section 10.4.) Will insurance be needed? Are permits required for various activities, etc.? This is the role of the operations screen.

Events often fall into two operational styles, volunteer or professional (although some have parts of both). For example, many events, especially in the personal, sporting and cultural categories, are run by volunteers. A volunteer committee may well consist of people who have had no experience of events before, or who have only their own experience and innate good sense to go on.

On the other hand, there are other events (particularly organizational, but also some sporting, cultural and some personal events) that are professionally run, or for which a professional adviser, consultant or Events Management Company (EMC) has been employed. The level of expertise available is, then, an issue for the operations screen, which indicates what events can be done within the style of organization preferred. As there are some excellent amateur organizations and some very inadequate professional ones (and vice versa), there is nothing to say that volunteer organizations are necessarily worse off than professional ones in putting on events. They may have less experience and (perhaps) lesser knowledge of what can be achieved, but it should not be assumed that professional organizations or companies know everything or will produce a perfect result. Any number of things may go wrong, including the professionals not paying sufficient attention to the brief or to key issues. On the other hand, volunteer organizations might be more enthusiastic, more resourceful with limited means, and have a better local knowledge than a professional events company.

Case Study 17 *Volunteer organizers and event screening: University College, Cork*

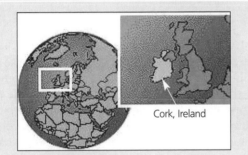

Cork, Ireland

Factbox

- University College, Cork, Ireland.
- Founded in 1845.
- 12,000 students.
- Almost 100 student clubs and societies.
- A large number of sports clubs.
- Men's Hockey Club run by a committee of seven.

Volunteer organizations are extremely common in events management. Clubs, societies, associations and charitable bodies often rely on volunteers to run the organization. Volunteers may have little or no training, but do have enthusiasm about and dedication to what they are doing. Many people have some experience of committee activity and voluntary organizations at college or university, where clubs and societies dedicated to a whole range of sporting, leisure, recreation and special interest activities are common. The Hockey Club of University College, Cork, is one such example. Its primary activity is playing hockey, but it also has an active social role.

The Hockey Club is very typical of many clubs and societies throughout colleges and universities. It plays matches and tournaments and has its own web pages within the website of University College, Cork. The club has an active social life, with its members take part in a whole range of student activities. Its committee organizes frequent events, both small and (relatively) large scale for its members and their friends and partners.

The choices of activities to end the 1999/2000 academic year produced a list of possible events that included a quiz night, a charity horse-race night, a buffet with disco, a formal dress ball, an American-style prom, dinner at a local restaurant or a fancy dress party. As the Hockey Club is a relatively informal kind of organization, these choices were bounced around members of the committee and the team and their friends. There was no complex formal process involved in deciding which event to have, only an informal process that involved the major stakeholders (the team and their friends) in the decision-making process. The choice reached was the result of a general consensus about what event they wanted. In this case, a formal dress ball, which members of the committee, together with a few helpers, organized.

The kind of process involved here is very typical of voluntary organizations and the limited market may mean that in-depth research is not required. However, the larger and more diverse the market, or the more unknown the style of event, the more likely will be the need to do a survey, or at least some pilot research work, to ensure the event is what the market is interested in.

Based on this case:

1. If you are a member of a club, society or association, what is the major event in the organization's social calendar?

2. How is this event organized and by whom, and how are the choices made about what kind of event it will be?

3. Can the process be said to involve any research or confirmation that the event is appropriate?

4. If you were the chair of a committee planning an event that the public has to pay to attend, what steps could you take to ensure your proposals would meet what the public wants to participate in?

Related website for those interested in University College Cork and its student life: www.ucc.ie/about

Source: Authors.

For events with a volunteer style of organization and volunteer staff, the matter of achievability is important. Does anyone within the organizing committee have relevant expertise? If so, they must be used to best effect. People with a financial background may be best suited to financial issues, people with design backgrounds best suited to design issues, and so on. In addition, volunteer organizations should not only look at members' jobs, but also at personal interests: creative people and good organizers are needed for special events. Clues about people's backgrounds, hobbies, interests and expertise need to be sought and could yield useful experience. However, volunteering is hard work and not everyone wants to do it. In the end, people may not have time to participate in the event, or may be called upon to deal with all kinds of occurrences or emergencies that they may not be equipped to cope with.

Equally important is knowledge of previous activities. Is the event a regular one, say, every year, and if so, who knows what has gone on in previous years? However, we need to recognize the boundaries of volunteer expertise – the person who has attended the annual flower show of a nearby town might be the only one in a volunteer organization who would know anything about how to organize a flower show, but the limitations of this approach must be understood. Going to a flower show (or any other event) as a visitor does not necessarily tell you anything about what goes on behind the scenes, how the event was organized or what effort went into putting it on. This is the issue of expertise, and when to know you need some. All kinds of special events have to start somehow, and the expertise to run them is often built up over many years, or at least the knowledge about where to obtain the expertise is. This expertise is key when issues of health and safety, legality or technology are important to an event.

The operations screen, then, is all about what can be achieved. From the original list it will have been possible to eliminate some of the activities on the basis that they are too difficult or complicated, or because there isn't the time, the staff or an appropriate venue. This can be done by using an events screening form (Figure 5.6), which will help formalize the screening, and several events might be written up in order to identify major problems and possible unforeseen issues in terms of licensing, regulations, and permissions or approvals needed.

Figure 5.6

Events screening form

OUTLINE EVENT DETAILS

Purpose of event:..

Suggested location: ....

Is the proposed event: ☐ A one-off event?
ㅤㅤㅤㅤㅤㅤㅤㅤㅤㅤㅤㅤ☐ Expected to take place annually?

Have you checked that the venue or location is available? ☐ Yes ☐ No

Details of the organizer or chair of the organizing committee:

Name: .... Phone Number: ....

Email: .... Mobile Number: ....

Address:..

....

Funding for the event:

How do you expect the event to be paid for? ....

....

What are the major costs of your event, and have you included insurance?................................

....

(A summary of the outline budget should be attached to this form)

Attendance at the event:

How many people do you expect to attend? ....

How many other people are there *(including organizers, crew, players, ushers, staff, etc)*? ....

Licensing, permissions, emergency issues:

Have you/will you be liaising with any of the following services, to establish their input to the event?

☐ Police ☐ Fire ☐ Ambulance ☐ Red Cross ☐ Licensing Authority ☐ Town Council
☐ Other:..

Will the event have any implications for local residents, i.e. noise, site set-up, parking, access, crowds, etc? ....

....

Will you need any specialist help with the event or other professional advice or input?

....

....

Signed: .... Date: ....

Source: kindly provided by Tendring District Council.

The financial screen

Almost all special events will have a budget of some kind, even if that 'budget' is only an approximate figure of what the organizers or clients can afford, based perhaps on similar events. For many events, the financial issues are cost-orientated. For a wedding, there is no discernible financial revenue to set against the balance of what might have to be spent. In this case, the organizers (the parents of the couple to be married and the couple themselves) will have some idea of how much they can afford, and if several ideas are being considered (for example, for the reception), the deciding factor might be the cost.

Not all events are 'cost only'; often there is a financial reason for putting an event on, such as fund-raising or economic regeneration. There are events that are expected to make sufficient money to cover costs and break even, or to make a small surplus. This is often the case with local volunteer events such as an annual town carnival – the carnival committee will be concerned with putting on a good show at a reasonable cost, and generating enough of a surplus to start next year's carnival properly.

Assuming the event has to make money (say, for fund-raising purposes), or at least to cover its costs, then the financial screen is all about identifying which possible events from the shortlist could achieve it. Two or three likely events might be compared using an outline budget. For this to happen, the organizers will need to come up with some basic financial information, both in terms of revenue (how many people attend, what can they be charged, what other ways revenue can be raised during the event, etc.) and in terms of costs (what are the likely costs of the location or venue, the staffing, the materials, the decor, the consumables, the insurance, the power, the food and drink, etc.), to assess whether a profit or surplus would be made from this. In some projects, especially large-scale ones, there are both capital costs and running costs. Think of the Olympics: the capital costs are about building the facilities, the infrastructure, the accommodation, etc. and the running costs are about actually operating the games. Will the revenue cover both of these, or, in the case of the capital costs, will some other benefit be the outcome – could the athletes' accommodation be turned into flats and sold afterwards? Could the stadium replace one that is old and needed replacing anyway? Crucially, will the event being planned take place within the appropriate budget?

In short, the purpose of the financial screen is to take the shortlist of possible events, preferably no more than two or three, and prepare an outline budget for each one, to help the decision-making process. A little later, as part of the detailed planning, the outline budget can be turned into something more detailed and accurate. For care in preparation, the outline budget should really underestimate revenues and overestimate costs.

Progressing the idea

In many respects, choosing the event, through the process outlined above, is the easy part. The sequence of brainstorming and then filtering ideas to see if an event is appropriate can be quite enjoyable. Serious financial and operational feasibility, if this were a major project, would then follow from the screening phase. The organizers or clients would also have some feel for the acceptability of the event, given their knowledge of who might be attending. In addition, for any event involving a significant budget or complicated organizational issues, a judgement of risks might have to be made. How vulnerable is the project financially and operationally? What issues might constitute a risk? Are there factors about fire, health and safety, crowd control, security, hazardous materials or activities that have to be considered? (See chapter 10 for risk management.)

Having found the preferred concept, the organizers might then wish to review the proposal again in the light of the objectives, and ask if the proposal still meets those objectives. Richards (1992) and Hall (1997) sought to identify some possible objectives for events (see Figure 5.7).

It is also quite common for events to have additional, subsidiary objectives, such as to educate, or to make money, or to leave a useful legacy. To take the idea forward there would have to be some building on the initial objectives, with a draft of the proposal containing the overall objective broken down into several aims, and then into the component parts for the event. Even relatively simple events may have several component parts. How will these be put together? Who will be doing the organizing and who is responsible for what? Where will the event be held and has more than one venue been approached? When will the event happen and are suitable dates and times available? What materials, supplies and equipment might be needed? What transport, parking or access? Why is the time schedule for achieving this important, and what are the deadlines?

All these questions will have to be answered. More work can be done later, but even if this is put into a few pages of notes it will be a useful start, and the planning can then be built from the initial ideas. The most important aspect of this pre-planning phase is to have enough time, not only to work up the detailed plans properly, but also to determine whether the event is achievable in the time available. In general, volunteer organizations may require more time to deal with complex events than professional or full-time organizations, but equally, those professional organizations are likely to have a far more realistic appreciation of the amount of work involved and the likely time it will take to achieve.

There may well be a 'critical path' (see chapter 10 for project management) of timing issues that will determine whether a project or event can be done in the

Figure 5.7

Examples of possible objectives for events

- Develop public involvement in the arts, sport or other leisure activities
- Fund-raise for a special project or charity
- Start a new event to create a tourist attraction, to extend the tourist season or to make better use of a resource
- Introduce a new idea to the market
- Attract more visitors to a venue or tourist destination
- Focus attention on a specified subject or project
- Create a sense of community, involve the community or strengthen its goodwill
- Advance and promote the community for the public benefit
- Promote political and cultural exchange
- Encourage participation in, or support of, an organization
- Support community or organizational objectives

timescale, which the unfamiliar organizer may think is easy, but may not be. Consider building projects as an example. Builders are often seen as overrunning the time 'allowed' for a project, but frequently this is due to an unrealistic appreciation of the complexity of the job, the need to get planning permission, the logistical problems, the delivery of long lead time, unusual materials, etc. Much the same is true of special events. An event that might seem very simple at first glance can become extremely complicated once someone actually sits down to write out all the parts. Nor is there any guarantee that what appears to be the 'critical path' of a project will be so. Suppose we are organizing a special prize ceremony for the best rose grower in the district. The organizing committee wants this to get some good local publicity, so has decided that the presentation should be made by the Mayor in the famous gardens of a nearby stately home. Several factors impinge on the timing: the event needs the stately home, the mayor and the local media (assuming there is to be no other activity after the ceremony). The critical path will emerge from one of the three elements:

- How long to book the stately home and are the possible dates available.
- How long it will take to get a slot in the mayor's busy diary and will this match the availability of the stately home.
- When is a good day for the local media.

For example, the lead-in to the critical path may be the last of these. Not all days are good days in media terms. If the local newspaper is published on a Friday, then they may be looking for good local stories several days before, probably Monday or Tuesday (not Wednesday or Thursday, as they have to write up a story and get the photos done in time to meet their own print deadline). This gives a framework for the best days on which to do this particular event. In all probability, both the booking of the stately home and the mayor's diary have long lead times, and whichever is longer (after preliminary enquiries) will have to be done first, as everything else can then follow. As a generality, the larger and more complicated an event, the more detailed the planning process will need to be and the longer the lead times will be. The key lead time is often booking the venue, as popular venues are booked months, sometimes years, in advance.

An experienced events organizer will be familiar with those issues that take time to get going, and those that can be done quickly. However, for the person who has never organized an event before, there is the problem of possibly overlooking something. Figure 5.8 gives an initial checklist for various issues and some useful things that can be listed at this stage of the event planning process. Nevertheless, all events vary in some way and the points shown in the list are not definitive, but are a possible source of ideas about what to check and what to do next. The information in the checklist, here called the pre-event planner, and of a type often found in a hotel 'Banqueting Order', is in three main sections. The first deals with contact information, who is organizing the event, and basic information about the date and type of event. The second deals with information about the possible venue, the event and any requirements for refreshments. The third section deals with requirements for the layout of the venue, design issues, entertainment and support activities, ranging from audio-visual equipment to car parking.

Figure 5.8

Simple pre-event planner

Pre-Event Planner

Target market:

Type of event: Date(s):

Organizer: Phone(s):

Address:

                                                         Staff required:

Client: Paid staff:

                                                         Volunteers:

Location / Room: Booking of venue done: yes ❑ no ❑

Start time: Finish time:

Number of participants / guests:

Number for meals and / or refreshments:

Menu: Menu printing / place cards / table plan

Bar / wine: Exhibition map / floor plan

Other refreshments: Contact lists

Booking deposit: €___   Deposit paid: yes ❑ no ❑

Final account: €___   Final account to be paid on ___

Room Layout:	For event / for fringe activities	
	For buffet / dinner / refreshment area	
Room Decoration:	Theme	Lighting
	Colour scheme	Special items
Entertainment:	Music	Fireworks
	Disco	TV / video / computers
	Other live entertainment	Crèche
	Games	
Special Equipment:	Audio	Exhibition stalls
	Visual	Signage
	Staging	Furniture
	Other items	Power requirements
	Costumes	Marquees / tents / toilets

Car parking notes:

Photography/video

Advertising required:

Any other remarks / special requests

Summary

At the beginning of the feasibility phase, a large number of ideas or concepts for an event were identified. These various ideas were then put through a series of screens: marketing, operational and financial, whose purpose was to filter out those ideas that were not really viable. Having done this, the organizers should now, at the end of the process, have a limited number of events to choose from; it is even possible that just one event may have made it. In fact, if the process is done in a very formal way, against set criteria for each part, there might be no ideal outcome, only the 'nearest fit'. Where there is more than one possible event, the objectives can be looked at again, and if there is still more than one special event on the shortlist, choose the one that would be most enjoyable!

References

Badmin, P., Coombs, M. and Rayner, G. (1992) *Leisure Operational Management*, Harlow, Longman, 2nd edn, vol. 1, p.106.

Costa, J. and Teare, R. (1996) *Environmental Scanning: A Tool for Competitive Advantage*, in Kotas, R. et al., *The International Hospitality Business*, London, Cassell, pp.12–20.

Forsyth, P. (1999) *Communicating with Your Staff*, London, Orion, pp.69–80.

Goldblatt, J.J. (1997) *Special Events: Best Practices in Modern Events Management*, New York, Wiley, 2nd edn, pp.3–37.

Hall, C.M. (1997) *Hallmark Tourist Events: Impact, Management and Planning*, London, Belhaven, pp.100–17.

Richards, B. (1992) *How to Market Tourist Attractions, Festivals and Special Events*, Harlow, Longman, pp.101, 103–5.

Seekings, D. (1999) *How to Organise Effective Conferences and Meetings*, London, Kogan Page, 7th edn, pp.21–9.

Tribe, J. (1999) *The Economics of Leisure and Tourism*, Oxford, Butterworth Heinemann, p.170.

6 Events Planning

Aims

- To examine the planning process for events.

- To consider the mechanisms for ensuring the effectiveness of the planning process.

- To consider operations, financial and marketing-related planning activities.

Introduction

Events are, by their nature, non-routine. The techniques used to organize and manage them, though, are just the opposite. The purpose of this chapter is to consider one of the most important aspects of events management – the planning process. Planning is vital to the success of events, because of their complexity, their unusual requirements (which may be considerably different from the regular or routine activities of an organization), and because of the possible unfamiliarity of those organizing an event with what is required. However, care may be needed, as organizations sometimes get so locked into the planning process that they never get to the doing part ('analysis paralysis'), or the plan itself becomes a cage from which they cannot escape. No plan will survive its first contact with reality, however good it is. Some change, however small, will be needed. Nevertheless, a plan is a guide and tool to measure progress against, and should not be lightly disregarded.

It can be argued that the planning process itself is the real key to what will happen. In having to sit down and prepare a plan, you have to think ahead about the event you are going to undertake, and therefore to identify the elements and issues that need to be sorted out. For this to work well, there has to be a systematic approach, because unless you break the plan down into smaller component parts, something important could easily be missed. The planning process, consequently, reveals both problems and opportunities; it should serve to get people involved and act as a mechanism to search the environment for information. It may be possible to find useful information to help with this process from a range of sources, not only those published in books and guides, but also from 'toolkits' that can sometimes be found on events-related websites. Two examples of these are the event organizational toolkit provided on-line for major sporting events, which was published in 2003 by UK Sport and which can be downloaded, and the volunteers' information sheets provided by the National Centre for Volunteering for more general use by organizations that use volunteers as a major source of staffing.

Having got some basic information together, planning has a number of benefits. These include better co-ordination, the creation of a focus, the experience of thinking ahead and the provision of a device (the plan) for effective control of the progress and outcome of the event. However, planning is time-consuming and necessarily involves thought and effort. Things may still go wrong, but as Reiss (1995) noted, 'this is a reason to plan, not to fail to'.

The planning process

The diversity and individuality of events can make them very labour-intensive, because of the effort involved in undertaking a non-routine activity. This is not simply a matter of how events are operated on the day, but is also a management and organizational issue. The management input to any event will be far greater than for a routinely manufactured product when management becomes essentially a supervisory function based around quality control, once the development phase is over, because the manufacturing process is being repeated again and again. Planning events, for the uninitiated or for an inexperienced organizer, is therefore rather more important and time-consuming than the equivalent processes for repetitive goods and services. Taking the example of a wedding, the actual wedding may be a ceremony of no more than an hour, followed by a reception and a buffet, but the planning may have taken several months and involved large numbers of people – families, friends, the venue management, the caterers, the florist, the dress hire company, the musicians, the car company, the religious authority or civil registrar, and so on. This complexity of planning is typical of events in general and is part of a whole cycle of interrelated activity

Figure 6.1

Planning as a
management
activity for an event

Event management activities

Objectives and getting started

Planning

Organizing and preparing the event

Implementing: running the event

Divestment / legacy

covering planning, action and control. The increased importance of planning is because of its key role in helping to deal with the uncertainties of events.

Planning is the process by which the manager or organizer looks towards the event to discover what various courses of action are available to arrange it, and which course of action would be the best. This is not to say that a plan is going to appear the moment someone sits down to think about it. The manager, organizer or planning committee may have run many events, or may have run none.

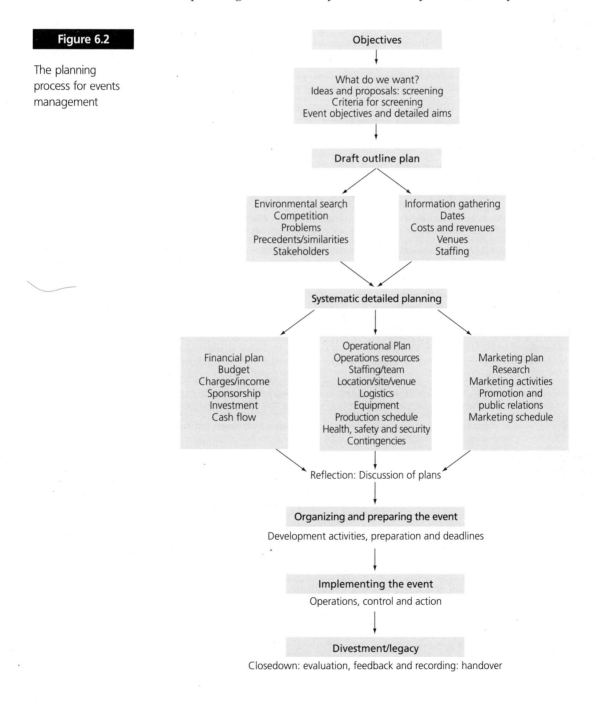

Figure 6.2

The planning process for events management

The advantage of having done it before is not only the experience, but also the existence of records and previous plans. On the other hand, with a new event, the plan, to start with, may be no more than a vague hunch or an organizer's intuition about what might be appropriate. However, this can be worked up very quickly into something more useful and relevant – a plan is essentially a predetermined course of action based on given objectives.

The objectives have to be carefully thought through, and sufficiently precise and clear to ensure that the purpose of the event is obvious to all those involved in it, from the chair of the organizing committee or clients, down to staff or volunteers at the operational level. Clarity at the beginning also helps the planning process and of getting everyone to pull in the same direction. The objectives should not be too complicated, perhaps consisting of only one or two primary objectives, although these can be broken down into a number of detailed aims; preferably not more than six, otherwise the point may be obscured, and simplicity is best at this stage.

Objectives, environmental search and information-gathering

The objectives are the starting point for the planning of any event – what is the event intended to do? Is it intended to celebrate, to entertain, to fund-raise? Given this, and some view of the feasibility of the event after the screening process, the organizers should have a reasonable idea of the kind of event that can be put on and whether it will suit the type of people coming to it (the target market). However, planning should not be seen as something that starts with a concept and ends on the opening hour. Even after the event has started the organizer is likely to be making changes, sometimes very major changes, in response to problems or to deal with an unforeseen crisis. One of the purposes of planning is to visualize potential problems and to have a plan that will take account of the environment of the event, the stakeholders, the circumstances in which the event is taking place and what might go wrong; or put more simply, there will need to be some contingency planning for emergencies, in addition to the main plan itself.

From the bare bones, an outline plan can be drawn up (see Figure 6.2), perhaps by brainstorming around the event idea and then listing the issues identified. This basic draft can then be added to in a more systematic way by the organizing committee and its advisers and helpers to cover headings such as operations, finance and marketing. This can include an 'environmental search and information-gathering' phase, a part of the process that involves collecting information relevant to the event. Facts such as available dates, suitable times, potential venues and useful staff have to be identified; checking has to take place to ensure there are no clashes with other, similar or competitor events. For major events, checking what else is taking place, or planned, can also be done using on-line listing services such as Foresight (www.fifi.co.uk) or Future News (www.futurenews.co.uk) as well as by paper-based methods, and, if the prospective market is not known, research should be done into what would like and pay for, building on the pilot research that might have been carried out at the screening stage.

The draft plan is really a place for initial ideas to be recorded, a kind of scrap-box for brainstorming and all your initial thoughts and concepts. Its headings should, importantly, cover six key issues, to give it some structure and form:

- Why the event is being undertaken?
- Who will be involved in the process and the event (and who may not)?
- What will take place and what information or research is needed to make decisions?
- How will it be done?
- Where will it happen (including the main location and any additional locational needs)?
- When will it take place (including dates and expected outline times)?

In addition, an environmental search is needed to pull in information about factors that relate to the event and will help it go well (or save it from going badly). This is part of the mechanism, like the screening process, by which an organizer seeks to identify potential problems at an early stage. Once all the ideas and information have been 'thrown in', the plan can then be reorganized to give it some proper structure. Always keep the first drafts, though, as sometimes they contain material that might be thought of as not very important, until, nearer the event, a problem of some kind emerges.

Case Study 18 *Environmental searching: the re-opening of the Scottish Parliament*

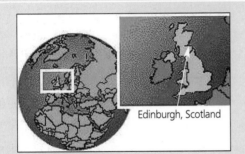
Edinburgh, Scotland

Factbox

- Re-opening of the Scottish Parliament, Edinburgh.
- First parliament in Edinburgh for almost 300 years.
- Ceremony combined old and new elements.
- Parliament opened by Queen Elizabeth.
- 'The Scottish Parliament, which adjourned on 17 March 1707 is hereby reconvened'.

On the 1 July 1999, the Scottish Parliament met for the first time in almost 300 years. It had been abolished after the joining of Scotland and England had removed political power from Edinburgh in 1707 and made Westminster the only UK parliament. The re-establishment of Scotland's parliament was greeted by considerable enthusiasm in Scotland.

The environment and circumstances of the planning stage

The nature of the opening of the parliament was a matter of some controversy during late 1998 and early 1999 in Scotland. There was a feeling that the ceremony would be too short and modern, and that the event would fail to include the heraldic flag-bearers of Scotland, who are traditionally associated with royal Scottish ceremonial events. In public, the reason given was that the ceremony needed to be modern, but the scathing publicity in the Scottish media about the absence of the flag-bearers suggests that the organizing committee was taken by surprise.

The committee initially failed in two ways: first, it had insufficient experience of Scottish public feeling, and second, they had not undertaken a proper environmental search. It was thought that the committee originally had no

▶

idea of Scottish traditions, because the reform had been initiated in London and the committee's 'starting point' had been London, not Edinburgh. There was therefore little recognition (due to inexperience and inadequate research) that a Scottish parliamentary tradition existed, let alone how it had worked. However, the committee (fortunately) listened very closely to public opinion in Scotland and these issues were addressed carefully and in time.

The stakeholders

The people and groups most concerned with the opening were its organizing committee; the political parties (notably the Labour Party, under whom the reform had been promoted, but other parties as well, including the Scottish National Party); Queen Elizabeth and the Royal Household; the Scottish Office (a government department); the national and local media; the people of Scotland; the army (as escort to the royal family); the Heralds and ceremonial officers of Scotland; The Duke of Hamilton (as Scotland's senior lord, responsible for the crown jewels of Scotland); and a very large number of people and groups involved in the ceremony, such as the orchestra, schoolchildren, poets, and so on.

The outcome was an event that was very well received (Engel, 1999). In the modern (and temporary chamber) of the Church of Scotland, the ceremony was opened with a fanfare played by the Royal Scottish National Orchestra, following which the Royal Procession entered with the Duke of Hamilton carrying the Scottish crown on a purple velvet cushion, followed by the Queen (Scottish protocol is that she is not Queen Elizabeth II of England, but Elizabeth, Queen of the Scots), and then the Lord Lyon King of Arms and the Heralds ('more Heralds than were needed to put on a Hollywood movie', the newspapers reported). This was followed by the opening speeches and, this being Scotland, by some poetry and spontaneous singing by the Scottish MPs.

The ceremony was hailed as a major success, not only in style but also in tone. It celebrated the need to open a modern parliament, and recalled the traditional way in which the old parliament, 300 years before, had been opened, thus fulfilling its objectives.

Based on this case:

1. Why is finding out about the environment and circumstances of your event important?

2. How can you identify the stakeholders (those people and groups that would take part or be interested in some way) for an event?

3. Why is doing this important, and what might happen if you do not identify them all?

4. Why is clarity of objectives key to running a successful event, and were the objectives for this event clear from the start?

Related website for those interested in the Scottish Parliament: www.scottish.parliament.uk

Source: authors

In many ways the environmental search/information-gathering process is also a search for opportunities (as well as problems). For example, another event in the same area and of the same type as your event might be seen as competitive, but could be complementary. The organizer, or in the case of a very large event, a professional researcher, will be looking for information about demand for the event and the capacity of the market; any competition; availability of technology, equipment and supplies; financing and sponsorship; organizations and the availability of staff; local cultural or social issues and precedents; and time issues in planning. This information can then be included (or put aside) and helps the organizers to plan and identify what else is needed, but assists also in the

Figure 6.3	State the event objectives, then;

Information-
gathering and
environmental
searching

Identify information needs ⟶ Competition around proposed date
Precedents and histories of previous events
Problems with similar events
Opportunities for this event
Suitability of the event for the market

Identify information sources ⟶ Local information and organizations
Previous years diaries, local newspapers, etc.
Upcoming events diaries, tourist information
Libraries, local societies, websites
Stakeholders and knowledgable individuals

Identify participants ⟶ Staff and organizers involved in the event
Allocate people to research information
Get interested individuals involved

Assign tasks ⟶ Give particular tasks to various team members
Delegate and spread the load
Try to ensure some overlap in searching

Collate and check information ⟶ Record information in minutes or a data file
Feed information to a specific person to cross check

Disseminate information ⟶ 'All hands' meeting to disseminate information
Summary sheet of main points and outcomes
Meeting acts as a check on results
Identify any problems or oversights.

Deal with any problems or oversights ⟶ Ensure gaps are closed wherever possible
Feedback from staff and other sources

Source: adapted from Costa and Teare, 1996.

organization and running of the event. Sometimes, however, the process of 'environmental searching' is not properly done and results in some major problems or mistakes which embarrass the organizers.

Demand and operational planning

For many events, the issue of demand may not seem directly relevant, and for personal events in particular it might be thought that demand is not a significant factor in the planning process, except to know roughly how many people are coming or will be invited to an event, such as a wedding or birthday party. (Yet even for personal events, some checking is needed. You might invite 100 people to your party, but this does not mean 100 people are going to turn up.) For almost all events, demand and the potential market are an issue. General public events can be difficult to plan for. What sort of people are interested? How many might attend? When would be a good date or time to put the event on? It can be difficult to assess this effectively, especially when no similar event has been run before. On the other hand, with many types of events, the potential number of attendees may be quite specific, or specific enough for the event manager to get a feel for the requirements. This can be checked by some research, either inform- ally such as 'talking to the locals', or by formal surveys and questionnaires.

Suppose we were organizing a fancy dress party for a university. We might already know a number of things about the market – the age group, the total number of students, their inclination to dress up, and so on. However, there may be a number of other factors to consider, especially about the date or timing of the event. If it is to be in the evening, then the total market may not be all the students attending the university, but only be the ones who live at the university, and then only those who have not yet made plans for the suggested date. Therefore, judging attendance becomes a fine art and both experience and research are needed to get it right. From an assessment of the whole market, the potential total of attendees and the timing, various other factors can then be considered. The competition may be significant as more than one event may be taking place around the planned date. There may be a gig in town or the University Rugby Club may also be plan- ning its annual party. As a consequence, the timing of the event may become key to ensuring maximum take up-of tickets (by avoiding the dates of the other events). In addition, searching the environment for other timing issues may still be needed, on the basis of other things taking place such as examinations or revision, another important local attraction, a big event on television, like the 'Euro 2004', or the launch of a major new film at the cinema. Also, importantly, whether there is a finance-related timing issue – the students may be better off at the start of term than at the end of it (but might still want to end with a good time). Comparative issues can be seen from this example, even in the case of public events. If a public event is perceived as expensive then it may be appropriate to schedule it only at a vacation time when discretionary income may be available, or when there are tourists around, or at a time of the month when many people get paid.

Moving onto some of the detailed issues of the planning process, the event will require a whole range of resources. It is easy to regard these resources as simply being staff and equipment. In practice, the single most important resource for event managers is time, because the brief for an event may allow only a very limited timescale. The brief (which is a specification or contract for an event, sometimes given by companies or organizers, for commercial and many other types of events) may not allow a realistic timescale in which to do it properly without incurring very high costs of management time, staffing and resources to 'throw at it' in order to get it done. Professional event managers may turn down some briefs on this basis. There has to be enough time to plan the event properly, to meet deadlines and cut-off points and to achieve the set-up, run the event and break down its various elements afterwards.

Case Study 19 *Demand planning: the opening night of the Millennium Dome*

The Millennium Dome, at Greenwich in London, took three years to build. The total cost of the building and its operations was some €1,200 million. It was opened at a ceremony scheduled to start on the evening of 31 December 1999 and run into the early hours of the morning of 1 January 2000.

The Dome was the culmination of a plan, first suggested in 1994, to celebrate a Christian (religious) event for 2000. Initially it was thought

▶

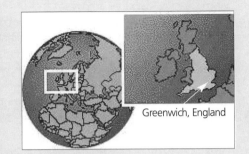

Greenwich, England

Factbox

- Millennium Dome, Greenwich, England
- Cost: in excess of €1,200 million.
- The Dome contained 14 zones.
- Much of the cost was covered by companies sponsoring the Dome and by Lottery grants.
- The opening night was reported as a disaster.

---

that Birmingham, in the English Midlands, would be the site. However, as the idea began to be adopted by the government, the concept changed from being religious (once the site was selected as Greenwich in east London), to having the purpose of regenerating a large area of derelict land on the Greenwich peninsula, overlooking the River Thames. In this form it was intended to be a trade exhibition, rather like the Festival of Britain of 1951, and its forerunners like the Paris Exposition of 1889 (see Case Study 4) but the idea gradually changed from this to an exhibition celebrating 'time' and the phases of life as its theme. The final outcome was the 'Dome', containing 14 zones, such as the mind zone, the journey zone, the home planet zone, etc., representing various life experiences. Each zone attracted sponsorship from national and international companies; for example, Ford sponsored the journey zone with almost €19.5 million of support (Nicholson, 1999).

The opening ceremony, despite every intention to make the event successful, was a shambles of haphazard ticketing, ineptly managed security and the unfortunate late arrival of guests. The results were not only tremendous stress and anger on the night itself, amongst those struggling to get to the event, but also massive public relations damage to the image of the Dome and to the organizing company. The cause of this shambles was inadequate planning and a lack of awareness on the part of the New Millennium Experience Company (NMEC), of scheduling, especially of the ticketing, together with the apparent lack of a thought-out timescale for the activities of ticket processing and security checks. Ten thousand people had been invited to the opening ceremony. A few days before the event, only just over half the tickets had been sent out. At this point, it was discovered that there would not be enough time to post the remaining tickets to the invited guests. The problem was compounded by a lack of a sense of urgency that this was a major material issue that, if not handled well, would cause serious damage.

NMEC showed no apparent significant managerial concern about the ticketing problem until the issue began to appear in the newspapers a few days before, by which time it was too late to get the tickets out. Consequently, guests were told to get themselves to Stratford underground railway station in east London on the night, where special arrangements would be made to get them onto the Tube (London's metro), which was running special trains to the Dome station at Greenwich. The Dome had been designed with almost no car parking, and access was by public transport only; this poor infrastructure was a major cause of low visitor numbers. Indeed, parking was often designated at car parks that were intended to be at public transport hubs, such as Luton Airport, some 70 km from the Dome. (In August 2000, after the Dome had further grants and loans of over €100 million, in addition to its original costs, and with continuing low visitor numbers, a car park with a capacity of 1,000 car parking spaces was opened at the Dome site, too late to save the peak summer season.)

The opening ceremony was to be performed by the Queen, together with the Prime Minister and the Archbishop of Canterbury, and with a large number of VIPs present, and there was to be tight security. In practice this meant that every guest was supposed to walk through an electronic security gate. The impact of 4,000 people turning up at the Stratford underground station, where there were four security gates (only one of which was working properly), had not been adequately thought about or properly checked. As the 4,000 ticketless but invited guests began to turn up at Stratford, in their best evening wear, dinner jackets and ball gowns, the outcome was complete chaos. In no way could 4,000 people get through one gate (Watt and Wells, 2000).

Management locations on the opening night

Senior Management in Greenwich at the Dome

↑

Supervisors at the Dome

↑

Junior contact staff

↑

Operations at Stratford

As the situation deteriorated and with an apparent blasé attitude on the part of the NMEC management, most of whom were already at the Dome and could not understand the magnitude of the chaos at Stratford, partly due to the filtering effect of layers of management and limited communications, as well as the distance, some efforts were made to get the guests to the Dome in time for the main ceremony, scheduled for midnight. Special buses were brought in, and eventually attempts at 'security' were abandoned, in an effort to get people to the Dome. By 10.40 pm, when the 4,000 unfortunate guests were at last beginning to arrive, all the food and drink (including 10,000 bottles of champagne) had been either consumed or removed, and further chaos ensued whilst people tried to find their seats. In this maelstrom the atmosphere of happiness intended for the evening was largely ruined, although the ceremony went ahead.

The following day, the managing director of the NMEC dismissed the chaos as unimportant. Unfortunately for the company, amongst the 4,000 invited guests who had been put through

the chaos at Stratford were several national newspaper editors and their wives, the director-general of the BBC and a number of the major sponsors. The company and the event were savaged in the media, and, together with the government, had to apologise. Within a month, and partly due to 'lower than expected attendances' at the Dome, the chief executive of the NMEC had been replaced. This was the price of inattention to detail in planning and a lack of conviction in management – for example, to avoid jokes about Disney, the NMEC had avoided seeking advice from the amusement park industry, which had the necessary experience of large scale outdoor events. The new chief executive, Pierre-Yves Gerbeau, appointed after the disaster, was from Disney in Europe and an expert in visitor park attractions and ticketing. The Dome closed in December 2000 and the post-event divestment of the site has had all the hallmarks of its dubious pre-event planning.

Based on this case:

Identify the key mistakes that NMEC made in its organization of the opening night of the Dome.

1. What are the likely background reasons for these mistakes?

2. What management tools or systems, used in event management, would have prevented the initial ticketing failure?

3. How did the shambles of the opening night impact on the public and media image of the Dome as an attraction?

4. Was this the only reason for lower than expected visitors to the Dome, or did the Dome have infrastructure and content problems as well?

5. What is the accounting convention known as 'sunk costs' and what might its relevance be to the Dome?

Search news website archives for media commentary on the Dome, such as: http://news.bbc.co.uk.

Source: authors

Event managers therefore need to be aware of key timing issues. The lead times of various event-related activities are often underestimated; hence the difficulty of getting a large number of tickets out for the Dome. But there are many other lead-time issues, from marketing and the production of brochures to the lead time of booking the right venue. Many venues will be booked up well over a year in advance. Popular dates and times of year often take the uninitiated by surprise and almost the first activity in planning will be to identify suitable venues and dates. Bookings can be made provisionally but will usually be subject to a deposit, even if the venue is the village hall. For events that are self-funding this may result in a chicken-and-egg type problem – what to do first: confirm the venue or sell tickets? This is usually resolved by having a cut-off date by which the event will be confirmed, and the venue paid for by selling a limited number of tickets early on. If cancelled, no money is lost before the booking cut-off date and it can then be returned to those who booked early.

Financial planning

The plan should now be starting to have some shape. The organizers should have been able to quantify the size of the event – how many people are coming, whether there is any competition or complimentation and whether the event is convenient in relation to this. Identifying similar events may also have given some feel for the prices people are willing to pay. However, price should not be determined by other events, but by what it will cost to put on your event and whether it has to be profitable (the issue of budgeting is dealt with in more detail later). This issue of pricing is very important, as inexperienced organizers typically underestimate the various costs. It is absolutely essential to sit down and list all the items required and cost them properly: 'a few balloons' may turn into a budget for decorations of several hundreds of euros.

There is a tendency on the part of everyone to say 'Oh well, it will cost about…', without actually checking. When someone does get around to checking the real amount comes as a shock. A good example is discos: someone on the organizing committee always 'has a mate' who does a disco and it will be 'really cheap'. No, it won't! The 'mate' will either not be able to do the date or will take various liberties with the organizers who will find out, after the event, that they could have had a cheaper disco by getting several quotes from firms in the phone book. The other serious mistake is for organizers to start off with a ticket price they have picked out of thin air: 'I think tickets should be…' This method, based on no reasoning whatsoever, is almost guaranteed to land the event in serious financial difficulties. If you decide the ticket price before the costing has been done, you end up cutting back on all the things that make the event special. The ticket price has to be based on accurate costings, and only then considered in the light of competition and what the market will pay (which should also be based on some realistic data, not on what the organizers 'think' the market will pay, which often underestimates reality). A further financial issue that should be included with the budget and cashflow statement, is a calculation about the break-even point of the event. For example, say ticket prices are €10 and costs are €500. For the event to break-even, this means that 50 tickets have to be sold. What if the venue only seats 45? You couldn't make a profit. In essence, once the full costs of the event are known, the ticket price can be calculated, bearing in mind that enough tickets have to be sold to cover all eventualities.

There are other, hidden, cost risks involved in event management. Breakdown and bottleneck costs can be very severe, and not apparent until they occur. The ticketing problems of the Millennium Dome could be thought of as having breakdown costs, with there being not only negative financial outcomes, such as having to pay compensation for the breakdown, and also the costs of damage to the company's reputation, which might turn out to be so severe that the company may not recover. These failure costs can be thought of as falling into three categories:

- Cost risks related to quality management and standards.
- Cost risks related to the expense of putting on the event.
- Costs risks related to the effective timing and scheduling of events.

A tension exists between these issues. For example, for the quality of an event to be assured, both adequate time and money have to be put in; if this is not done, the outcome may not be as intended. This was the case with the Dome's opening night. There was the failure of not having planned enough time and given enough resources (such as expertise, management and staffing) to despatch 4,000 tickets. The breakdown resulted in a quality failure and a cost failure (the simple cost in terms of getting people to the Dome by special buses, and the severe and complex cost afterwards of the public relations damage). What action could have been taken to deal with the problem is open to debate, but it should have been possible, for example, to courier tickets out to more than one location for distribution; to arrange for people to meet at more than one place for their onward transport, as well as to have more than one operating security gate at these different locations. Doing this would have cost money to sort out, quite a lot of money. But it would have saved the reputation of the NMEC. The lesson is to pay enough attention to the services being provided for the event and what the guests are saying. In doing so, the cost of solving a problem as it develops may be less than the cost of trying to put the damage right afterwards.

Marketing planning

All events require marketing planning. We might think some events that are not intended as public activities (such as those for our immediate family and friends), might not need marketing. But think what you do when you invite your friends to a party – you want to make it sound good so people will come, so you are, in effect, doing some marketing. The issue of how to market an event does become significant, even if we are only 'marketing' within a group of friends or neighbours or to a small organization, rather than to the public as a whole. Arguably, we are looking at several marketing-related activities: research (if a public event: who is our market? What will they pay? What are their interests? How will they get to us? etc.); internal marketing, within the organization, both in respect of the people involved in preparing the event and in respect of those people within the organization whom the event would be for; and/or external marketing, for public events or events where some external public relations would be a benefit.

Assuming the event organizers wish to obtain some publicity or public relations coverage, it is necessary to plan the marketing activities that would produce this. For some kinds of activities, such as product launches, the budget available for promoting the event might be very large indeed. For other events, such as a village fête, there might be a modest budget, so, the marketing for it might have to be based on effective public relations rather than on advertising or expensive promotional tools. In working up a marketing plan, the event organizer will have to identify what the available budget is. There are essentially two ways of doing this. One way is to say, well, here is the income, marketing can have so much (after which the marketing team will take fright and probably have to see what they can get for limited money). The other, more preferable, way is to look at the event objectives and work up a marketing budget based on what needs to be done.

The next stage will be planning the marketing effort in terms of time. We can call this a marketing action plan, or even a launch plan. It is a schedule of activities leading up to the event (other activities may take place afterwards, such as getting pictures of the event in the local newspapers). The marketing team will need to

Figure 6.4
Simple example of marketing lead times: Middleburg Sports Day

Outline marketing plan: August/September 2004, week 1 to 4. To raise money for the church bells. Middleburg Sports Day to take place on Saturday 8th September 2004, including a sack race, three-legged race, tug of war, knockout games and 'guess the weight of the big church bell' competition. Various traders and stalls will be booked.

Week	1 MTWTFSS	2 MTWTFSS	3 MTWTFSS	4 MTWTFSS
Write Plan, check costs etc, Book venue	XXX			
Make sure Mayor Beaumont is confirmed to open the event	X			
Send sponsorship request letter to local businesses		XX		
Promote event competition in the town newspaper, public notice boards, library, and halls		XX		
Design a poster		XX		
Write media release		XX		
Send media release			XXX	
Put up poster in key places			XXXXX	
Vicar to go round local businesses to follow up sponsorship letter				XX
Post out invitations on mailing list				XXX
Open sports day				X
Work out what money was made for the bells fund				X
Have a glass of Alsace with Mayor Beaumont				X
Make a note of any problems for next event; send letters of thanks				X

identify the key lead times for each activity. Suppose a printed programme is required. It will be important to find out not only how long it will take to collect the information to include, but also how long the programme will take to print; how long to be proof-read and checked; and how long to be delivered. Many marketing teams have come unstuck with programmes or brochures because a vital piece of information is not ready ('Oh yes, the committee is meeting next week to decide that.' 'But we need to get the programme proof to the printer today.' 'Oh sorry, you'll just have to wait.' 'But it takes six weeks to print…'). In consequence, the key to the marketing programme is to allow enough time and to know who is making relevant decisions and when. Things that often appear simple are not, or take much longer than expected. Comments such as: 'I rang up the radio station to tell them about tomorrow's fireworks…they said they needed to know three weeks ago, in order to get it into the right schedule' are very typical for the inexperienced organizer. It is essential to find out, genuinely, how long marketing and public relations matters will take, and then to plan accordingly.

There are many lead-time issues that relate to the marketing function. These may include, for example, printing: of tickets, posters, menus, programmes, banners, etc.; ordering of equipment: often the more specialized the longer the lead time; advertising and promotion: even local radio may need two or three weeks notification of an event to ensure it is given good coverage; liaison issues: where relevant, with police, highways departments, health and safety, and so on, especially where large numbers of the public may be attending. In essence, the longer the lead time before an event the better, although this is not to say it is impossible to put on an event very quickly, but to do so may need professional help or may result in higher costs.

Getting it together

At the point at which the organizers have gathered all the information, written the plans and sorted out the major issues, there should be a pause. This may happen naturally between the planning and the event, or it may have to be built in. It is needed because there should be sufficient time to reflect on the progress of planning the event so far, because of the need to check the status of the plans, and because time is needed for discussion and feedback and for people and organizations to respond. This is one of those points when everyone should meet to see what else has been done, to discuss what still needs to be achieved and to participate in further arrangements and final checking. Organizers must handle this phase sensitively. It is not necessarily there for them to tell people what will be done, but is to jointly and openly explore progress, and is a characteristic of good events planning, an opportunity to pause and listen.

Throughout this process, the event will be getting closer and closer. There will be deadlines to deal with, and in due course, the event will take place. With careful planning, modest (or major) success should be the result. After that, a short 'wash-up' session should take place, for feedback on the event, to write up the accounts, complete the records and make any notes of importance to the planning of a similar future event.

Summary

Planning, and the planning process, plays a key role in the organization and management of special events. It is a tool that organizers can use effectively or, sometimes, badly. Even the simplest of events, such as a birthday or dinner party, will need to be planned, or at least given some forethought. The larger and more complex events become, the more detailed and systematic the planning will have to be. Care, time and effort at the planning stage of an event will yield many benefits, the most important of which is ensuring the most positive outcome for the event. The issues of planning, in terms of finance, organization, marketing and managing the event are dealt with in much more detail in the chapters which follow.

References

Costa, J. and Teare, R. (1996) 'Environmental Scanning: A tool for competitive advantage', in Kotas, R. et al., *The International Hospitality Business*, London, Cassell, pp.12–20.

Engel, M. (1999) 'Opening of Parliament', London, *Guardian*, 2 July, p.5.

National Centre for Volunteering (2003) Volunteer information sheets, London, NCV, www.volunteering.org.uk/workwith/sheets.htm (4 February 2004).

Nicholson, A. (1999) 'The Theatre of the Age', London, *Sunday Telegraph* 'Magazine', 5 December, pp.11–45.

Reiss, G. (1995) *Project Management Demystified*, London, E&FN Spon, 2nd edn, pp.27–43.

Richards, B. (1992) *How to Market Tourist Attractions, Festivals and Special Events*, Harlow, Longman, pp.21–43.

Stokes, D. (1995) *Small Business Management*, London, DP Publications, pp.210–11.

UK Sport (2003) Major Sports Events: The Guide, London, UK Sport, www.uksport.gov.uk/generic_template.asp.id=12237 (4 February 2004).

Watt., N and Wells, M. (2000) 'Falconer apologises for Dome fiasco', London, *Guardian*, 3 January, p.1.

7 Financial management and the budget

Aims

- To provide an introduction to some of the financial planning, control and budgetary issues in running events.

- To consider the budgetary organization of events in terms of break-even, monitoring and recording of revenues and costs.

- To discuss additional financial issues such as raising income, public funding, concessions and sponsorship.

Introduction

Financial planning and good financial control are important aspects of the event management process. Even if we are only organizing a small personal event, we need to know how much can be spent. For the vast majority of events, there will be both an income and expenditure. The careful monitoring, recording and control of these incomes and expenditures is a significant concern of clients, organizers, co-ordinators and finance officers of all kinds. For the professional finance officer, this chapter will seem a very general outline of what has to be done, but for the person new to the job of volunteer treasurer or financial officer of an event, it should prove a helpful starting point. As such, the purpose of the chapter is not to deal with the entire financial management subject related to the area; for this the reader may wish to look at Wiseman et al. (1996) or Owen (1998). The recording of the financial aspects of events, ranging from the purchase of items to the final budgeted accounts, is potentially much more complicated than the summary here. Good financial control is important to the success of events, even those not intended to be profit-making, but there are many useful accountancy practice books (as noted) and considerable software available for those who wish to expand their expertise.

For events that are revenue generating, as well as those where the recording of outgoings against a client's budget is needed, we can begin to see the necessity of normal accounting processes, rather than simply being able to list the costs on a sheet of paper. Even the scouts of Middleburg with their car wash fund-raising idea can serve to illustrate the fact that events exist whose primary purpose is to make money with a minimum expenditure (a few buckets of warm water, some sponges and a large number of happy scouts being all that is needed), but it is still essential to know what money has been made. So while we might have events that are entirely cost-oriented on the one hand, or entirely income-oriented on the other, there are a very large number of events that require both these things and have to be financially managed in a conventional way, with careful assessment of potential income, expenditure and profit, surplus or break-even, depending on the type of event.

In all cases, some effort needs to go into providing an overview of the financial aspects of the event, both at the planning stage, during the event itself and at the end. In the case of the wedding or the scouts' car wash, this might simply comprise a list of what has been spent or what has been made (it is better to do two lists – of what is planned and what actually happened – both forecast and actual). Clearly, if the wedding was planned to cost €5,000, but €10,000 was spent, someone had to find the money. Equally, if the scouts planned to raise €1,000 from washing cars but raised only €500, then perhaps the new roof and redecoration of their hut might have to be reduced to the new roof. The function of financial control is to tell us what happened, but it also takes place before and during an event. Beforehand, a budget will be needed so the organizers can judge whether the event is likely to be a success, and afterwards as a guide to see whether the event could be judged successful against its financial objectives. Additionally, we will look at ways in which the potential income for an event could be increased, and also at the public funding of events and sponsorship.

Objectives and financial planning

The setting of objectives is important for the entire event and also the key to what has to be done financially. Event organizers may be faced with a range of financial choices depending on what has been decided about the objectives (see chapter 5, about the financial screening process). Care, time and effort will need to be expended at an early stage to ensure good financial management, and that all the possible kinds of expenditure and income have been identified. Small personal events, whose objective is simply the enjoyment of the participants, may have little in the way of financial management, except an awareness of the potential spend in the most general terms. For very large events on a regional, national or international scale, the financial aspects may have to become the subject of financial feasibility studies based on a range of possible techniques, from cost-benefit analysis to assessing the tourism multiplier of a total event project (Hall, 1997). Such techniques are, however, rather beyond the boundaries of this book and we will concentrate on the more common aspects of financial management in terms of budgeting and control, which are appropriate for the popular range of events.

One key to the effective financial management of events is the appointment of someone responsible for it, in the same way that members of an organizing committee might be responsible for bookings, organization, staff and publicity. It is rather typical of events (particularly those that rely on volunteer staffing, as many do) for their financial aspects to be relatively poorly understood, especially in terms of cashflow (that is, the relative timing of income and expenditure). Many events organizers do not fully appreciate the financial implications of the decisions they are making and are consequently surprised, when the accounts are done, how little profit has been made or how big a loss has been incurred. Even apparently unrelated decisions can have a major impact on revenue. A good example might be the timing of an event. If this decision is wrong, and perhaps the event clashes with a similar one at the same time, then the target market might not be able to attend both, with a consequent loss of ticket sales, income and other revenue, which may result in a forecast profit becoming an actual loss. For this reason, a numerate and capable person should be appointed to oversee the accounts.

It is also useful to understand the links between the original setting of the objectives and to follow those through into the financial management and budgets. It is no good saying in the objectives (as in the example in Figure 7.1), that a key objective is to raise enough money 'to rebuild the city stadium', if it is not known how much that would cost, and whether the budget for the event will actually be able to cope with it. Similarly, it is no good saying that the objective for a wedding is to spend less than €5,000, if this is not properly written into the budget, or if someone goes out and blows €4,500 on the pre-wedding party, leaving only €500 for the whole of the actual wedding ('Oh, nobody told me we only had €5,000'). The objectives and the financial management are intimately linked. It is essential that the organizers make the links clear (remember the SMART acronym [see page 165]: the budget is about measuring).

Figure 7.1	**A leisure event**	
	International city athletic competition:	
Examples of various event objectives	Primary objectives:	• To develop sporting talent in athletics
		• To bring a large number of visitors to the city to watch or participate
		• To improve the city's image
	Financial Objectives:	• To make enough money (surplus from the event) to rebuild the city stadium
		• To provide some additional housing once the competitors have left (Based on the financing of the athletes' village in conjunction with developers)
	A cultural event	
	Village fête:	
	Primary objective:	• To hold an enjoyable annual celebration for the village
	Financial objective:	• To make enough money to break even and to buy a new bench to put beside the village pond
	An organizational event	
	Sales manager's team-building day:	
	Primary objective:	• To improve the team skills of the sales department
	Financial objective:	• To keep within the budgeted cost allowed for staff development
	A personal event	
	Family wedding:	
	Primary objective:	• To celebrate the wedding and have a good time
	Financial objective:	• To cost less than €5,000

Cashflow issues also tend to be serious, particularly for events that involve pre-booking, such as a fund-raising dinner. Some expenditure or investment may well have to take place before any income is generated or tickets sold, thus exposing the organizers to risk of financial failure. Venues for events often have long lead times for bookings and require money up front to hold or confirm the booking. When this is the case, the treasurer (or finance officer of the organizing committee) will have to ensure sufficient money is available to pay for the various costs before the deadlines, or risk losing the booking and the event. This will mean careful attention to issues such as debt collection and credit periods. (For example, if an agent has agreed to take a certain number of advance tickets for an event, when do you, as finance office of the event, get paid for them? If the period between booking the tickets and payment is too long, your event might go bankrupt in the meantime, because you have to pay money out but have not got enough cash coming in) (see Figure 7.2).

Suppose a town festival committee has booked a marquee for a medieval banquet as the climax to its annual town pageant. Although the festival might not take place until August, the marquee company, the caterers and the musicians may all want a booking fee. Suppose these booking fees add up to €1,000. The capacity of the marquee is 250, and the booking deadline is the end of June. In a very basic way, the financial manager will either have to find €1,000 from existing funds (if the event has been run before and generated a surplus in previous years), or, in the case of there being no existing funds, would have to get 250 deposits of €4 per person (or equivalent) to cover the booking costs by, say, a week before the end of June, to have a chance of the event running; or funds from other methods, such as sponsorship, donations or borrowing (e.g. a

Figure 7.2

Cashflow at events

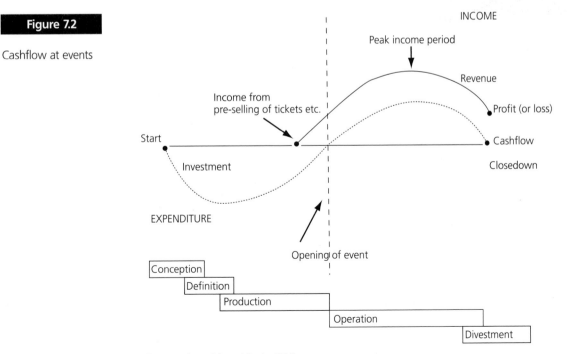

Source: adapted from Morris, 1994.

bank loan, bearing in mind that this would have to be repaid with interest, probably against some form of security). This might be only the first of several financial deadlines and serves to illustrate that cashflow and deadlines could mean the difference between whether an event runs or not.

Creating a budget

For commercial organizations, senior management or a head of department might do the preparation of a budget for an event. However, in the case of many events, run by volunteers, committees, individuals or families, who may have no experience of how to make an event work in financial terms, the preparation of a budget might involve several people, or a volunteer with some financial or organizational background suited to the task. For the person new to the financial aspects of running an event, the planning of a budget may not be as easy as it first appears, since a great deal of information has to be collected, and many new techniques learned, which might not be obvious at the start. However, the time and effort put into careful preparation of a budget is extremely important to the success of the event, and to the financial and general control of what is going on.

The budget for an event may be no more complicated than a list of revenues and costs, or it may be vastly complicated. Either way, it has to be determined with the objectives of the event in mind. It is no good setting a budget in which a large profit is forecast, if the event is supposed to be for public entertainment and only intended to generate a small surplus or to break even, because making a large profit might result in having to charge too high a ticket price. So, what is the financial objective? Is the event intended to make money or simply to cover its costs? If it is to cover costs, what is the total amount that can be spent, specified either by the clients or by the organizing committee?

The ticket price issue is also a frequent source of heated debate, sometimes before any attempt has been made to identify costs. This is a very common mistake, partly because organizers wrongly see it as the most important issue.

Figure 7.3

Some common budgeting mistakes

- Ignoring the objectives of the event when setting the budget.

- Plucking a figure out of the air for ticket sales *before* finding out how much the event is going to cost (a serious and regrettably frequent mistake).

- Not involving everyone concerned in the budget preparation and failing to identify the full range of costs accurately.

- Being over-optimistic about demand for the event, or failing to find a venue with enough capacity to do it properly.

- Overlooking subsidiary issues such as the costs of ensuring safety and security, or the effect of having to add tax.

- Not having enough capital or start-up funds to get the event off the ground, given the need for deposits or advanced payments of various kinds.

- People spending money but not getting receipts or invoices, so the money is unchecked and you have no control evidence that they actually spent it.

The ticket price might be an important issue, but it simply is not good enough to say 'We must make it cheap or no-one will come'. This is usually based on someone's private opinion, not on a carefully budgeted assessment of the costs, let alone on an objective view of what the target market would really pay. In essence, costs need to be listed first and accurately (not just, 'My mate said it would be the same as the one they did last year at the football ground'). Quotes or actual prices need to be obtained for all aspects of the activity. For the football ground, for example, by getting the quote from the ground manager, not from 'your mate'. In some cases there would need to be more than one quote. Quotations should be made on like for like basis, and the criteria decided (do you want the cheapest quotation, or the best quality of good or services, etc.?). From there, the expenditure can be assessed and then, and only then, should a ticket price be estimated, bearing in mind the numbers expected to come (Bowdin et al., 2001).

In the case of certain types of events there might also be differential pricing of tickets (e.g. at sporting events, where the best seats have a higher price). Differential pricing also allows us to provide a range of tickets at a range of prices, for example, family tickets, group tickets, full price or off-peak tickets. This requires careful understanding. Suppose our event needs to sell 120 tickets at €10 each to make our target profit, but our estimates of what the target market will pay show that only half the people we expect to attend will pay the full price, even though we are expecting an attendance of 120 people. What do we do? Perhaps we might have to cancel. On the other hand, we might find that the rest are willing to pay €6.00 for tickets (we will call these 'contribution price' tickets). Does this help, even if we have said ticket price must be €10? It depends on whether the €6.00 will be enough to cover our fixed costs, and if enough people paying full price still want to come. Fixed costs might be €5.00 per person (this is very simplified).

Full profit is €1,200, and in this case, break-even required is €750 (i.e. total fixed and variable costs)

We can sell 60 full price tickets at €10 = €600

We can also sell 60 contribution price tickets at €6 = €360

The total income would thus be €960 and the event would make a profit, even though we couldn't sell all our tickets at the full price and make the full profit. You will have noticed that I didn't use the word 'discount' in this example. Forget 'discount', as it gives you the wrong idea, since the contribution tickets still have to cover all fixed costs, and we still have to sell enough of all tickets to cover our total costs. This is why you can go to, say, a leisure centre or a theme park at an off-peak period and pay less than you would at a peak period. It is about having differential ticket prices for different times, for different target markets (see chapter 9) and different groups, in the knowledge that not everyone will pay full price, at any given time. Airlines do it too. You might have got the last two seats on a plane at €50, when everyone else has paid €500 a ticket, but that is because the plane is covering its total costs, and they might as well have two people with cheap seats, rather than two empty seats. On the other hand, if everyone paid €50, then they probably couldn't afford to taxi the plane along the runway. This is also true of events, and can lead you to do some creative ticket pricing, if you have to. But only if you have to.

Figure 7.4

Outline budget form for quotations

PRELIMINARY BUDGET FORM

Proposed event:..   Date today: ....

Date of event: ....   Days to go:...

Forecast number of people expected: ....   *(paying guests/paying visitors)*

Capacity of venue:..

List of costs

Venue hire: total amount: € ....

Deposit amount: € ....   Deposit due by: ....

Staff/labour: number of volunteers needed: ....   Number of paid staff needed: ....

Total staffing cost inc. staff feeding: € ....

Example Overheads	Total amount €	Best price quotation given by:
Advertising	....	....
Pricing/posters/tickets	....	....
Signs/place cards/menus/programmes	....	....
Custom T-shirt/uniform/badges	....	....
Equipment hire	....	....
Food	....	....
Drink	....	....
Entertainment	....	....
Music	....	....
Decorations	....	....
Linen/linen hire	....	....
Prizes/complimentary items	....	....
Floristry/plants	....	....
Security/crowd control/guides/info point	....	....
Insurance	....	....
Refuse removal/cleaning	....	....
Power/heat/ light/air conditioning	....	....
Ticket distribution/stationary/postage	....	....
Licence/licence application	....	....
Audio-visuals/sounds	....	....
Phones/mobiles/radio links	....	....
Photographer/video company/press kit	....	....
Other items	....	....
Total costs, including venue and staff	_____	

Total costs divided by number of paying guests (including venue hire, staffing and any other items not listed here but known, expected or planned):   € .... (Costs per person)

Profit/Surplus required?   € .... (Profit per person)

List any additional deposits or prepayments required:

....

Does your list include VAT? (sales tax) ....

A major issue for event organizers is knowing how many people will attend. In order to prepare a reasonably accurate budget, the estimates of attendance may be based on surveys of the market, attendance at similar or previous events, knowledge of the size of the available customer base, and so on. From the point of view of budget preparation, an organizer might want to be optimistic about attendance, but, given the potential problems about booking deadlines and deposits, it is important to be realistic about how many tickets can be sold and whether the venue can be filled, or whether the budget should estimate to break even, if, say, half the venue is filled. Optimism is very nice, but the real test is often when the organizing committee or sales team go out and try to sell tickets and find that 'no-one wants to buy them yet'. There are ways in which this kind of response can be influenced, such as by asking for a deposit (once people have committed some money they are generally likely to pay the balance when the time comes), or by offering discounts for advance purchase (rather like advance purchase airline tickets), or by selling tickets to key opinion formers as a way of generating interest.

Break-even is a key issue and sometimes not well understood. Say an event will cost €500 to put on, and the venue will accommodate 100 people. At first glance you might say, we need to sell 100 tickets at €5. But if you did this, you would make a loss even if 99 out of the 100 tickets were sold. You have to consider what your realistic break-even point is. To make €100 profit in this case you would have to sell 100 tickets at a ticket price of €6, not €5.

Other difficulties arise due to unforeseen costs or subsidiary issues, a common one being whether tax has to be added to ticket prices. For most small-scale or family events, this is irrelevant, but for big events it would have to be checked with the correct government department, as there is a minimum threshold for payment (in the UK, this is the Department of Customs and Excise and the UK VAT threshold at the time of writing is £52,000 before registration is required).

For those new to events budgeting, the Outline Budget Form in Figure 7.4 will help you understand what is needed and what information may be missing. It may also show that once you have identified all the costs, your first ideas about how much to charge as an entry fee or ticket may be completely wrong. Most important of all, it may also be evident that there is no margin of safety in running the event between its revenue and its forecast costs. In simple terms, there have to be enough people attending and paying to cover the costs and make sure there is a profit or small surplus. (Although some events are not intended to make a profit.)

Suppose our total costs are €1,000. We forecast that 100 people will attend, so the cost would appear to be €10 per person. This, however, is not a safe position to be in, as even if 99 people come to the event it will still make a loss. The budget should be worked out based on the idea that more people will come to the event than are needed to cover the costs, for example, 125 people at €10. Or that the ticket price is higher, for example, 100 people at €12.50. In this respect it is also necessary to take into account not only how many people we expect to attend, but whether the venue capacity is appropriate. If the venue will only accommodate 75 people but we need 100 people to attend in order to cover our costs or make a profit, then the event is not viable at that venue. It is possible, on the basis of various cost estimates, for the organizing committee or finance officer to prepare some comparative outline budgets to help the decision-making process, where an issue, like the venue, needs to be compared with others (see Figure 7.5).

This first attempt at providing an adequate outline budget will help us identify what further information is needed to prepare a more detailed budget forecast. The detailed budget can be based on a given number of attendees, or we can have alternatives showing worst case and best case. It is necessary, probably crucial, to have a good idea of the point at which the event will break-even and make a profit. For this we have to bear in mind that some costs are fixed and some are variable (Wilson and Chua, 1993). For example, for whatever number of people attend, the cost of hiring a marquee for an event would be fixed, let us say €1,450. The marquee will still cost €1,450 whether one person attends our event or whether 100 people attend – this is a *fixed* cost. On the other hand, the cost of the food might be variable in relation to the number of people: let us suppose a sit-down meal costs €20 per person. In the case of the meal, if one person attends the cost is €20. If 50 people attend the cost is €1,000 and if 100 people attend it is €2,000. This is a *variable* cost (see Figure 7.6).

In terms of expenditure and costs it is essential that we have properly calculated the total costs and have included every cost that might be involved. It is very important to ensure that all the costs have been checked and that the list is genuinely complete.

Figure 7.5 Example of comparative outline budgets for a proposed company party			
Venue	Luigi's garden bistro	Rolf's bar and marquee	Rumours nightclub
Venue capacity	60	100	120
No. of guests expected	50	50	50
Costs			
Venue hire	0	1,450 *(marquee)*	500 *(deposit)*
Staffing costs	0 *(included in meal)*	0 *(included in meal)*	100 *(door/costs)*
Printing	50	50	50
Menus & place cards	50	50	50
Food	1,250 *(sit down meal)*	1,000 *(sit down meal)*	750 *(buffet)*
Reception drinks	300	300	300
Band	500	500	500
Raffle prizes	100	100	100
Total estimated costs	2,250	3,450	2,350
Ticket price if 40 people attend	€45	€69	€47

Figure 7.6

Break-even chart

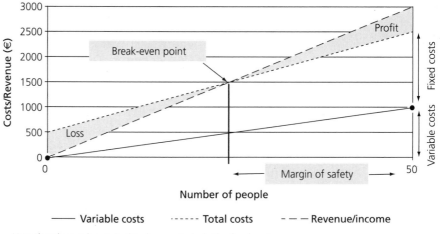

Note that the total costs in this diagram include the fixed costs

Case Study 20 *Event break-even: the annual dinner of the Ecclesbourne Valley Railway*

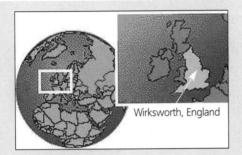

Wirksworth, England

Factbox

- The Ecclesbourne Valley Railway.
- 14-km heritage railway at Wirksworth, near Derby, England.
- Runs a number of public events each year.
- Annual dinner targeted at members and shareholders.
- Purpose of the event: to raise money for the railway.

The Ecclesbourne Valley Railway is typical of the many heritage railways and railway museums in the UK and in other parts of Europe. It is a 14-km privately owned railway line in the English Midlands, providing a tourist experience for people interested in railway history, steam locomotives, and historic railway equipment and artefacts. As a tourist attraction run largely by volunteers, it not only raises its revenue through ticket sales, retail activities, catering and other commercial means, but also through events of various kinds, charitable grants and donations and local authority contributions. This range of fund-raising is necessary to keep the railway operational and to help restore and maintain its historic artefacts.

In the 2004 event season the following annual dinner was costed. This type of dinner, often called a fund-raising dinner or 'Sportsman's' dinner, is very typical of this sort of event. Such dinners are common amongst all kinds of charitable, voluntary and sporting organizations, and in the case of some of the smaller organizations, a dinner of this kind may be the major social event in their calendar. In most cases the objectives are as follows. Primary objective: fund-raising (either in general, or for a specific reason, e.g. new kit for a rugby club; refurbishment of the club's premises; new fencing, etc.); secondary objectives: social meeting of an organization's members and supporters; raising of the organization's profile amongst potential supporters and sponsors; opportunity to invite honoured guests, contributors or sponsors by way of thanks for their interest in or help given to the organization.

In the case of the Ecclesbourne Valley Railway, the primary purpose is to raise funds for the maintenance and repair of historic rolling stock (engines, carriages, wagons, etc.). The secondary purpose is to provide a social opportunity for the railway's shareholders and members, the budget for the event being based on a maximum number of 150 guests and a break-even point of 38 guests.

There are some interesting issues in considering this data:

First, unlike our text examples, the fixed costs for this dinner can be reduced somewhat to lower the break-even point. For example, this could be done for the guest speaker's expenses by not having a guest speaker. Thus, if demand for tickets were very low indeed, but those attending still wished it to go ahead without having a speaker, some fixed costs could be saved here. Some further fixed costs could be saved by not having the menus and place cards printed professionally, but simply printing one menu per table on a home computer. Also, the cost of mailing out final tickets fall if there are fewer of them. So if the organization wanted the event to go ahead for secondary reasons (in this case social reasons), this could still be done, even though very little profit could be made.

Second, further money could be raised during the event itself, separate from ticket revenue.

Venue: the Garden Suite, Midland Hotel, Derby, England. Event date: Friday 24 September 2004

Maximum capacity of the venue: 150 diners. Ticket Price: €45

	For 150 people	For 38 people
Fixed Costs	€	€
Venue hire	300.00	300.00
Guest speaker's expenses	150.00	0.00
Menus and place cards	75.00	2.25
Mail-out to shareholders promoting the event	285.00	285.00
Photocopying of booking form for mail-out	60.00	60.00
Photocopying and mail-out of booked tickets	51.75	30.00
	921.75	677.25
Variable Costs		
Cost of dinner per head €26.40	3,960.00	1,029.60
Total Costs	4,881.75	1,706.85
Revenue at ticket price €45	6,750.00	1,710.00
Profit on event	€1,868.25	€3.15

This is very common at charitable dinners and is done by holding raffles, playing bingo, having a range of money-raising games (e.g. tops and tails, etc.) or holding auctions of donated gifts or pledges. Third, the very act of holding the event might bring in new sponsors, advertisers or useful contacts. In consequence, if organizers at any fund-raising dinner had to make a decision about whether to run their dinner in the case of only break-even on ticket sales, they might still wish to carry on because of the secondary benefits.

Based on this case:

1. Suppose the above event had three additional revenue-earning games, a raffle, a bingo game and an auction of a prize, which respectively brought in €350 per activity, what would be the total profit of this event at its maximum capacity?

2. Consider any fund-raising activity or dinner you have attended. How has the main revenue been earned and what additional sources of revenue have the organizers found?

3. The guest speaker's expenses in this case were very small, the speaker being a local man with an interest in railway history. What might the costs have been for a 'celebrity' or professional speaker?

4. Might these costs have wiped out the potential profit of this event? How could this be overcome?

Related website for those interested in the Ecclesbourne Valley Railway:
www.ecclesbournevalleyrailway.com

Source: authors, 2004.

Figure 7.7

General budget
form (summary
sheet)

(Summary) EVENT BUDGET

Event: ....

Date of Event: .... Date of this budget: ....

Attendance (Paying guests) Forecast: .... Actual: ....

Income/Revenue	Budget €	Actual €
Ticket Sales	....	....
Catering	....	....
Income from concession stand rental	....	....
Raffle/games	....	....
Other (Specify)	....	....
Total Income	€	€ ....

Expenditure	Budget €	Actual €
Venue hire	....	....
Staff/labour	....	....
Advertising	....	....
Printing/posters/tickets	....	....
Signs/place cards/menus/programmes	....	....
Custom T-shirt/uniform/badges	....	....
Equipment hire	....	....
Food	....	....
Drink	....	....
Entertainment	....	....
Music	....	....
Decorations	....	....
Linen/linen hire	....	....
Prizes/complimentary items	....	....
Floristry/plants	....	....
Security/crowd control/guides/info point	....	....
Insurance	....	....
Refuse removal/cleaning	....	....
Power/heat/light/air conditioning	....	....
Ticket distribution/stationary/postage	....	....
Licence/licence application	....	....
Audio-visuals/sounds	....	....
Phones/mobiles/radio links	....	....
Photographer/video company/press kit	....	....
Other items	....	....
Total costs, including venue & staff	€	€ ....
Surplus (profit) or deficit (loss)	€	€ ....

The detailed budget

It would be very easy to use the common financial term 'budgetary control' at this stage. However, 'control' often concentrates financial managers' minds only on costs or expenditure, and clearly, in event management terms, revenue generation and the 'whole' picture are equally important. If the event objective is about quality rather than profitability, then over-concentration on costs might well damage the success of the event, because cheap materials would be bought rather than good quality ones. We have already noted that certain types of events can be more revenue-led than cost-led.

A budget is a forecast or plan, which helps to regulate the operation of an event (or any business) over a given period of time. In the case of a business such as a hotel, the budget might be an annual one. In the case of an event, because events are one-off and time limited, the budget will normally be for the time period of that event. A budget is also a management tool by which responsibility for various activities (e.g. sales or the control of costs) can be seen, in much the same way as the general event plan. The budget, both a forecast of what is intended to happen and a record of what is happening (or, after the event, of what had happened), acts as a means of comparing the forecast with the reality and sets targets that the organizers can strive to achieve.

The advantages of having a budget are that it is a detailed forecast of what should be happening financially, and as such it helps planning. But, as with any other element of a plan, it should not be a single controlling factor. A budget is just that, a financial guide, not a straitjacket. The budget should result in better co-ordination between the organizers of an event. For example, the budget could be split into revenue budget, as a target for the ticket sales staff to achieve; a publicity budget for the marketing staff to keep within and an operations budget for the events manager to ensure that he/she has not overspent on printing, decorations, staff, equipment or other resources. The budget is intended to act as a measure of performance between that which is forecast and the actual outcome which the organizers are responsible for. This forecasting may often be difficult for events because of their unique nature, and be simply an approximate estimate. On the other hand, some events may have occurred before, in similar circumstances, or in previous years, and a new budget can be created from the actual outcome of the last event, with a little adjustment.

Budgeting is also a method of controlling expenses and costs, because it should help to establish clear lines of responsibility about who can or cannot spend money. Related to this, the budget should also make managers aware of costs and revenues, so that they do not become over-enthusiastic in spending money, or fail to exploit an opportunity to make money or generate revenue from some aspect of the event. For example, it might be very nice to have a media celebrity open a carnival or present the winners of a sports competition with their prize, but most media celebrities charge a major fee for appearing, and if this has not been budgeted for, it should not be done – it might result in an event that should have made money making a loss.

The budget, because it is helping the planning process, should also seek to ensure that the resources the organizer has are most economically or efficiently used, thus helping to keep costs under control or to ensure a profit or surplus is made. For example there is no point hiring 20 ushers all day if they are only

Figure 7.8

Budget: detailed
income and costs –
final outcome
summary

DETAILED EVENT BUDGET SUMMARY AND COST BREAKDOWNS

Event: ....

Date of Event: .... Date of this budget: ....

Attendance	Forecast:	Actual:
Paying visitors/Guests	....	....
Complimentary/Hospitality visitors	....	....
VIPs	....	....
Press	....	....

Opening balance (at bank) € ....

Income/Revenue	Budget €	Actual €
Ticket sales		
Individual	....	....
Family	....	....
Group	....	....
Discount/Elders	....	....
Catering		
Restaurant food	....	....
Restaurant drink	....	....
Arena coffee bar	....	....
Arena hospitality area extras	....	....
Income from concession stand rental		
Ice cream stands	....	....
Retail Stands	....	....
Raffle		
Saturday raffle	....	....
Sunday raffle	....	....
Other (specify): parking	....	....
Total Income	€	€ ....

Expenditure	Budget €	Actual €
Venue hire	....	....
Staff/labour		
Staff wages	....	....
Staff feeding	....	....
Staff insurance	....	....
Staff uniforms	....	....
Volunteers feeding	....	....
Volunteers gift bags	....	....
Volunteers sashes and armbands	....	....
Advertising		
Local radio 6 adverts (10 second)	....	....
The Telegraph 3 adverts (1/8 page)	....	....
Banners (2)	....	....
Newspaper insert (10,000)	....	....
Artwork for leaflets	....	....
Leaflets (10,000)	....	....
Etc.	....	....
Etc.	....	....
Etc.	....	....
Total costs	€	€ ....
Surplus (profit) or deficit (loss)	€	€ ....
Closing balance (at bank)	€	€ ....

going to be needed for the first ten minutes, and costs like this might well show up in the forecast as being out of line with the rest of the budget. The budget can be made more or less detailed depending on the needs of the organizers or clients. For a small event, it might be enough to include minor costs (cost of ushers, for example) in the budget line about staffing. On the other hand, we might want to have full and complete details of all items. To do this, the general budget, with its list of incomes and costs, can be broken down into extra information (see Figure 7.8).

Who spends what

We have now prepared our detailed budget, it has been approved by the clients or the organizing committee, and the serious preparations are about to begin. People will want to go out and spend money, but before they do, it is vital that we have a control system in place to record who is spending what, when and how. Each part of the budget needs to have someone responsible for it (not just the finance officer who wrote it). The revenue part of the budget might be the responsibility of the marketing department, together with their own expenditure. For example, the advertising expenditure budget might be €1,000, but in giving the marketing department this amount to spend, we expect them to attract 500 people to the event, paying €10 a ticket. Therefore the marketing department must have its own clear targets about how its money is best spent to attract the 500 people. Similarly, if we expect the catering department to make money, say, €500 on beverages, it needs to have some idea of what kind of beverages it is going to sell, and how many it will have to sell and at what price and profit to make the expected €500.

An important issue is who is allowed to spend money. If a department has a budget, normally it will be the department head who has the authority to spend it, and the key question is how much and who else can authorize this. Events management depends on the ability of managers and events organizers to solve problems, often very quickly. If they do not have the funds to do this, or the ability to take decisions quickly, then the event may fail (the ticketing fiasco at the Millennium Dome opening night is an example – the inability to deal with the problem of not being able to get enough tickets out to enough people might have resulted from the ticketing manager's lack of authority to spend enough money to get the tickets out in time). Also, in normal circumstances, many items for events are pre-ordered, and for this to take place properly not only are purchase specifications needed (which describe what sort of item is being ordered in detail, so you get what you ordered on the day, e.g. 500 blue stacking chairs, not 250 green armchairs), but also purchase order numbers for any item above a given amount (see Figure 7.9). In this way expenditure can be properly recorded (Lucey, 2002).

Similarly, for small items, petty cash may be needed and a system will have to be set up to issue it (petty cash is a small amount of money for items that have to be paid for in cash, say at local shops, also minor items and those that are too small to be bought in bulk). Normally, an amount of petty cash (perhaps €500) might be held by the event co-ordinator and issued on petty cash vouchers (see Figure 7.10),

Figure 7.9

Purchase order form

MIDDLEBURG EVENT COMPANY

Festival Park Street
Middleburg
0044(0)1786123456

to:
Red Dragon Furniture Hire
Ty Gywn
Fford Uwd
Abertawe, Wales
SW5 6RE

Order nr: 48519
date: 14 August 2004

Dear Sir/Madam,
Please supply and deliver the following items to the address and on the date stated below:

Quality	*Size*	*Description*	*Cost*
500	Standard	Stacking chairs (type 2000) Blue only	€5,600 (incl VAT)

Delivered to
Mr Kevin McDonald
Events co-ordinator
At: Middleburg Music Festival
Festival Park Street
Middleburg

On
28 August 2004
(before 1 pm)

Yours faithfully,

Anna Murray

Purchasing officer
Middleburg Event Company
anna@middleburg.co.eu

Figure 7.10

Petty cash voucher

Petty Cash

Petty cash requested for:

_____

_____

Amount issued:

€_____ / ___ cents

Issued to (signature):

_____

Date:

_____

Print name

_____

Authorized by (signature):

_____

Receipt attached for items

Cost: amount used

€_____ / ___ cents

so that people can be sent out quickly for things that are needed. ('Oh, we've run out of teabags.' 'OK, here's a 20, go and get a box. And bring me the receipt.') At the end of the event, the various petty cash vouchers and receipts, together with the major receipts and invoices, will be collated to make up the final accounts.

The budget is also a mechanism for showing what is going wrong. If the budget shows a forecast expenditure of €1,000 on seating, but the real cost is €2,000, you need to find out why, and to do so quickly. The reasons might be legitimate and necessary, and you might have to adjust the rest of the budget to take account of this, perhaps by increasing prices or cutting back on something else. On the other hand, the reason may not be legitimate and you will have to take very rapid action. Someone may be defrauding you, or theft is taking place, or any number of other problems, which the divergence between the budget forecast and the actual might show.

Other sources of income

So far we have assumed that income is derived from people buying tickets. It is important to bear in mind that there might be other sources of income or revenue besides the ticket sales. These sources may be other revenue-generating activities, or sponsorship-related activities. Nevertheless, it is important to bear in mind that a large number of events, especially corporate events, have a predetermined budget as part of their brief, as the event is not intended to raise money, but to perform some other organizational function, so that income (or revenue) is simply a matter of the use (or application) to which the budgeted figure is put.

Special events are such diverse activities that it can be difficult to generalize about them, especially in financial terms. Additional income is often needed for events, even those where there is a defined ticket price. For example, we might wish to run a charity or philanthropic fund-raising race night and charge tickets at €15. This might raise a good amount, above and beyond what was needed to break even. But more money might also be generated for charity by having other activities going on besides the races. There could be a raffle, or an auction of pledges, there could be games such as 'hit the whisky bottle' (with a large denomination coin, whoever gets the closest wins the bottle, and the rest of the coins are collected for the charity), there could be a cash bar, in addition to, say, wine included in the ticket price. A little careful thought can identify many good,

Figure 7.11

Sources of additional revenue in addition to ticket or admission prices

Programmes / brochures / guidebooks

Catering / fast food / sales stalls

Retail / souvenirs / clothing / merchandising

Corporate hospitality areas / lounges / chill-out areas / crèche

Photography charges / photography sales / video

Car parking / transport services

Concessions / stalls / stands / pitches / franchises / rentals / contracting

Raffles / lottery / tombola / games

Broadcast rights (usually major sporting events only)

The use of 'membership'-type subscriptions to encourage repeat visits (where appropriate)

simple, money-raising activities, thus helping to increase the income of an event (see Figure 7.11). (Control needs to be exercised over loose cash, though. Money should be recorded properly if going through tills. If being collected in some other way, e.g. for charity, it needs to be collected in *sealed* containers, which should only be opened with two people present. In this way it can be counted and recorded legitimately.)

This is not to say that the financial manager of an event should not be actively seeking external or additional ways of raising money to support an event. In fact, the generation of additional revenue is often a key failure of many events, especially volunteer events, because it is wrongly seen as less important than financial control. It is easy to see who is responsible for cost control within budgets, but the raising of additional or extra revenues is often overlooked: no-one is made responsible for ideas about it or for carrying through such ideas and consequently opportunities to raise extra income streams are lost.

Events vary considerably in how they are funded. It is important to recognize that many events have more than one source of income or revenue – in fact there might be as many sources of income as there are costs associated with the event. Equally, we should not regard the term 'income' as necessarily meaning revenue. The 'income' for operating an event may simply be a budgeted amount that an organization has to spend, funded by the organization itself. Similarly, events put on by government or councils may depend on a budgeted amount, which is funded by tax nationally or locally. The purpose of tax is to provide public

Figure 7.12	
Types of event funding	

Leisure event:

International city athletics competition
Funding: Possible range of funding including from government agencies such as sports councils, local government funding for sporting events, support from sports sponsors and broadcasters, together with income generated from ticket sales, concessions selling food, drink and sports-related merchandise.

Cultural event:

Village fête
Major income might be from entrance tickets, parking, income from renting pitches for the various stands, money raised from a raffle and various games, also sponsorship of activities on an organizational or individual basis, charitable donations in money or in kind (gifts).

Organizational event:

Sales managers' team-building day
No direct income as such. The event will be paid for within a particular budget determined by the organization and operated by the Sales Department itself (for staff training) or a related department such as personnel, according to the appropriate organizational objective.

Personal event:

Small family wedding
No direct income as such. The event would be paid for by the people getting married, and/or their families, with donations of presents and other useful things 'in kind' e.g. friends decorate the church, or help make a buffet, contribute flowers, etc.

services, of which sporting, cultural, ceremonial or tourist events might be one example (in the same way that rubbish collection, street lighting and hospitals are public services paid for out of taxes). Certain types of events can require start-up funding. This can be sought from all kinds of bodies who might have an interest in the event, not just government, councils or agencies, although there are official bodies (and some sponsors) who often have limited funds for this type of activity(but many calls on them).

Sponsorship and public funding

One of the common misconceptions in the design of events is the view that an event will easily attract sponsorship. In practice the attractiveness of any given event to potential sponsors is very limited. The time and effort that the organizers might waste trying to get (elusive) sponsorship could well be better used elsewhere, perhaps in developing secondary income streams for the event, such as catering or retailing, as mentioned earlier (Hall, 1997). The most important aspect of sponsorship is for event organizers to remember that potential sponsors have to get something out of the event, and are extremely unlikely to provide money for nothing ('Oh, but you can have an advert in our programme...' 'Really? Why should I need that?'). Therefore it is important to keep in mind what the event would do for a potential sponsor (Watt, 1998). There are several aspects to this. First, the event and potential sponsors should be looking at the same target market. It is no good trying to get a hearing aid manufacturer to sponsor an annual student ball. Second, the issue of media exposure: what are the publicity and public relations plans for your event, and will the sponsor benefit from them? Thirdly, will the sponsor get some direct benefit besides media coverage? For example, some places at a table in the gala dinner; free admission to the event for the sponsor and a colleague or partner; complimentary VIP seats in the hospitality box. Without some or other of these benefits to give to potential sponsors, events organizers will have significant problems attracting sponsorship.

Case Study 21 *Sponsorship and the Tour de France*

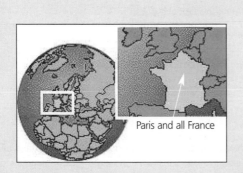

Paris and all France

Factbox

- Begun as a newspaper publicity stunt, it celebrated its centenary in 2003.
- 22 teams, of nine riders, compete for €3 million in prize money – €400,000 for the winner.
- Coloured jerseys (each sponsored), distinguish the leader on time; leader on points; 'King of the Mountains'; best climber and best young rider.

The Tour de France began as a 2,500 km bicycle race in 1903, as a means of boosting sales of *L'Auto* newspaper. Controversy dogged the race from the start and the `gamesmanship' of the 1904 race (such as fans sprinkling nails in the tracks of their competitors, or competitors using cars and trains to gain ground) nearly forced *L'Auto* to call it off. By the 1920s, it was seen as the world's toughest bicycle race, in which manufacturers' teams battled it out. At that time the course was over 5,500 km long and under severe rules, although, some felt, even then, that overt commercialism overshadowed the cycling.

In 1930, the competition amended its rules so that manufacturer teams were replaced by national squads (of eight riders, picked by the organizers and paid by the Tour itself); everyone rode identical bikes and a publicity caravan was introduced, to make up the cash shortfall from the manufacturers and their teams. For the first time, radio covered the race. It was first televised in 1952, television being new then.

During the 1960s, national teams were once again replaced by sponsored teams. In 1978 riders went on strike over split stages and transfers. Concerns over drugs became an issue when Pedro Delgado won in 1988, having tested positively for a substance banned at the Olympic Games, but not by the Tour's organizers.

In 1998, it was thought that one third of France's entire population lined the route, but the event was remembered, not for the immense public support and interest, but for another media scandal about drugs. The banned substance EPO had been found in one team car, days before the race, and the testing of staff and competitors lead to various teams being withdrawn and a string of arrests, including riders, team officials and doctors, prompting sit-downs and go-slows amongst the riders. The Festina team suffered the worst publicity, but sponsors stayed loyal to the event. Despite the Festina team being at the centre of the media attack surrounding this race, the watchmaking firm has continued its sponsorship with confidence and remains a sponsor to the present day.

Since the days of the manufacturer teams, the Tour de France has been attractive to sponsors and they have stayed consistently loyal. For example, the US Postal Service began with a small team and a fairly low-key presence, but after 1997 replaced Motorola as the leading US team, expanding into a multinational effort that included Nike within its family of sponsors and confirming its involvement to 2004, despite domestic criticism in the USA of a public organization spending 'millions of dollars' abroad.

The Tour de France attracts many major national and international companies as sponsors: Nestlé, Champion, Credit Lyonnais and Ford formed the Club du Tour de France for the centenary event, whilst Astra, Coca-Cola, Festina, Nike, POMU, Sodexho and France Telecom were Official Partners. The sponsorship family extended to embrace a further 13 official suppliers. To consider one of these in a little more detail:

Nestlé Aquarel has become a major supplier of bottled mineral water, particularly after having taken over Perrier in 1991. Nestlé use sponsorship of the Tour de France as a strategic communication tool for developing the Nestlé Aquarel brand. Nestlé regards the race as extremely significant as the Tour enjoys very significant recognition levels in all Nestlé Aquarel markets, attracting several million spectators each year massed along the roads of France. The Nestlé strategy is to sponsor the white jersey and prize for the best young rider; to have strong visibility of its logo boards along the last 25 kms of each stage of the race; to distribute the product to racers and spectators at the finish line (amounting to some 400,000 litres) and at the caravan (no ordinary caravan, this); and with a further 12 vehicles to distribute up to 500,000 samples. Associated promotion takes place at sales outlets, and several million bottles bear the Tour de France logo throughout the European sales area. There is an extensive public relations and corporate hospitality effort associated with the sponsorship, and some 1,000 of Nestlé Aquarel's major customers were invited to attend the Tour. This is a huge brand in Europe. Some 100 million litres were sold in the first year of its launch in the initial target market of six countries. In the 2002 season, the interactive nature of the promotion and sponsorship was stressed in the strategy. The local fire brigades along the route were provided with supplies of the product and encouraged to spritz the crowd with it; local newly-weds were spritzed, as well as Miss France. Coverage of the 2003 Centenary Tour amongst the media also saw extensive awareness of the product, thus fulfilling Nestlé's efforts in its sponsorship. The 2003 Centenary Tour finished on Sunday 27 July at the Champs Elysées, Paris, after some 3,350 km of cycling.

Based on this case:

1. How do cycling and the Tour de France compare, as sponsorship opportunities, with other sports and events?

2. How has the heritage of the race, including some of the negative aspects, affected the outlook for event, team and personal sponsorship?

3. What implications are there for ensuring that each of the several sponsoring companies gets an optimum return?

Related website for those interested in the Tour de France: http://www.letour.com/

Source: authors, 2004.

Sponsors will be looking not only for hospitality opportunities, but also for events that raise their image (for example, as an organization that actively supports its local community) or supports some other marketing objective. In short, to get sponsorship an event organizer must fit (conveniently) into the sponsor's own plans, as well as matching the event's objectives. We must also be clear that sponsorship is, effectively, a commercial promotional technique, and not a method of obtaining donations. As such there are various mechanisms for seeking sponsorship, rather than just posting a letter and hoping for the best. Sponsorship agencies are now relatively common, and can be found by searching the web or the phone directory. These agencies, for a fee, will seek to match potential sponsors with causes requiring sponsorship (for an example, see www.sponsorshiponline.co.uk). In addition, there are a number of trade-and-business related bodies with an interest in promoting relationships between commercial organizations and those seeking sponsorship, patronage or other support. In the UK, Arts and Business (formerly the Association for Business Sponsorship of the Arts) is one such example (www.absa.org.uk). There are also bodies and trade associations that have an interest in corporate responsibility and take an active role in community activities, and seek to promote an ethical and social approach to business, which may encompass in sponsorship or patronage activities.

In cases where an event is sufficiently attractive to sponsors that it obtains one or more of them, the job is not over. An event organizer, having succeeded in getting the desired sponsorship, must then be able to service the sponsor, that is to fulfil the sponsor's expectations of the event and its outcomes for the sponsor's business or brand. To do this a Sponsorship Agreement is needed (sometimes called a Sponsorship Business Plan). Quite simply, there are costs and benefits attached to servicing sponsors. Both the event organizer and the sponsor will wish to get the best from this arrangement, and to achieve this someone from the event organization will need to be responsible for liaison with sponsors, ensuring that the sponsorship agreement is fulfilled and that the objectives are achieved and measured. Elements of this plan would include: a Heads of Agreement, stating the objectives of the sponsorship on the parts of both the event organization and the sponsor, and the person in each organization who is ultimately responsible for ensuring the success of the sponsorship activities; a Marketing Statement, laying out the target audiences and stakeholders, and listing the methods by which the sponsor's name or brands will be placed in the public eye before the target audiences (target market); a Budget, dealing with how the funds received from the sponsorship would be allocated, e.g. on prizes, equipment, kit, gear, buildings, etc. and also dealing with what supporting funding would be available for promotion (the sponsor would, no doubt, wish their name to appear on poster boards, publicity material, programmes, brochures, signs and any number of other items associated with the event). Where there is more than one sponsor, that respective areas of promotion are allocated in the sections of the agreement. An evaluation section will also be found here, dealing with how the impact of the sponsorship would be measured, for example, in the keeping of press cuttings, minutes of exposure obtained in TV or radio news or other media and whether participants' awareness of the sponsor had been raised.

In addition to this plan, the event organizer's liaison officer or team will need their own checklist to deal with those items needed to support the sponsor – liaison officer's time, allocation of corporate hospitality funds for sponsor's support, costs for publicity, printing, signage, VIP parking allocations, travel and other expenses, and ticketing arrangements for sponsors. In fact, this type of checklist can also be used to work up an estimate of what costs are associated with servicing a sponsor, and thus how much money in terms of sponsorship is actually needed above and beyond operating costs for a sponsorship proposal to be worthwhile. Quite simply, if the costs of servicing a sponsor are going to be more than the sponsor is actually paying, then other sources of funding will be preferable.

Sponsorship is not the only potential alternative income source for an event. The range of sources depends a great deal on the type of event. Local authorities or other funding agencies might be willing to put money into an event (for example,

Figure 7.13

Sources of patronage, grant funding and other income for events

- 'In-kind' arrangements, mutual benefit exchanges of goods or activities, volunteer work or donations

- Grants from local, regional or national governments or the European Union

- Grants from charitable bodies; development agencies; arts, leisure or heritage bodies

- Lottery grants or subsidiary (matching) funding

- Fund-raising activities related to the event

- Commercial borrowing (from banks, etc. – this will have to be repaid with interest)

- Funding from trusts or other philanthropic bodies, often listed in national directories of funding agencies and trusts

- The provision of funds or donations from a patron, commercial sponsorship

a sporting or tourism event) if an appropriate and suitable case is made for it and if such a case complies with the objectives of the funding body. It might be that there is some kind of social regeneration, or other benefit to holding an event that could be of interest to the funding body. The event might, for example, attract large numbers of tourists, or have an arts impact for which arts trusts and foundations might consider grants. It should be noted, though, that funding from public bodies not only requires time and care in applying, but the response of many public funding bodies is notoriously slow (Pick and Anderton, 1996). Let us repeat the word, 'slow'. Indeed, even after this slow process, your application for a grant may not succeed. Similarly, funding from philanthropic bodies has the disadvantage of being rather difficult to obtain as essentially you are seeking money from a patron or body that needs to have a personal or direct interest in your event. The short-lived nature of some events makes this a problem. There simply is not enough time to build up the relationships needed for philanthropic giving for many kinds of events. However, if we are dealing with repeat editions, this may change, and especially so with arts-related events, which have a long tradition of attracting patrons through relationship marketing. Philanthropy can also be found in the strangest places, as even some of the most commercial companies have a strong awareness of their social responsibilities, resulting in company policies with very definite philanthropic outcomes (Harrison, 2000).

Any proposal for sponsorship, philanthropic (or other) funding would have to say much more than,'This will attract a lot of participants who will spend money on your product after they attend the event'. Measurement and quantification of the benefits will have to be stated. Does the type of event being put on match the social or community objectives of the patron? Will there be a positive outcome in terms of public image? Will it result in, say, employment? These are the types of questions which will have to be dealt with, very often, in order to get funding. In return, patrons should gain some personal or organizational benefits. Events patrons often gain preferential seats; admittance to VIP areas of the event; invitations to launch parties or to meet celebrities; attendance at a patron's lunch or VIP dinner, etc. In some cases patrons may wish their name on some aspect of the event, but this is by no means always the case; some patrons may wish to remain private supporters of an event, and to avoid the publicity associated with them.

Summary

Effective financial management of special events is increasingly complex. The financial implications of organizing even a relatively simple activity or celebration or a small personal event can be are significant. The extent to which external funding, such as via sponsors, may be available could be more limited than organizers foresee. This makes careful budgeting for regular income sources and proposed expenditure extremely important. The careful monitoring, recording and control of these incomes and expenditures is a significant concern of clients, organizers, co-ordinators and finance officers of all kinds. The recording of the financial aspects, ranging from the purchase of items to the final budgeted accounts, is potentially important to the success of events, even those not intended to be profit-making. Therefore, even those new to event organization should regard good financial management as necessary and vital.

References

Bowdin, G.A.J., McDonnell, I., Allen, J. and O'Toole, W. (2001) *Events Management*, Oxford, Butterworth Heinemann, p.185.

Hall, C.M. (1997) *Hallmark Tourist Events: Impacts, Management and Planning*, London, Belhaven, pp.50–59, 148–56.

Harrison, S. (2000) *Public Relations*, London, Business Press, pp.140–50.

Lucey, T. (2002) *Costing*, London, Continuum, 6th edn, pp.27–38.

Morris, W.G. (1994) *The Management of Projects*, London, Thomas Telford, p.245.

Owen, G. (1998) *Accounting for Hospitality, Tourism and Leisure*, Harlow, Longman.

Pick, J. and Anderton, M. (1996) *Arts Administration*, London, E&FN Spon, pp.78–87.

Watt, D.C. (1998) *Event Management in Leisure and Tourism*, Harlow, Longman, pp.52–59.

Wilson, R.M.S. and Chua, W.F. (1993) *Managerial Accounting*, London, Van Nostrand Reinhold, 2nd edn, pp.99–114.

Wiseman, E., Edmond, J. and Betteridge, D. (1996) *Finance in Leisure and Tourism*, London, Hodder and Stoughton.

8 The event: venue-finding, logistics and ambience

Aims

- To discuss the preparation phase for events, including logistics.

- To identify the range of support functions for events.

- To consider the key components of celebrations, including the creation of the appropriate ambience and atmosphere.

Introduction

The preparation and development phase for events is not necessarily separate from the planning phase, and the two mostly run hand in hand. However, the business of getting an event ready involves considerable time, effort and hard work. At the point where the event is starting to be implemented, the number of people and the quantity of resources involved will begin to increase, with the workload. The pace of preparation and development will also increase once the venue has been identified and orders begin to be placed for equipment, facilities and services. The logistics of ensuring that all these items arrive in time for the event, in their proper place, in good condition, and in the style or format they were ordered, represents a considerable effort on the part of the event co-ordinator.

Support functions, such as food and drink, music and entertainment, technical and related activities and services, can be very complicated, depending on the size and importance of the event. If you consider the sheer complexity of the preparations for even a modest family wedding, it becomes evident how crucial careful logistical preparations are. Different types of events will require different support functions, which can be supplied directly by the organizers or contracted out. Where support functions are contracted out, the need for careful specification of the service being purchased is particularly relevant.

Getting everything in place for an event is not only a matter of the behind-the-scenes efforts in terms of logistics, organization and preparation; it is also crucial to the atmosphere and ambience that will be created. Events may be simple or complicated; in the modern world it is more difficult to impress an audience with an event, because the general public is very much more used to seeing events in the media and to attending events. This means that the efforts that may have to be put into creating an attractive ambience at a venue, in circumstances that might make its staging quite difficult, but still ensuring an enjoyable atmosphere, may have to be very considerable. This stage of the process may have to take into account the venue and its environment, as well as the design, decor, lighting, music, colour scheme and a whole range of other incidental factors. Nevertheless, we must bear in mind that at the vast majority of events it is the guests or visitors themselves who will help create the atmosphere, simply by their presence or by their participation and involvement. The issue for the event organizer in creating an event that is well organized and enjoyable, is to work smarter, not harder. To do this, a range of techniques are discussed in this chapter and in chapter 10 (on project management), to help ensure the event runs efficiently.

Finding the venue

At this point in creating an event, we may not yet have identified the venue, let alone what other facilities and services we will need. But hand in hand with planning will be the early exploration of issues such as what our key requirements are, including those factors that will be critical to success. These might include the location of the event, the range of potential venues available, ease of access, and the ability to ensure that all the necessary items of equipment, resources, personnel and visitors can get to the venue easily. The preparation phase of the process will therefore consist not only of venue-finding, but also of logistics. Logistics is the discipline of planning and organizing the flow of goods, equipment and people to their point of use. Logistics are important to events because of the need to concentrate resources on a particular location for a particular time (even if that event is multi-site and taking place over a fairly long period). Without careful planning of this activity, the supplies needed to undertake the event may not arrive correctly.

In logistics terms, our supplies are not simply products and services; they also include the flow of customers and customer services. For example, when we choose a venue we must ensure that our potential customers, visitors or participants are able to get to it easily, using their typical mode of transport, and also that there is suitable and adequate access, both for them and for goods, and in case of emergency. The Millennium Dome opening night served to highlight several logistical problems, including the supply of tickets, the unnecessary queuing, and the lack of car parking at the Dome site itself. We can see from this that logistics do not simply refer to on-site activities.

Venue-finding is probably one of the most important aspects of the development phase of an event. In some cases an event organizer might know exactly which venue to choose. In other cases the choice of venue may be extremely limited, especially in rural areas. In general, however, a reasonable choice of venue will be available. The first question an organizer will normally ask will be, 'What location is required?' (bearing in mind the objectives of the event), and then, 'What are the available venues within that location?' (noting any criteria that were set up about selection in the screening process). Early on, a number of

Figure 8.1

Venue-finding
checklist (see also
website:
www.conferences
direct.co.uk)

Event: ....   Date: ....

Name of venue: ....   Address: ....

Phone number: ....

Fax number:....................................   ....

General manager: ....   Event contact:...............................

GM's email: ....   Contact's email: ....

What are the objectives of the event in relation to the venue? ....

....

....

What factors are critical to the success of the event in relation to the venue?
(What do you need?)

Factor 1 ....

Factor 2 ....

Factor 3 ....

Does this venue satisfy these factors?

Factor 1: ☐ Yes ☐ No   Factor 2: ☐ Yes ☐ No   Factor 3: ☐ Yes ☐ No

Site inspection: venue environment and location:

General environment: *(e.g. leafy countryside, city centre)* ....

Access:	Good	OK	Poor	Comment
By road *(car & taxi)*	☐	☐	☐	....
On foot / cycle	☐	☐	☐	....
By bus / tram	☐	☐	☐	....
By rail	☐	☐	☐	....
Nearest station:				
By air	☐	☐	☐	....
Nearest airport:				....

Identify any access problems related to loading / unloading / mobility-impaired visitors / limitations of parking: ....

Site Inspection: Venue facilities and services:

Capacity of main area: ....   Capacity of support areas: ....

Capacity of parking:.............................   Capacity of kitchens: ....

Area (sq metres) main:..   Area (sq metres) support: ....

Is internal access for entry and exit of visitors, loading and the mobility impaired adequate?

....

Is a scale plan of the venue available? *If so, obtain one. If not, measure main features.*

State ceiling height: .... m   State access door height: .... m   State access door width: .... m

Has the venue power? ....   How many power points? ....   Lighting / Dimmers ....

Has the venue gas? ....   Air conditioning? ....   What sort of heating?

Attach a copy of the fire procedure to this checklist. In relation to the needs of your event, what other specialist facilities / services are available: *(e.g. sound system, presentation equipment, etc.)* or are missing?: ....

Comment on your impression of the venue and the venue management:

....

....

....

questions have to be asked about the potential venue, and whatever we know about the type of audience for the event, and the event itself, will inform our judgment about the venue. For example, if our event were to be a national sales exhibition, then the venue would probably have to be large and central to the whole country. If it was to be a town carnival, then the venue might cover several locations in the town, as well as suitable areas for the assembly and dispersal of the carnival procession. Organizers themselves may have a good local knowledge, but if not, a visit to the area will be necessary to look around. Alternatively, a professional venue-finding agency can be used; these are quite common and can be identified in the telephone book under 'conference/event organizers'. Normally an agency or organizer will come up with a shortlist of three or four possible venues. These can be visited and a checklist made about the particular requirements of the event in terms of the venue (Seekings, 1999). Whichever venue best matches the criteria, bearing in mind price considerations and the professionalism of the venue management, should be chosen (see Figure 8.1).

Site visits are useful, but the organizer needs to have a reasonable idea of the event requirements before visiting venues (if you go with a poor idea of what you need, you give yourself problems later). Visits should be arranged via venue managers, or for larger sites, the venue sales team. Where a professional venue-finding agency has been used the agency may also be able to provide an organizer with professional help to inspect venues, for a small fee. It is important for organizers to make out a list of questions to ask each venue before going, in addition to a checklist of criteria. Much depends on the event. For example, is a band required during the party? Is a stage needed? Will sound equipment be needed? Can the venue provide these?

First impressions are important. The first impression an organizer gets may well be the same that visitors and guests get. Organizers should pay attention to all their senses. What does the site look like? What are its surroundings? Is it attractive? What can be heard: is it quiet, noisy, under a flight path, does it have good acoustics (clap your hands to hear the echo, or listen for dead areas in sound transmission)? What does it smell like: is it neutral, does it smell of stale food? Does it have gardens? Are the toilets clean and fresh? Touch the furnishings and some of the equipment – do these feel clean? Do your shoes stick to the floor or carpets?

At your first visit you are probably not able to taste anything. But if food is an element of your event, then once you have chosen the venue, you may wish to try samples of the food you have selected, especially if the event is large or involves VIP catering, in order to see if the kitchen is up to the job. On your visit, try to make sure you see all the areas your visitors will use, not only the main room, site, arena or hall, but also the entrances, corridors, car parks, toilets and food service areas. Are these places well kept? Is there evidence of activity, cleanliness, good maintenance? All these are indicators of an active and capable management at the venue. The more capable they are, the easier your job will be.

Logistics

Once given a venue, the event co-ordinator or logistics officer can address some of the major licensing and official preparation activities, such as permits and insurance (see chapter 10). In logistics terms, services that have a long lead time must be considered early on. The event may have special power requirements, it might need additional utilities laid on (e.g. telecoms, gas, water, sewerage, waste removal), all of which have typically long lead times to arrange, especially if groundwork has to be undertaken to put them in. The logistics officer has to be conscious of those event activities that have the longest lead times and that have to be dealt with first. A logistics plan, showing the various needs and plotting them into order, may have to be prepared.

It is useful to recognize that the nearer the event deadline, the less able one is to make big changes without having to expend enormous amounts of money and effort. In short, there is a cut-off point at which the contractual arrangements have to stand (this varies, depending on what supplies or services are being provided and how long they take). Logistics officers will need to draw together a potentially wide range of support functions for an event to work properly.

Figure 8.2	
The events management process: the organizational and logistical activities	Objects ↓ Planning ↓ Organizing and preparing ...

Figure 8.2

The events management process: the organizational and logistical activities

Objectives

↓

Planning

↓

Organizing and preparing

Development activities, preparation and deadlines: timing / preparation schedules

Venue-finding

↓

Venue preparation arrangements

Licence and permit applications / insurance / booking and contracts

Risk analysis / set-up of emergency procedures (see chapter 10 for details)

↓

Logistics and supply functions

Special power and utilities supplies

Specialist supply items / equipment hire / food and drink ordering / linen hire and uniforms /

signs / audio-visual requirement / backdrop and staging / security / decoration supplies /

Dressing rooms / public and crew facilities

↓

Implementing the event

Operations, control and action

Communications, problem-solving on the day

↓

Divestment / legacies

Close-down: evaluation, feedback and recording

Refuse, equipment and services removal / cleaning / contracts acquittal and payments

Site restoration / handover

The key to the implementation phase of the event (i.e. running the event itself) is good communications. It is helpful to commit ideas and important issues to paper. With a large number of people to manage, it is impossible for one individual to communicate 'in person' with them all. Therefore many forms of communication may be used to help ensure people know what to do: briefings about plans, the event programme, the emergency procedures, etc., must take place. A useful tool in the range of techniques available to an event organizer is the preparation of an event production schedule (see Figure 8.9). This is essentially a list of the activities that the event involves, in time order. This production schedule should be as detailed as possible for events where timing issues are essential to a positive outcome. At this stage, the production schedule may go through several editions before the final one emerges and is agreed upon. In several cases the production schedule will also state who is responsible for the given timed activities and what methods are to be used to carry them out.

Case Study 22 Co-ordination of local efforts: the Festival of St John, Oporto

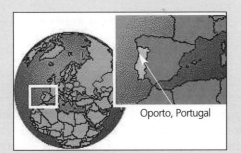

Oporto, Portugal

Factbox

- Festival of St John.
- Has taken place for over 500 years.
- Religious in origin.
- Local people make large numbers of 'cascatas', which are dioramas or models about the life of St John, using miniature figures.

Oporto, situated on the River Douro in northern Portugal, holds a number of attractive and colourful events during the year. Its biggest is probably the long summer festival in June, celebrating the festivities of a number of saints, including St Anthony, St Peter and, largest of all, St John. Such festivals are common in many parts of Europe and are extremely historic and traditional.

Staging the St John's festival is a combination of local informality, with people decorating their own houses, courtyards and streets, and formal organization – the practicalities provided by the city authorities and by the religious authorities related to St John's Eve. Local people build miniature theatrical scenes (dioramas) with figures to celebrate some aspect of the saint's life. These are displayed all over the city, which is decorated with flowers and greenery, especially with leek, basil and bunches of other aromatic plants. At the peak of the festivities, the summer solstice, people flood on to the streets in the evening in their best costumes for the traditional celebrations.

Preparations therefore involve three main groups. First, local people, with traditional efforts, such as making diorama models ('cascatas'), decorating residential areas and dressing up. Second, the city council, which co-ordinates the activities, promotes the event and deals with the clear-up afterwards. Third, the religious officials, who deal with the formal activities associated with St John in the city's cathedral and churches. The department responsible for the co-ordination of this effort is the Commission for City Festivities.

▶

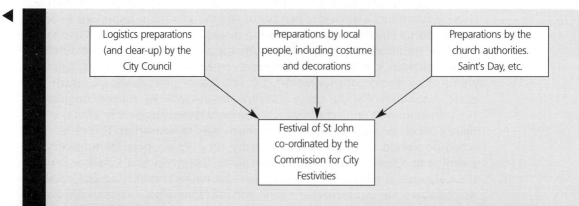

Based on this case:

1. The advance preparations for the festival of St John at Oporto are extremely informal, and led by local people. How do they know what to do, and how have such traditions been maintained over many centuries?

2. The logistical preparations for the event do not, at first sight, involve any great complexity.

Why is this, and is this approach suitable for other types of events?

3. Oporto is a world heritage site. Do the preparations for the festivities and the festivities itself help to attract visitors to the city in large numbers, or would visitors come anyway?

Related website for those interested in Oporto: www.porto.pt

The logistics officer, working with the marketing officer and the overall event co-ordinator, must also organize pre-event meetings and use tools such as site maps, bulletins and newsletters to help get across major issues to staff, crew, artists, volunteers and helpers, to achieve co-ordination of effort.

Supplies, transport and distribution

We have said that logistics is the discipline of planning and organizing the flow of goods, equipment and people to their point of use. Therefore logistics in events terms includes activities such as ticketing and enquiries (in co-operation with the marketing department), arrival and departure of visitors, the flow of people, equipment, suppliers, artists and crew around the venue. Within this, the preparation, opening and running of an event (whether it is a wedding reception or a coronation) depends on getting all the elements to the right place in time for a range of deadlines. This can be a complicated process, and individual staff and departments will be expected to prepare their own order lists of requirements. Where events are being run by professional management companies, these organizations will keep on computer database a general listings of supplies and suppliers used for previous events, which can be easily adapted according to the particular needs of the one being prepared. Supplies can be ordered and deliveries checked, usually at a central arrival point, and the supplies distributed as required to the parts of the site where they are needed.

At a small event such as a village fête, most supplies could be accommodated in a store once they have been delivered by the local suppliers. These can then be laid out or sent to the kitchen, service areas, stands, stalls or whichever department requires them (see Figure 8.3). For a large event such as an International Air Show, the logistics task is huge. Many companies will be involved and the integration of the whole operation will be a significant task. The air show may have 20 or 30 catering companies supplying visitor catering or hospitality pavilions. These pavilions, have to be set up, supplied regularly and wound down. Pre-planning may take nine months (perhaps following a previous year's event); detailed planning and ordering another three months; site set-up three weeks, including pavilion erections and the provision of utilities. This would be followed by the public opening, three days of inputting goods and services, one day's breather, then three days of stripping out of goods and finally equipment. Lastly, a week of clearing up followed by site restoration, all done to a carefully organized timetable.

There will also need to be clarity, in the logistics officer's list of suppliers, about who should be contacted at a supplier in case the wrong items turn up, when checked, together with a list of alternative suppliers in key areas, in case of serious problems. The logistics officer should never forget to bring the local phone directory to an event! (See Figure 8.4.)

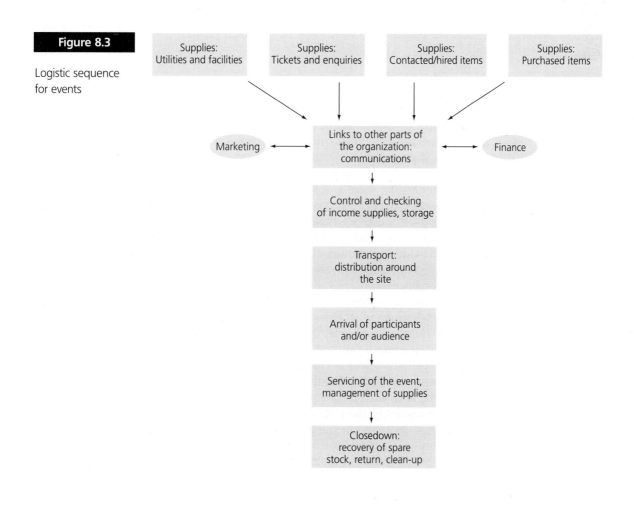

Figure 8.3

Logistic sequence for events

Figure 8.4

Middleburg Festival
equipment receival
form (goes with
Figure 8.10, the
contact list)

Item	Size/Type	No	Supplier	To go to	Received/Checked
Furniture					
Stacking chairs blue	Standard 2000	450	Red Dragon	Park arena	☐
Stacking chairs blue	Standard 2000	50	Red Dragon	Catering tent	☐
Office chairs blue	Operator	10	Red Dragon	Park office portacabins	☐
Round tables	1m	6	Red Dragon	Catering tent	☐
Square tables	1m	6	Red Dragon	Catering tent	☐
Trestle tables	2m	2	Red Dragon	Catering tent	☐
Trestle tables	2m	2	Red Dragon	Park office portacabins	☐
Trestle tables	2m	1	Red Dragon	Park entrance gate tent	☐
Utilities					
Mobile toilet block	M/F Type 20	1	T Crapper & Co.	100m west of catering tent	☐
Power	'3 phase'	2 lines	Mid Electric	Arena stage	☐
Power	8 socket supply	1 line	Mid Electric	Catering tent	☐
Mobile chiller room	32 m²	1	Coolfridge Hire	Back of catering tent	☐
Tents and Shades					
Marquee white	Deluxe 50m	1	Grand Tents	Catering tent as marked	☐
Tent white	Standard 5m	1	Grand Tents	Park entrance tent as marked	☐
Equipment					
Plates white	Dinner 25 cm	450	National Equip	Catering tent	☐
Plates white	Side 10 cm	450	National Equip	Catering tent	☐
Etc.	Etc.				

Catering

Having created a suitable event venue for those attending, one issue that will certainly colour visitors' view of their experience is the provision of food and drink. Event co-ordinators should bear this in mind and ensure there is sufficient time and space built into events for this important aspect, if catering is to be provided properly.

The organization of catering varies considerably according to the type of venue, but as a generality, there is a choice between in-house catering as practised by the banqueting departments of hotel-type venues, and contracted-out catering as practised by the other types of venue, ranging from public halls to sports stadiums. There are advantages and disadvantages to both methods and the method provided by venues to handle their catering may have as much to do with historical precedent in that venue as with matters of profitability, flexibility and convenience.

Having found a caterer, of whatever type, the basic questions and the starting points to determine what the visitor will have are the same. These are questions about the number of people, the refreshment times, the budget and the visitors themselves. It could be argued that one of the chief failings of catering at events is an insensitivity towards the type of people attending. There is a tendency towards standardized and rather predictable menus, which, whilst convenient for kitchens and sales co-ordinators, may be inappropriate for certain types of visitors. Increasingly, the public attending events is better educated in food and drink than at any time in the past. The range of services on offer may be built around continuous provision throughout the event, rather than the traditional presentation of breakfast, lunch and dinner. The layout for café or buffet-type service also needs to be given careful thought. Bear in mind that people are inherently used to lining up in queues. In an unfamiliar situation (such as at a new event), they will naturally revert to this method. To plan catering outlets at events to be 'free flow' may therefore be counter productive; people may be confused and irritated, especially if there is a log-jam at the cash desk (see Figure 8.5).

In cases where there will be a large number of people at an event, queues at catering outlets can be relieved by having smaller outlets that deal only in drinks and small food, to help take the weight of demand away from major food counters. The same kind of rules apply to cafeteria service as to buffet service – think carefully about how many people your counter can handle at once. Add more counters or small outlets to ease the crush.

Buffets are popular at events, and there are commonly two types: finger buffet or fork buffet. With the former, guests normally stand, with the latter, guests normally sit, and the buffet food may be hot or cold or both. Timing is an important issue. Many people will politely queue at a buffet, which naturally takes time and must be taken into account when laying out the buffet. More than one direction or side of a buffet table should be available. It will take the average diner 20 seconds to load his/her plate – multiply that up by the number of people and you will understand why more than one buffet flow is needed for a large event. It should also be borne in mind that buffets are often understaffed, which leads to chaos, inability to restock and inability to clear tables. The normal buffet service ratio is one staff to 30 diners. This can be raised to 35 if serving international delegates, as they are somewhat less likely to queue and this must be noted when laying out the buffet. For international delegates, it should not, generally, be laid out in a linear fashion, but similar dishes can be laid out in various sections of a buffet table.

Where events may feature a particular element, such as a gala dinner, organizers should ensure they have provided a seating layout for the event that will best suit the client (Shone, 1998) (see Figure 8.6). For a full service meal, the typical service ratio is one staff to between ten and fifteen diners, plus one member of drinks staff (for wine service) to every 30 diners.

Menu composition and the range of food provided is significant not only in terms of the menu, but also in terms of what is within a venue's capabilities. For example, a range of individually priced dishes may be suggested to the

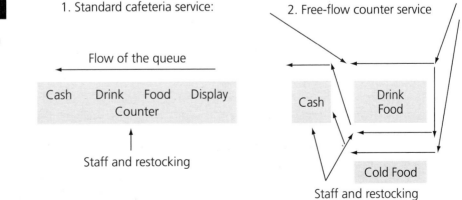

Figure 8.5

Alternative cafeteria flow services

1. Standard cafeteria service:

Flow of the queue

| Cash | Drink | Food | Display |

Counter

Staff and restocking

2. Free-flow counter service

Cash

Drink Food

Cold Food

Staff and restocking

organizer, who then chooses a selection to suit the likely visitor profile. This is based on the view that organizers know something of the style, likes and dislikes of the public. However, not all do, and organizers often pick dishes they themselves like, only to find that visitors criticize their poor judgement. Menu composition is, therefore, not simply a technical issue, but also a serious question that organizers should ask themselves. What are our potential visitors like? What are their demographics? What are their most popular styles of eating?

The chief 'back of house' players in catering operations are the head chef and the bars manager, in the sense that they are responsible for food and drink costings, pre-planning, ordering and preparation of food and drink. Nevertheless, it must be remembered that the initial enquiry and first meeting between the venue and the organizer will probably take place with the venue sales manager or sales co-ordinator, although a number of organizers will ask for the chef to be present, to find out what the venue's caterers are able to produce.

The alternative is to contract out the catering to a specialist organization (Cracknell et al., 2000). These vary from large national operations with many contracts, to small individual caterers with only one contract or *ad hoc* business. Catering of this kind is common in many venues. Contractual arrangements vary. Some venues may have one approved caterer who provides all the food, drink and related services for that venue. Alternatively, venues may have an 'approved' list of caterers whom they are happy to work with and who are familiar with the venue, its operation, management and typical requirements. Some venues, such as public halls, may allow any caterer, including the event organizers themselves, to do the catering.

The advantage of contracting-out is that the organizers do not need to concern themselves with the technicalities of food and drink provision. They simply making the best contractual arrangement possible and act as a link between the client (or the visitor) and the caterers. The disadvantage is a certain loss of control: a contract caterer interested in cutting costs may have no incentive to provide a quality service. A related disadvantage is less well-known, but probably more serious – loss of flexibility. An in-house catering function is often, in practice, highly flexible and can provide peripheral activities that contractors do not (e.g.

Figure 8.6

Examples of some seated meal layouts (there are many others)

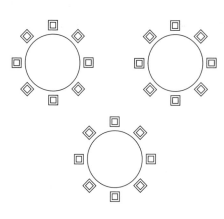

Rounds

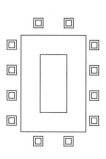

Boardroom

an 'on the spot' VIP dinner for a key client). The chief problem is that contracts are often badly written, ignoring a wide range of needs, some of which may only occur occasionally but are nevertheless vital, and which a contractor will charge extra for.

The number of visitors attending and expected to eat may not be the same. At some kinds of events visitors may bring in their own food, for example to a summer evening open air concert. For the caterer it is also of importance to know approximate numbers up to two weeks before the event and final numbers two days in advance, in order to enable accurate food, drink and equipment ordering. A deadline must be enforced for bookings where the event has elements such as sit-down gala dinners as opposed to continuous through-the-day catering. The time of refreshments should also be checked between the organizers and the caterers on the day.

Visitors and some sections of the public attending events may be traditional in their tastes, but they are no longer uneducated in food. Travel abroad, ethnic and specialist restaurants at home and wide-ranging food programmes and articles in the media have engendered a far greater range of public taste. Venues and even hotels are not always in the forefront of change when developing menus, nor perhaps would the public necessarily wish them to be; but it is essential that the food presented is of a suitable standard, and appropriate to the type of people at the event (see Figure 8.7). Sometimes this is not the case, partly due to insufficient attention to the type of customer or visitor, or to a lack of competitor analysis, and perhaps complacency on the part of venues, which fails to do what in other industries would be called benchmarking. Older banqueting managers and caterers may recall the days when it was *de rigueur* to eat in competitor establishments, or at similar events. This is now extremely rare amongst modern managers, and the quality of event food sometimes suffers for lack of knowledge of what competitors are providing, or lack of awareness about how competitor's efforts might reasonably be exceeded.

There are other common weaknesses in event dining, some of which are training related. Event dining often relies on casual staff, even on volunteers,

Figure 8.7
 	
Issues in determining menus and refreshments
	• The number of visitors attending and expected to buy refreshments, and how many refreshment opportunities a visit to the event might represent.
	
	• The number of staff or crew which have to be fed and at what times.
	
	• Details about the visitor group themselves:
	  – Who they are
	  – Typical food interests, and styles of eating
	  – Age group
	  – Male/female balance
	  – Special dietary needs (e.g. vegetarians).
	
	• Whether there is a budget for refreshments, or whether food is exclusive of the ticket price.
	
	• The expertise and ability of the catering staff.
	
	• The type of catering facilities, storage capacity and equipment available at the venue.
	
	• Whether the food / drink is brought in from outside and how it is brought in.
	
	• What utilities and mains services are available at the venue.

and this is a particular difficulty. Such staff may have limited food preparation knowledge, or poor hygiene training, or may have gleaned their meagre knowledge of food and drink service from other staff or from *ad hoc* demonstrations by a the head waiter(ress) or head cook. Some considered effort needs to go into training, even if, for waiting staff, this only amounts to a half-hour briefing before service about the food, the drink, whom to serve first, what colour the vegetarians' place cards are and how to look around for diners trying to attract staff attention. Nevertheless, where professional caterers are present, either in-house, or contracted, the standard of staff training is generally very good.

Meals are often intended as the highlight of an event, perhaps in the form of gala dinners or theme dinners. Regrettably, they can be badly done, with poorly cooked food, indifferent service and poorly presented staff. Style and content at many events is as important in this environment as in the fine restaurants of great hotels, and guests often expect the same standards of service at an outdoor event as they would receive in a fine restaurant (Lillicrap et al., 2002). The problems of delivering this for outdoor event caterers may be extremely severe: anything from having no main services, electricity, drainage, etc. to having to bring in fresh water in sealed containers, fresh food in chiller lorries, or even having no proper access to muddy fields where outdoor events are being held, except by farm tractor or golf buggy (Konopka, 1995).

A further issue is the feeding of staff and crew, especially volunteers. This should be a charge supported as part of the budget. How many staff and crew need to be fed? With what? At what time and by whom? When will the staff dining room be open, if there is one? Do staff and crew pay for reasonable refreshments in such a dining room? If not, where and how are the staff and crew to be fed? Is food and drink for volunteers or staff entirely free, or subsidized, as part of the event, or as a contribution for their help?

On a final catering note, it is far better to plan activities (such as food re-stocking) as a matter of professional routine, than to allow something to go wrong and have to expend inordinate effort putting it right. This can be called the 'salt pot' syndrome – if a function is badly prepared and not checked, there will be things waiting to create maximum disruption: the missing salt pot will be discovered by a guest about to consume their main course, and who will, rightly, demand one at the busiest point of service, causing widespread disruption. Typically there will be no salt pots in the function area, and the staff will have to go to the wash-up area to get one – a location where, mysteriously, there will be no salt pots. This will necessitate the slowest washer-up in the entire site having to search for, wash, dry and fill a fresh salt pot, taking the maximum care, because it is now a 'special' salt pot, and thus taking the maximum possible time. The guest's food, now cold, will have to be returned to the kitchen, and the guest will have to wait for it to be heated up. In the meantime, the rhythm of service for the whole function will have been destroyed.

This kind of unprofessional shambles can often be seen in catering operations where staff have not been trained to maintain the flow of key supplies as they go along, or where there are a depressing number of staff behind a counter, none of whom are actually serving, to the considerable anger and distress of a large number of potential customers, who are watching them do anything and everything except serve (see Figure 8.12). Poor managers and lazy staff may regard good preparation as a nuisance, but it is the bedrock on which all else is built.

Drinks Services

Bars for events are essentially of two types: paid and cash. Paid (or account) bars are those where the client or organizer has arranged for some element of payment for guests, let us say for the VIPs, to have free drinks, because the client or organization is paying. In some cases, organizers may specify that guests may cover their first drink by this method. However, such arrangements must be made clear. It is far better simply, to serve a pre-determined aperitif (e.g. juice, a spritzer or a fizz) than attempt to monitor who is 'just' having their first drink. The alternative method is to set a bar limit, which the organizer will pay for, and after which delegates pay for their own. Again, this method has severe limitations and could result in an undignified scrum at the bar to get as many free ones as possible before guests have to pay. It is far easier, and much more normal, to have a cash bar. Guests pay for what they drink.

Bars at events should normally have a ratio of one member of staff to every 75 drinkers (for example, at a pre-dinner reception). These ratios can be subject to variation. For instance, experience of a particular event may conclude that guests on previous visits have been particularly heavy drinkers, thus requiring a strengthening of the staff. The importance of this latter point is that the manager responsible for the food and drink service at an event meal must be flexible. It is far too easy to assume that a pre-set standard will do for all functions. This is an easy approach, but leads to a lack of attention to the detail of staffing and to potentially serious mistakes such as under- or over-staffing.

There is also the related issue of drinks served during a meal. The most common method is for organizers to include an allowance of one or two glasses of wine (or half a bottle) or juice with a meal for guests. Thereafter, diners may buy their own wine on payment to the sommelier (wine waiter/ress); similarly, liqueurs are usually on a cash basis. One bottle of wine (70cl) will normally serve six persons; with a common ratio of three to one in favour of white to red in northern Europe, depending on the type of guest. Spirit service is of the order of 28 (25ml) measures to a bottle. In addition, jugged iced plain water should always be put on the table before the meal arrives. There is a belief that diners will not drink alcohol if water is put on the tables. This is fallacious, and it always results in tables asking for water and service being disrupted to get it. Such disruptions reflect an amateur approach.

Figure 8.8	• Have licences for alcohol and food sales *(e.g. from stalls)* been applied for, and given?

Further considerations in food and drink services

• Have licences for alcohol and food sales *(e.g. from stalls)* been applied for, and given?

• Is there sufficient space for food, drink and equipment storage, preparation and service?

• Are these areas easily accessible, do they have the necessary utilities and comply with hygiene regulations?

• What are the set-up, opening, closing and departure times?

• What cleaning and clearing arrangements are there?

• Are there selection criteria for a mix of catering providers, and what arrangements are there for them to pay for their concession, pitch or stall area?

Technical facilities

The technical services that events co-ordinators and venues are expected to provide are becoming increasingly sophisticated, to the extent that events co-ordinators may choose to outsource the hi-tech needs of clients to production or multimedia companies. The larger and more important the event, the greater the likelihood of a need for specialists, although a contributory difficulty is that some venue managers may not be sufficiently knowledgeable about the capabilities of production companies and of the latest developments in contemporary technology.

Multimedia can include video, computer-generated text and graphics, transfer of pictures from digital sources and the insertion of sound or video into presentations. Similarly, rapid development in communications has seen some use of video conferencing and, at large-scale events, satellite links from one continent to another, enabling the presentation of a speaker in, say, Frankfurt, to be made on a video wall in Bilbao. There is also the issue of the image a client may wish to foster amongst the audience. Consequently, there has been a significant adoption of theatrical scene-building techniques to provide backdrops for events. Larger-scale integrated staging and backdrops are mainly the province of theatrical or event production companies.

The other common technical issue is that of sound and the need for sound re-inforcement, at all but the smallest events. Sound re-inforcement is provided by microphones, amplifiers and loudspeakers. Technical skill and careful preparation can achieve a very effective presentation. In terms of a soundtrack, there are issues of copyright for music and video, and in venue terms the quality of the facilities and the acoustics of the venue need not be taken into account. The development of technology to entertain an audience has moved extremely fast, from the point at which, 20 years ago, the highest level of technology would have been a 16 mm film projector, to a whole range of presentation methods ranging from the laser projector to the laptop display.

If venues have suitable equipment available, venue management and technical staff should request that presenters come and test their material at least a week prior to the event. This applies particularly to computer-based presentations. Not all systems can be compatible and minor glitches such as cabling problems, or insufficient attention to text size for projections, are as much a problem as compatibility (or lack of compatibility) of the equipment and software itself. It is unreasonable to expect that hi-tech presentations will work first time unless the speaker and venue are regular partners. In addition, the level of technical skill required to solve the simplest of equipment problems is not always available on the spot. Increasing sophistication of communications is also permitting advances in how, and where, events can be held. However, the resources required to do this may have to be brought in specially.

Backdrops and staging

Whilst technical support may be thought to be essentially aural or visual reinforcement (additional sound or lighting systems), it is also the case that event organizers (on behalf of a more sophisticated public) are looking for a standard that is extremely high, and are willing to pay for it. The backdrop, or staging, is of major concern. It not only provides the location of a screen, but is also the place where a corporate or marketing image is demonstrated (Goldblatt, 1990). The backdrop may, of course, be simple: a contained screen with banner and a little special lighting. On the other hand, the backdrop may be a matter of

Figure 8.9

Example of a logistics production schedule

Middleburg Festival Production Schedule 2001

Start at: Production: Finish by:

Preparatory Work

Monday 27 August

08.00	Co-ordinator's briefing at Park House, welcome volunteers, coffee	08.30
08.30	Site checks of festival park	09.00
09.00	Mark out parking, arena, market, marquee and tent sites	11.00
11.00	Hold meeting with emergency services, council representatives and others	12.00
12.00	Lunch on Park House terrace, delivered by Anna's Bakery (at 11.30)	13.00
13.00	Co-ordinators to assist afternoon deliveries of tents, utilities, portacabins, etc.	
17.00	Hand over to night security man (and complete any outstanding set-ups)	17.30

Set-up and Rehearsals

Tuesday 28 August

08.00	Co-ordinator's briefing at Park House, coffee	08.30
08.30	Co-ordinate arrival of supplies, check arriving items, direct to correct area	12.00
12.00	Lunch on Park House terrace, delivered by Anna's Bakery (at 11.30)	13.00
13.00	Organize volunteers to set up arena, market, catering and entrance tents	16.00
16.00	Check completion of set-up, arrival of supplies, chase outstanding items	17.00
17.00	Volunteers' tea on Park House terrace, delivered by Anna's Bakery (16.30)	18.00
17.00	Issue volunteers with T-shirts, badges, site maps and answer any questions	18.00
18.00	Test all services, list items not working for attention Wednesday am	19.00
19.00	Middleburg Festival Orchestra rehearsal	22.00
22.00	Hand over to night security	22.15

Festival Event

Wednesday 29 August

08.00	Co-ordinator's briefing at Park House, coffee	08.30
08.30	Attend to outstanding problems, get volunteers to their posts, check signs	09.30
09.30	Check festival market	10.00
10.00	Check Middleburg Band is ready near Venetian Bridge	10.10
10.10	Welcome mayor, provide coffee in Entrance Tent	10.25
10.25	Go with mayor to Venetian Bridge for opening speech and tape-cutting	10.45
10.45	Festival opens, band plays light music, festival market opens	10.45
12.00	Volunteers and band lunch (rotation) in catering tent	13.00
14.00	Afternoon concert by Middleburg Band	16.00
16.00	Parade by Middleburg youth organizations	17.00
17.00	Various music soloists and small groups scheduled to play in catering tent	19.00
19.00	Guests arrival for main evening concert	19.30
19.30	Main evening concert in arena, seats and picnic places	22.00
19.30	Festival market closes down	20.00
20.00	Volunteers dinner on Park House terrace (supplied by Catering Tent)	21.00
21.00	Catering tent closes after concert intermission	21.10
22.30	Co-ordinator hands over to night security	22.45

Closedown

Thursday 30 August

08.00	Co-ordinator's briefing at Park House, coffee	08.30
08.30	Suppliers arrive to remove utilities, tents, return equipment	13.00
12.00	Volunteers lunch on Park House terrace, delivered by Anna's Bakery	13.00
13.00	Volunteer litter pickers, site cleaners complete clearing	15.00
15.00	Hand over site to park keeper, site repairs and lawns restoration begins	17.00

considerable technical expertise incorporating stage design elements (Holt, 1993). These elements may range from the preparation and construction of stage flats (Reid, 2001) to back projection and theatrical-style lighting. Gobos (light projectors) are often used for backdrops. These project screen designs which can both be provided from a range of prepared formats, such as cityscapes, starfields, etc. or, more commonly, be purpose-made with a logo or theme to use as a backdrop.

It is also more common for large-scale events to use video walls composed of a bank of TV monitors. This has been a feature of special events at concerts and gigs for some time, to enable very large (often outdoor) audiences to see the performers. Where backdrops are constructed and set up by a production company, the company may work regularly with a particular venue (many of the large venues have links with local production companies), but where this is not the case, the production company will have to undertake preparatory site work to assess factors such as available space, power, structural capacities and access to the hall or arena in order to do the job properly. The company will also work closely with the event co-ordinator or logistics officer to ensure everything gets to the right place when it is needed. For this, a production schedule will be drawn up (see Figure 8.9).

Lighting

The lighting of venues has a number of purposes. In terms of function rooms themselves the main purposes are to provide ambient lighting, to highlight artists or speakers, to light backdrops and to enhance the atmosphere. In the other areas of venues the lighting has to provide adequate background illumination in both public and support areas, and some decorative illumination, particularly in VIP rooms, dining areas and foyers. The final lighting issue is one of provision for safety, and to help people feel secure, particularly in terms of exits and traffic routes in and around the venue or site.

Diffused illumination is necessary in the public areas of a building. Corridors, toilets, foyers and reception areas should be well-lit, although not harshly so. This is necessary to enable the proper functioning of these areas, to ensure safety and security, and to maintain a pleasant general ambience. Consideration must also be given to lighting control systems, dimmers and sensor switches. Typically, the scalar illumination of public rooms should be of the order of 200 lux, with corridors and background areas having approximately 100 lux (Lawson, 1995).

Emergency lighting is essential, and a legal requirement, in public buildings. This is usually provided by secondary battery-powered lights lasting up to three hours, activated by the fire alarm system or a power failure. Exits should be clearly illuminated and the emergency lighting sufficient to allow adequate means of escape. In some modern buildings, floor lighting strips are provided along exit routes, similar to those provided on aircraft floors to direct people to emergency exits. Security lighting is also necessary for areas containing expensive equipment, such as computers. Externally, particularly in car parks and around the building, good lighting is needed to ensure visitors feel secure. Lighting should be provided throughout the venue from the various public areas to the place of final exit.

Sound and communications

Historically, the sound system at venues was, at best, a microphone and a couple of loudspeakers, and if you were lucky, an amplifier and a mixer. This tends to be inadequate for current needs. Consequently, provision of professional sound systems is often necessary. Not only is there the need for the audience to be able to hear the proceedings, there are also issues of sound re-inforcement needed to go with visual tools and multimedia presentations, to accompany sets, to provide atmosphere, as well as provide the full range of aural stimulation for an audience at an event.

Notwithstanding copyright law (which imposes various requirements, including payments, for public entertainment and public performance), music may be played from CD, minidisks or whatever system is available. Major venues are usually equipped to provide modern sound equipment, but, whilst almost every home has a disc player, not enough small or municipal venues are so equipped. Organizers wishing to incorporate good quality sound often have to hire-in the equipment to provide it. Companies providing equipment are able to provide equipment packages that will include not only public address (PA) systems, but also complete music systems. Given the complexity of this technology, a package,

Figure 8.10 Logistics: communications contact list	

Contact List

Add contacts to the list as you make them (in alphabetical order):
Telephones: M [mobile]; W [work]; H [home]; S [site]

Date / Time of this list: 24/03/2004 14.05

Internal Contact Network

Name	Job	Base Location	Phone	Radio
Jo Example	Event co-ordinator	Site office	07720 123456 (M) 01234 234567 (H)	Yes
Marc Sample	Volunteer leader	Catering tent	None	Yes
Mike Specimen	Stage technician	Stage	01334 654321 (S)	No
Etc.				

External Contacts and Suppliers

Name	Address	Phone	Fax	Email
Catering Equipment:				
National Equipment	Arboretum Hall 12 Castle Hill Middleburg Scotland SG1 3PQ	01786 123456	01786 123457	jock@catering.com
Furniture:				
Red Dragon Hire	Ty Gwyn Fford Uwd Abertawe Wales SA6 5RE	01792 123456	01792 123457	Rhys@reddragon.co.eu
Marquee Hire:				
Etc.				

including the hire of a technician (again an element that not all venues are able to provide) is often necessary.

A loudspeaker system may, in some cases, be built into a room such as an arena or large hall, but may also be in the form of quite large portable loud-speakers. These would normally be set up between presenters and audience, and would also usually be quite high up, at least head height for a seated event, to reduce the amount of sound absorbed by the audience. Most loudspeakers will be stand- or floor-mounted, but in purpose-built venues they can often be ceiling-hung from gantries designed for them. There are some issues of aesthetics to be borne in mind, and increasingly loudspeakers are screened by some means such as lightweight curtaining, floral displays, or careful illumination around them, so that the loudspeakers themselves are in relative seclusion.

Where an event is extremely large, and takes place in an arena-type venue, there may also be a need to allow communication between more than one tech-nician and between co-ordinators. For this purpose it is preferable to provide a communication ring. Whilst this can be done using radios or cell phones, there is a danger of these interfering with other systems and of failure in an emergency. In consequence, the communications ring must be a land line. Sufficient time must be allowed for crews to set up systems in the case of a large event, and to obtain frequencies for events radio communications, if these are needed. The logistics officer should, when planning the provision of communications, prepare a contact listing, both for internal and external contacts. This acts as a kind of event phone book and saves trying to track down contacts from bits of paper, and should be built up as the event is being created (see Figure 8.10).

Amenities and cleaning

Cleaning and clearing are issues sometimes neglected in the servicing of venues, sites and events. It is essential that when there is a break in the programme, or at any other convenient point, the opportunity is taken for minor rubbish clearing, bin emptying, replenishment of consumables and other stock. This should be planned to happen at regular intervals and can be regarded as 'preventative' action. Cleaning equipment and materials must be available and accessible to the support staff. It may be a simple case of needing to clear up a broken glass. On the other hand, a guest may have over-indulged at dinner and in the bar and proceeded to throw up in a grand manner on the way to the toilets, resulting in multi-coloured vomit all over the corridor. Delay in responding to these crises, major and minor, is typically due to lack of correctly placed equipment, material and forethought.

In terms of the provision of amenities, the general rule is to provide one toilet for every 75 people (of each gender), which can be increased for VIP events. Portable toilets, for example, can be hired in blocks, different standards of facility can be also hired, as well as shower blocks if required. It is essential to provide servicing for event toilets, and supervision to ensure that effective cleaning is done. Admittedly, difficulties of maintaining cleanliness in portable facilities that are not only used for ablutions, but which might possibly be used by drug users or by people to have to sex in. Nevertheless, proper systems for servicing and supervision is as much a necessity as any other support service. As with most other activities, this can be contracted out if necessary.

Creating the ambience

Ambience is often significant to the creation of a good event. An event with the right ambience can be a huge success. An event with the wrong ambience can be a huge failure. At a personal event, such as a birthday party, the ambience may be created simply by the people who are there, without the need for anything else – good company amongst friends can make an excellent event.

Case Study 23 *The ambience of events: Glastonbury Festival*

Glastonbury, England

Factbox

- Glastonbury Festival, England.
- 112,500 'weekend tickets', for the three-day event sold out in 24 hours – capacity is set at 150,000.
- Employs some 1,700 during the event (excluding volunteers and pre-event contractors).
- Admission price in 2003 was €155.
- Famous for its informality – and its mud.

In a number of large fields on Worthy Farm in Somerset, nestling in the rolling green English countryside, 100,000 people gather to listen to bands playing anything from hip hop to jazz. This is Glastonbury, put on by Michael Eavis, a large number of volunteers and some paid staff almost every year at the summer solstice. Not quite every year, because sometimes the land needs to be given a rest. This is a farm and it has real cows. In fact, at the first festival, the admission price included free milk, for the 1,500 people who attended it then, in 1971. Since 2002, the

'Mean Fiddler' events organization has been involved with the festival's management, in conjunction with Mr Eavis.

Glastonbury has, over the 30 or so years of its existence, become internationally famous. It has played host to hundreds of bands and individuals. It is 'peculiarly British' in the type of people it attracts, a cross-section of the music-loving public, and is relaxed in a hippy, New Age kind of way. It is well known for the nature of its portable toilets and, in rainy summers (this is England), its sea of mud. Although there are headline bands each year, the programme is not especially fixed, but might contain over 50 bands or acts over the three days, who play on several sound stages throughout the farm area. There is a tendency for much of what goes on to be impromptu, and because of its rural situation it plays all night (to the annoyance of a few local residents).

The general theme has tended to be dance music, which makes for an enjoyable environment. The social inclusiveness of the festival also means that considerable charitable funds are raised for Greenpeace, Oxfam, Campaign for Nuclear Disarmament and other local and national charities. The audience is catered for by facilities such as the festival markets, which include over 700 stalls in five or so main market areas, laid out in pre-sold pitches (in effect, a way of licensing stalls). These markets are grouped together around key services such as water, electricity and toilets. Camping, in the open, in tents, vans, motorcaravans, caravans and big motor homes is a feature of Glastonbury, and the campsite fields have various facilities including cafes. In the

▶

evenings the warm glow of campfires in the summer dusk contributes to much of the festival's atmosphere, also created by its location in a beautiful valley extending towards the Tor (rocky hill) at Glastonbury itself. The music also impacts on the festival atmosphere, depending on which bands, players and sets are performing and when. The mood can be raucous or peaceful. For example, it was reported by Dorian Lynskey (of the *Guardian* newspaper) that the 2002 event did not have one of the great line-ups of the festival in terms of range of bands, but that the massed singing during the Coldplay set of their piece 'Trouble' was some of the gentlest mass singing ever heard.

The festival has also had a number of impacts. Its informality (as well as sound) did not go down well with some locals, to the extent that in 1981 the local Conservative ('Tory') Member of Parliament tried to stop the festival by creating a law (via the British Parliament) requiring all festivals in Britain to be licensed by a local authority (council). The intention was to stop the Glastonbury Festival, but the local Mendip Council approved the licence. A delay in granting a licence for the 2003 event related to concerns over security in the wider area; partially, reflecting the success of the festival in improving its on-site security by the provision of a 'superfence' around the site, in 2002. The fence prevented gatecrashers and meant that, for the first time, ticketing arrangements worked properly; the downside was a sense of increased crime in the local area outside the fence. It was this that led to the refusal of the licence in December 2002. Views differ as to whether the Regulatory Board can be criticized for its lack of understanding of the festival management's success in regaining control of festival admittance, or whether crimes taking place outside a venue should be linked to an organizers' licence application. The festival attracts a large number of visitors and participants and injects a significant amount of money into the area and into local businesses associated with it. These are also significant considerations.

Based on this case:

1. In what way does the setting of Glastonbury have an impact on the atmosphere and style of the festival?

2. Identify the major features of the surroundings and of the communal lifestyle that predominates at Glastonbury. Is the atmosphere due solely to the type of music, or are a range of other factors in place?

3. Can these factors be successfully transferred to other festivals?

4. Which features make the Glastonbury Festival unusual in organizational terms?

5. Having spawned a host of imitators, how should Glastonbury be competing with them?

Related website for those interested in Glastonbury: www.glastonburyfestivals.co.uk; for media material, search the websites of the news media, such as *Guardian* newspapers: www.guardian.co.uk/Archive/

Some events, however, may need a little help to go well. As at a birthday party, there might be the need for decorations, music and games, as well as food and drink. But it is important to understand that the presence of these elements does not in any way guarantee that things will go well. There can be a wonderful environment, expensive themed decor, large amounts of excellent food and drink, yet the event might still not be quite the success that the organizers intended. However, one of the roles of an events co-ordinator is to try and ensure the event succeeds by careful attention to detail and by attempting to encourage the desired outcome. Berkley (1996) illustrates some components in trying to create atmosphere at an event, as do Bateman and Hoffman (1999) in their discussion of the physical environment of service operations. In rather simpler terms we can regard the staging and ambience of an event as comprising a number of interlinked features (see Figure 8.11).

The physical setting of an event, which deals with various design and staging activities, is primarily intended to look after the events surroundings and the visitor's responses to them. Visitors respond to stimulus of their senses of smell, sight, touch, hearing and taste. The physical responses to a pleasant meal environment are well understood, and much the same applies to an event environment.

An event environment can be probably quite complicated in certain situations. Suppose we are organizing a mediaeval theme night. In order to be effective, its planning and execution night will have to appeal to all the senses, in order to provide a themed environment that would be convincing to the guests. This might require the careful selection of a venue, as it would be easier to adapt a suitable building than to create a total mediaeval experience in a marquee (although this could be done, with enough time and resources). After this, all the elements of the theme could be prepared, from the decor to the costumes.

The physical elements, of surroundings, backdrops, props, layout, equipment, personal artefacts, etc., go towards making up what Bitner (in Bateman and Hoffman, 1999) refers to as the 'Holistic Environment'. This environment, together with the cognitive, emotional and physiological responses of the guests (as well of the as staff, crew, artists and musicians) help make up what people feel about the event, and will also help determine how the guests interact, how they respond to staff and whether they stay and enjoy themselves.

In addition to the setting of the event and its surroundings, there are various service factors as perceived by the guests. Many events are run by amateurs and volunteers, and this may be a key part of the experience. If the client is paying a

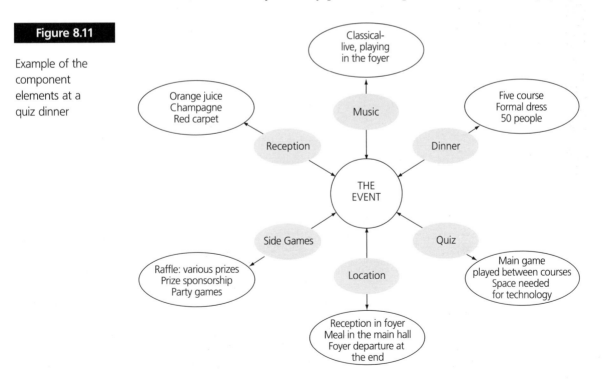

Figure 8.11

Example of the component elements at a quiz dinner

Figure 8.12

The event service experience

1. Chilly reception: A bad day in the catering tent

Procedural	Convivial
Slow	Insensitive
Inconsistent	Cold
Disorganized	Apathetic
Chaotic	Uninterested
Inconvenient	Bored

The guest thinks: 'Why is this a shambles? I waited for ages'. (Or, 'Where is the damn salt pot?')

2. Get 'em in and ship 'em out: The production line at the burger stall

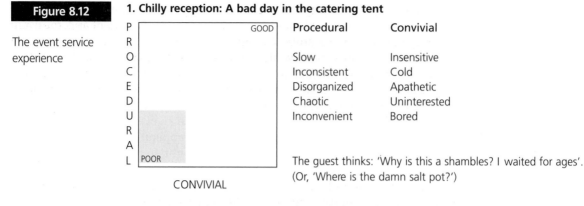

Procedural	Convivial
Timely	Insensitive
Efficient	Cold
Uniform	Apathetic
By the book	Uninterested

The guest thinks: 'That was quick, but I didn't enjoy it much'.

3. An amateur production: A funny day at the fête, happy people and cold coffee

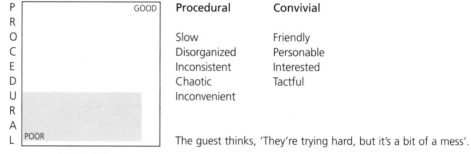

Procedural	Convivial
Slow	Friendly
Disorganized	Personable
Inconsistent	Interested
Chaotic	Tactful
Inconvenient	

The guest thinks, 'They're trying hard, but it's a bit of a mess'.

4. Satisfaction guaranteed: A professional event

Procedural	Convivial
Timely	Friendly
Efficient	Personable
Uniform	Interested
Adaptable	Tactful
Visible management	

The guest thinks, 'Wow, I didn't expect it to be so good'.

professional to put on a mediaeval theme evening, he/she is likely to have certain expectations of the event and its service standards. If, on the other hand, the event is a co-operative one, put on by volunteers in their spare time and by their own efforts, the expectations of the event and its service standards may be quite different. Service at events might be thought of more in terms of procedural and conviviality characteristics, as shown in Figure 8.12. (We are grateful to Rudi Drost, formerly of the Colchester Institute, for expressing this concept in relation to events.)

Summary

This chapter has sought to discuss the preparation and support activities for events, including logistics and the ordering and supply of goods, equipment and the other items needed to ensure everything is ready at the correct time and is in the correct place. All these elements have to be assembled in a way that will help the event co-ordinator create the right kind of event, not only in terms of the efficiency of organization, but also in terms of its ambience and atmosphere, so that visitors will regard the event as having been enjoyable to attend and well run.

References

Bateman, J.E.G. and Hoffman, K.D. (1999) *Managing Services Marketing*, Fort Worth, Dryden, 4th edn, pp.135–49.

Berkley, B.J. (1996) 'Designing Services with Function Analysis', in *Hospitality Research Journal*, vol. 20, no 1, pp.73–100.

Cracknell, H.L., Nobis, G. and Kaufmann, R.J. (2000) *Practical Professional Catering Management*, Basingstoke, Macmillan, 2nd edn, pp.292–95.

Goldblatt, J.J. (1990) *Special Events: The Art and Science of Celebration*, New York, Van Nostrand Reinhold, pp.65–68, 73-77, 107–17.

Holt, M. (1993) *Stage Design and Properties*, London, Phaidon, pp.36–51.

Konopka, C. (1995) 'The Big Event', *Caterer and Hotelkeeper*, 18 May, pp.64–66.

Lawson, F. (1995) *Hotels and Resorts*, Oxford, Butterworth Heinemann, pp.295–98.

Lillicrap, D., Smith, R. and Cousins, J. (2002) *Food and Beverage Service*, London, Hodder and Stoughton, 6th edn, pp.337–64

Reid, F. (2001) *The Staging Handbook*, London, A&C Black, 3rd edn, pp.33–52.

Seekings, D. (1999) *How to Organise Effective Conferences and Meetings*, London, Kogan Page, 7th edn, pp.94–96, 135–207, 304–6, 333–35.

Shone, A. (1998) *The Business of Conferences*, Oxford, Butterworth Heinemann, p.93.

9 Marketing and public relations for events

Aims

- To explore some of the key marketing issues of events management including budgetary and timing issues.

- To suggest appropriate marketing and public relations techniques which events organizers can use.

- To consider some of the marketing needs for both new events and for further editions.

Introduction

As with many aspects of events management, the breadth and range of types of special event make it hard to generalize about how to market events, when those events are intended to fulfil very different objectives and may be targeted at very different markets. The key to how an event will be marketed is the target market itself – knowing what kind of people will attend, where they live and how can they be influenced to attend. Marketing is not simply pushing out a few posters and hoping for the best. We need to know as much as possible about the target market, and be able to split it into convenient segments in order to best understand what techniques would make them aware of the event and attract them to it, as well as considering issues of differential pricing for the different segments of the target market. People have limited discretionary or disposable income, and limited time. This being the case, events compete for the public's attention, money and time, against all kinds of other activities and attractions, from eating out to engaging in sports and hobbies.

Careful marketing planning and effective marketing are required for activities that will help to ensure the success of what we are doing. As with other activities, there will be finite money, time and staff available for marketing, and these resources need to be planned carefully and used effectively. At the initial stage, marketing was one of the filters, or screens, through which various event ideas could be put, in order to identify ideas that were appropriate. This filtering process should have given the events organizer a firm basis to work on, and a starting place to consider some of the more detailed aspects of marketing, beginning with research. Research may be required about the target market, as well as a thorough assessment of the competitive environment the event is operating in. Once this information is known and objectives have been set, work can begin on the budget and on the marketing schedule.

One of the key functions of the budget will be to obtain the most effective marketing impact for possibly limited money. Not all marketing is expensive. Indeed, some types of activities, such as public relations (PR), may have quite modest costs and be as effective as large-scale expensive advertising campaigns. The budget, therefore, has to relate to what needs to be done, and can either be calculated as a percentage of the overall budget, or built up from 'zero', based on what needs to be done and how much that will cost. Some commentators suggest that events should have quite a substantial marketing budget compared to normal kinds of products, perhaps as much as 10 per cent of the total event expenditure, as opposed to 3–4 per cent for most other goods and services, because of the short duration and unique profile of events, compared to other, longer-lived, types of goods and services. Of all the marketing planning activities, the marketing schedule is the one most likely to surprise people new to the job. The lead times for preparing some marketing activities can be shockingly long. It is not possible, for example, to bang out a brochure in a day or two, as you have to decide what you need to say in it, and find suitable pictures or graphics for it, and it has to be laid out to look attractive, proofed, checked, returned, amended and checked again. This all takes time, if the end result is going to be professional.

This chapter also looks at events marketing in terms of the considerations needed for new, or 'one-off' events, as these will need more detailed research and preparation work, due to the uncertainty of the target market and the questionability of the success of the event, if a new concept has not been tried before. This can be compared with the marketing of repeat editions of an event, where the event has run previously, perhaps for many years, and where a great deal of experience has been accumulated about it. In these cases the market, its participants or visitors, may be well known, although – especially where an event has been organized by volunteers – the information recorded might not be especially complete or particularly detailed. A case is therefore made for the kind of information that a marketing officer would find useful to record for the marketing of further editions.

The target market

In our case, the term 'target market' refers, in the main, to the people who would be coming to a particular event. We should bear in mind, however, that for some events, a target market could be watching it on TV, or via the Internet, or follow it as a recreational interest (e.g. sports events). In the most general way, we can see that the target market for a rugby tournament would be very different from one for a heritage pageant, or a motor show, since different people like different things. The issue for the events organizer is how much is known about the potential target market for a given event, and whether this can be used to marketing advantage. In addition, it might be wrong to think that an event could only have one target market, as this may not be the case. Take the village fête. The main target market might be people who live in the village itself; a secondary market might be those who live in the surrounding area; and another secondary market might be tourists who happen to be visiting the village on the (hopefully) sunny summer day when the fête is being held.

In asking various questions about the potential market, the answer will help us decide what has to be done next (see Figure 9.1). For example, if the answer to the question: 'Is your event targeted at the general public?' is 'Yes', then the next step is to consider how this knowledge helps us. It provides some focus around which to work, indicates what techniques can be used and what marketing approach might be best for that particular target market, given the resources we have. Appreciating the limitations of the target market concept is also important. The larger an event, the more likely it is to attract a more diverse range of people, for which more comprehensive market segmentation might be needed (Swarbrooke, 2002). Also, there might be 'stakeholders' in the activity and opinion leaders who themselves could also be regarded as separate or discrete target markets, at least from the point of view of public relations.

Figure 9.1

Key questions to ask about the target market

- Who is your potential market?

- Is your event targeted at the general public, or at a specific group?

- What sort of age or lifestyle segment will your event attract?

- Will your event appeal to special interest groups?

- Can you identify different segments to attract?

- Are the different segments likely to be responsive to different prices?

Source: adapted from Richards, 1992.

Figure 9.2

Catchment and origin

- Where is your catchment area?

- Where do most of your target market live?

- From how far away will people come to your event?

- What is the most likely distance (or time) people would travel to your event?

- Can you say how many people in your various target markets are in each catchment?

- How will these various groups travel to your event?

Part of the process of identifying the target markets for an event involves knowing where your visitors will be coming from. This is easy if you are organizing a student ball, as the catchment area is the campus – students and their friends. Similarly, if you are organizing a wedding anniversary, catchment is not really an issue, because the target market is simply the friends and relations of the couple. However, for many events an understanding of the catchment area is useful for the marketing officer. The target market might have been determined, say, for a horticultural show, to consist of gardening enthusiasts and those in the general public in the 55-plus age group who are retired and enjoy gardening. If this is a village show, the catchment might be quite small – people from the village and mainly those within walking distance. But for a larger show or event, a typical travel time of one hour might be seen as reasonable to define how far visitors might travel to visit the event, to be involved or entertained. As a ground rule, the more important the event, the larger its catchment area (see Figure 9.2).

Travel distances in the catchment are often influenced by the time it takes to get to and from the event from various population centres. An hour's travel time on a motorway may cover 100 km, but an hour's travel on a country road might cover only 30 km (see Figure 9.3). These limits in terms of time, rather than simply distance, are what will determine the outer limit of the catchment area for the event. It would then be possible to calculate the size of the catchment area in population terms from census information, or from other sources such as from local newspaper 'rate and data' information (local papers often keep information on population structure and social groups in their area, in order to help sell advertising space), or from companies who provide market research assessments, or local council economic development departments. Combining this information about social group size and catchment area should give an idea of the potential size of, say, the working population, or that section of the population in a particular age group, although not all information will have been collected in a way that makes it useful for event marketing officers. Nor will all the people in the selected target market attend your event. Attendance will be influenced by a whole range of things, from effective (or ineffective) marketing to personal preferences, the opinions of friends, or something else going on at the same time.

Figure 9.3

Example of a catchment area: the Middleburg Music Festival

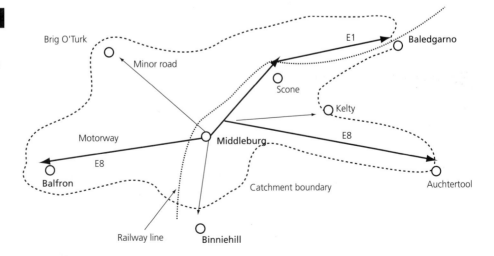

More detail could be added to the catchment as a better picture is built up; for example, if the special event were, say an opera, a large-scale map could be drawn up showing areas of upmarket housing (given a presumption that opera goers would live in those districts, which is not necessarily correct, but serves to illustrate the point). Clearly, different towns, and different areas within a town, have different population compositions, and a thorough knowledge of the target market and the areas in which its members live would help focus the marketing effort on those areas.

Case Study 24 *Marketing catchment areas: Lake Vyrnwy Marathon, Wales*

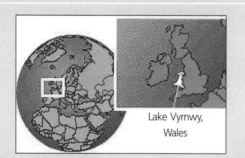

Lake Vyrnwy,
Wales

The race takes place during the afternoon, starting at 1.00 pm, with the fastest runners able to get around the course in about an hour and ten minutes, and an average time of an hour and a half to two hours. The race has over 12 classes, depending on the age and sex of the runners, with a number of awards for the various classes and overall winners. The race is organized by the Oswestry Olympians, who also organize various other races and competitions in north and mid-Wales, for example:

Factbox

- Lake Vyrnwy Marathon, Powys, Wales.
- Attracts some 1,200 runners.
- Runners from over 200 clubs take part.
- Entry is about €12.
- Takes place on the third Sunday in September.
- Involves runners, friends, race-watchers and marathon staff and stewards.

Race	Location race	Type of race	Type of participant	Type of runner	Date
Park relays and 10k	Oswestry	Relay race		School years 5 and 6	1 July
Mynydd Hill run	Trefonen	Recreational run		Under-18s short run Over-18s long run	29 May
Gobowen pentathlon	Gobowen	Pentathlon		Club members Individuals	4 August

Running is a very popular sport, with large numbers of road races, marathons, multi-terrain races and related activities such as triathlons taking place throughout Europe. There are a very large number of clubs associated with the sport, which also has quite a lot of sponsorship activity attached to it. The Severn Trent Lake Vyrnwy Marathon is an extremely popular event attended by some of the best runners in Wales, around a good course known for its fast scenic route.

The target markets for this type of activity are:

- Amateur and professional runners
- Members of running clubs
- Recreational (occasional) runners
- Individuals interested in trying the sport, but not wishing to do a whole marathon
- Race-watchers and sightseers
- Friends and family of the runners

▶

The catchment area for this race is quite large. It is a well-known race, in popular scenery. It attracts runners from a catchment area covering the whole of Wales and the north and Midlands of England, from where the drive time is about two hours to Lake Vyrnwy, which is about 20 km west of Oswestry and Welshpool. Consequently, the race is marketed locally and regionally in newspapers and by poster promotions, as well as in national running magazines, and by flyers to running clubs and other relevant locations (such as leisure centres) in the area.

The catchment area for those watching the race is rather less than the catchment for runners. Apart from friends and family of the participants, running is not a huge spectator sport on the scale of soccer, but nevertheless, people interested in running as a recreational activity do go to watch the race. Because of its scenic location, there is perhaps a one hour travel time for spectators. There is no separate marketing programme for spectators.

The issue of catchment and travel time must also be seen in the light of accessibility. If we were to say that catchment was an hour on motorways, this would cover a far larger area, because you can drive further and faster on a motorway than on minor roads. This means that catchment areas are unlikely to be circular, but will vary according to the quality of roads and access to the event location. (This can be seen from the shape of the example catchment pattern shown in Figure 9.3.).

Based on this case:

1. Take a map of Wales and the surrounding area. Consider the road network around Lake Vyrnwy. How does this affect the potential catchment for runners?

2. If this race was held in central Birmingham, how would the catchment compare, and why?

3. Consider an event you have recently attended, what different types of people were there and how could they be classed into various target markets? How would this information be useful?

Related websites for those interested in the Lake Vyrnwy Marathon:
www.oswestryolympians.co.uk

How to influence the target market

There are several reasons why a knowledge of the target market is important to the events organizer; the most important is that this knowledge enables some thought to be given to how to promote the event to a particular group, as well as knowing what kind of activities they would enjoy, or what publicity material they might respond to, i.e. what they read, what they watch on TV, or aspects of their lifestyle that the marketing officer could use as a marketing mechanism (see Figure 9.4). This also helps us understand the likelihood of their coming to our event. In all probability, our marketing plan will have to contain a range of activities both to raise awareness of the event, and to convert possible visitors into definite visitors.

For the marketing officer who might feel that once you know who your target market is, and what their media habits and buying habits are, all you have to do is to get the promotion or advertising right for them, a word of caution: there are a range of influences on why a target audience might or might not attend an event. Sometimes such reasons are straightforward, like the weather. On the other hand, for an event to be popular it might be necessary to have a critical mass of people showing an interest in attending. This critical mass might only develop through word of mouth via a reference group (that is to say, the people we know). For example, suppose the event is a student summer ball. Ticket sales might not have reached the break-even point needed by the break-even deadline, in spite of advertising in the student magazine, posters around the campus or other sales efforts. The reason for this could be that the reference group (other students) might not have shown a wish to go, perhaps because of other events planned on the same night, or of a lack of immediate interest, or other reasons (Hill et al., 1995).

| **Figure 9.4** | • How can you influence people to attend? |

Influencing the market

- How can you influence people to attend?

- What are their media habits, what newspapers, magazines, etc. do they read?

- Can you use direct mail or newspaper inserts to influence them?

- Do they watch TV, go the cinema or listen to local radio?

- How can you influence them if they are not engaged by the media (not everyone is)?

- What public relations activities could you use for these groups?

- Who are the opinion leaders and how might they be influenced?

Figure 9.5

Determinants for participation in an event (the 'buying process')

- Whether your friends might go (cultural, personal or other 'reference' groups)

- What decision-making time is available, or what lead time is there before you have to buy a ticket?

- Whether the price is a major concern ('price sensitivity' – high cost, low cost, total package, and value for money)

- Whether the event will be good enough – the perceived quality of the event

- Access factors – e.g. local, regional, national, international: do people in your area go to this type of event? How easy is it to get to? What are the opening times?

- One-off or repeat sales opportunities – is this annual, biannual, occasional? Will the event happen again, or is this the only opportunity to go?

- Familiarity – people's knowledge and awareness: have they been to one before, or something similar?

- Propensity to join in community activities (high, low)

- Inclination to join in the activity due to personal interest, education, entertainment, relaxation, status, etc.

- Considerations of personal enjoyment, arousal or other satisfaction from the event

In general, the determinants of why or whether a visitor would come to an event are very varied (and not just about whether we can advertise or promote our event in front of their noses), and some understanding of this process (the buying process) can help us in deciding how best to promote our particular event. In general, these motives can be seen as relevant to the marketing of other activities and products, not just events (Kotler et al., 1996). It is also useful to remember the points made in chapter 2, about some of these motives being more important than others – primary and secondary motives – because we need to know how best to promote the event given what we know about why people will come to it. For example, a primary motive may be social, because the person knows that many of their friends will go. A secondary motive might be to be entertained. This process is also influenced by other determinants, such as whether the event will be repeated, whether it is easy to get to, etc.

It can be seen that there are some differences in the 'buying process' between, say, the purchase of the weekly shopping or of new clothes, and the purchase of a ticket for a special event. In the case of certain types of event, no purchase may be taking place. If you have been invited to a dinner party, you are not 'purchasing' the event – you don't buy a ticket, you go because you enjoy the company of your friends. This is true of many types of event: no buying decision is involved, only a social decision (although there is the hidden cost of time and effort, which might be interpreted as buying factors). On the other hand, many special events, particularly in the sporting and organizational categories, will involve a buying decision: whether to buy the ticket, whether it will be value for money, whether the event will be enjoyable, would all be part of the buying decision in such a case.

A number of determinants can be seen as being specific to an 'events buyer'. This is rather a tricky term to use, as the 'buyer' may be a whole family having a day out; a group of people in a minibus going to a sports competition; or one person buying a ticket for a beer festival. If you were the marketing officer for an event, it would be important to have an understanding of who was doing the buying, of who gets the ticket and how you might influence them to do it (Russell and Cotton, 1999). What places would you advertise in? What are the benefits of the event you are promoting, to the attendees, visitors, guests or participants? What price would be charged for tickets? Where could people actually buy the tickets?

For the marketing officer, perhaps a significant issue is the benefit that a visitor or attendee gets from the event. This may also be related to the question of expectations. If the visitor expects an excellent, well-organized, enjoyable and good value event, then the level of satisfaction he/she would have would be very high. On the other hand, if the visitor is led to expect these things, but gets none of them, then the outcome will be not only dissatisfaction, but possibly bad publicity for the organizers. Marketing, then, is not just about getting people in through the door. It is, at least in part, about ensuring they get the kind of satisfaction from the event that they have been led to expect (see Figure 9.6).

Leading on from the issue of what motivates and influences people to attend or participate in an event, we have to recognize the difficulty of marketing what are essentially unique, one-off occasions to a diverse market – and very possibly, a diverse market of people who do not know they want to attend or participate. In terms of personal events, there are no conventional marketing issues in getting people to a private party. These events are 'invited', not marketed; in fact, in some cases, the problem is to stop people coming to events where they might not be wanted. Gatecrashers are an example of this. We can organize a party for friends, only to find that they turn up with people we might not expect, perhaps even do not like, or that word has got around to people whom we would not want at our party. This happens not only at some types of personal event, but also at high profile public events, which involve celebrities or film stars. Various people might try to blag their way into an event by all kinds of unscrupulous means, such as emailing the organizers to say they have not received the tickets they were promised (when no one said they could have tickets); trying to get in by hanging around, in the hope someone will recognize them and take them in; trying to buy tickets from touts, and so on.

For most events, in the leisure, cultural or organizational categories, the issue will not be how to stop people getting in, but how to encourage people to come. For a local charity fund-raising event, the issue will be both how to get a good crowd in and to make some money for the charity concerned. For organizations selling products, there may well be a clear need to market the event, so that a lot of people come to see the product and hopefully some of them will buy it. This is especially the case with events such as trade shows and exhibitions, but the need to market an event applies to a large range of activities. An example of the decision-making process is shown in Figure 9.7. There are some key marketing issues in this scenario. In promoting an event, it is necessary to create an awareness of it amongst the target market. In this example the method is posters, and the market is students. The interest phase is about stimulating the interest of the target market. In any target market, people who are considering attending the

Figure 9.6	• What are the benefits of attending the event? Will it be enjoyable, entertaining, diverting, educational, stimulating or exciting?

Individual's expectations of an event

• What will be the style and standard of the venue; distance from home; closeness to transport; convenience of getting there, parking, ease of arrival and departure, facilities?

• What will be the likely standard of the event? Will it be professionally done – even by amateurs or volunteers – will it be well-organized, will it be value for money, or will it just be a jolly, convivial, if moderately disorganized shambles? (This latter may be a *normal* expectation held by a potential visitor…)

• What will the people be like? Can we expect excellence, commitment, enthusiasm, knowledge (or otherwise) from staff, volunteers or other participants?

• What is the price (or value) in comparison to other uses for the money – other possible events, other days out, meals or other leisure or social activities?

• What range of activities is available, what interaction, sights and sounds, inclusiveness?

• What is the reputation of the event if it has been held before? Is it friendly, safe, happy?

• How easy is it to get information, buy tickets, or have questions answered?

event will be seeking a reference mechanism for confirming that the event is what they want.

For many people, the reference mechanism is word of mouth from people they know. One of the biggest difficulties facing the marketers of events is that for one-off occasional events, the word-of-mouth support may not exist, as no-one has been to the event before, or been able get a view of how good or bad it is. They then have to rely on external referents, such as the quality of the advertising material, or the views of critics (as of a new play or film). In some respects, events marketers can try to generate word-of-mouth support by targeting opinion formers, but this is problematic and only suitable for certain types of events. Thereafter, what we are seeking to create is desire for the product, through encouraging people to feel that the event will fulfil their particular needs and by generating a positive 'buzz' about it. From here onwards it should be easy. The prospective attendee simply takes 'action' and buys the ticket, and the event, of course, goes wonderfully well.

The marketing plan

The marketing plan, like the operational plan and the financial budget, will be developed from the event objective, in a number of stages (McDonald, 1995) (see Figure 9.8). Marketing techniques employed by events organizers vary, and the range of approaches is extremely wide, because of differences in the types of events being put on and the different characteristics of target markets. Nevertheless, the nature of the event buying decision and the influencing factors make targeting potential visitors relatively complicated for certain types of event (although not all – a village fête would have a relatively simple target market in the catchment area (of the village and its immediate surroundings).

The event marketing officer's expertise and resources in selling the event may not always be large, often depending on volunteer effort and small budgets,

Figure 9.7

Event decision-making process for a university ball

Attention
Saw poster at university for the summer ball
Instinctive consideration of whether the date and the cost would be OK

Interest
Talked to friends in the class (or other reference group) to see if anyone else was interested
If lots of people interested, do the benefits outweigh the cost (being a student with limited money)?
Is there anything else going on?
If not, why should I go?

Desire
Primary motives for going: Have a good time, get drunk or get laid
Secondary motives for going: Don't have to watch awful television in study bedroom; Food is included.
Reasons for not going: May be too difficult to get a ticket.

Action
Ticket seller knocked on the door, so bought a ticket

perhaps tending to rely on general awareness and word of mouth, or responses to enquiries, rather than expensive advertising. For this reason, public relations (PR) may play a greater role in promoting some events than paid advertising. However, this should not prevent careful thought and planning about marketing

Figure 9.8

Creating the marketing plan from the event objectives

Review of the event objectives, filter out unsuitable ideas, identify preferred event.

↓

Marketing audit of the external environment, internal environment and expertise.

↓

Statement of marketing objectives and general marketing strategy, including an overview of the results that would be expected.

↓

Preparation of the detailed marketing plan, including target market summaries, the schedule and what the budget is likely to be spent on.

↓

Identification of the system for measuring effectiveness.

Figure 9.9

Elements of the events marketing plan

Objectives

↓

Systematic detailed planning

Elements of the marketing plan

1. Statement of purpose and objectives including expected results
2. Analysis of the environment, competitors and similar events
3. Summary of the event component product(s) or service(s)
4. Overview of the target markets
5. Marketing budget
6. Marketing schedule for promotions, public relations and advertising

↓

Organizing and preparing the event (marketing-related issues)

Development activities, ticketing and enquiry systems, preparation and deadlines

↓

Implementing the event

Organization of key ceremonies / activities
Recording of incoming marketing information

↓

Closedown: divestment / legacy

Collation and analysis of data, post-event marketing evaluation and feedback
Recording for the next edition (where appropriate)

as a whole activity, nor should it prevent due consideration of the need for public relations to focus on internal as well as external communication (Harrison, 2000).

Marketing for a new event

Objectives and analysis of the environment

If the marketing of an event has to be started from a blank sheet of paper, the marketing plan will have to be written to cover six main elements (see Figure 9.9). Some of these should have been identified early on in the event planning process, and should be easy to summarize in the first few sections of the marketing plan. These are the sections dealing with the purpose of the event, which might be written as one line or sentence, and can then be broken down into several smaller objectives. To make this as simple as possible there should be no more than about five aims for the event (there might be only one, remember), because the more aims you have, the more difficult it will be to achieve them all adequately. In addition, either too much complication, or too much vagueness, about the objectives can render the marketing and public relations effort meaningless (Barry, 2002). This is followed by the analysis of the environment in which the event will operate (covered in chapters 5 and 6), what competition there might be, what other things are going on at the same time that might take some of the potential target market away and whether there have been, or are, similar events that could be seen not so much as competitors, but as complementary to your event.

Event components mix and target markets

The summary of the component products and services of the event is a list of its respective parts (which might also be called the product/service mix), that might attract different parts of the target market. In the case of a garden show, this mix might comprise the main garden exhibition itself; seminars on gardening given by experts to visitors; the prizegiving ceremony for the best flowers; the catering tent; the sales and retail stands; the prize draw competition to win a garden makeover from an expert; and the children's crèche.

When preparing the summary of the event's components, the ability to cross-reference the products and services being offered against the likely target markets, will help to identify which parts of the event might turn out to be the busiest, and will also indicate how the marketing and promotion effort might be targeted at individual markets (rather than the general whole), by showing

Figure 9.10

Events components and target market matrix

Market	Exhibition	Seminars	Prizegiving	Catering	Sales	Draw	Crèche
① Families	X			X	X		X
② Pensioners	X		X	X		X	
③ Hobbyists	X	X	X	X	X	X	
④ Tour groups	X			X	X		

which elements of the event's components mix could be highlighted in specific literature or other promotional material for a given market segment or target (see Figure 9.10). At this point in the marketing plan, the target markets can be isolated and described in some detail, together with information about the catchment; the kind of marketing tools that will be used to influence each target market segment to come to the event; what media habits each target market has: and what other promotions or public relations activities might also have an impact on the decision to attend. From this list, the most effective marketing tools can be, and as the marketing budget is assembled, these can be given priority as the potentially being most effective.

The marketing budget

One of the largest single costs in terms of marketing budgets for professionally run events is the staffing cost of the marketing department itself, as almost all larger professional events have marketing or sales teams, or co-ordinators. The advantage that volunteer-run events have is that there is no staffing cost, but equally, for a volunteer-run event, the marketing budget might be very small.

In normal circumstances, the student of the events business would probably automatically think of advertising as the major marketing tool available to organizers – all you do is advertise in the right place and visitors or participants come flocking in. Would that it were so easy. Advertising has its place and plays a significant role in raising awareness and helping to support an image for an activity. It is particularly relevant on a national scale for events organized in the corporate sector, or by voluntary associations in the national market. However, the wide range of potential events can take a wide range of approaches, which may include not only advertising and public relations, but also the use of a variety of other marketing tools.

Individual events can also attempt to entice the public, visitors, attendees, participants and even potential staff by providing pre-event activities, or a series of awareness-raising promotions to help familiarize people with the main event. It is also important to keep the target market 'warm', i.e. to call and talk to opinion leaders, or invite them to familiarization or hospitality events. In this way, some

Figure 9.11

Examples of marketing expenditure items

- Print items: tickets, posters, brochures, leaflets, visitor maps (design costs, display costs)
- Direct marketing: sales visits to opinion leaders / event organizers / agencies / mailings
- 'Advertorials': journal/magazine inserts or advertising copy pieces
- Hospitality: familiarization visits, Pre-event days
- Exhibition material for local promotions, stands, site models
- Paid advertising: newspapers, magazines, radio, TV
- Websites, CD-ROMs
- Payments for celebrity guests
- Press kits, photography and artwork activities
- Banners, signs, etc.

Figure 9.12

Event marketing
budget form (adapt
as required)

Marketing Budget Proposals

Event: ....

Date of event: .... Date of this Budget: ....

Target market segments:	Target numbers:	Ticket price:
Individuals	....	€ ....cent
Families	....	€ c
Children	....	€ c
Concessions / Students / Elders	....	€ c
Groups	....	€ c
Complimentary / Hospitality / VIPs	....	Nil
Press	....	Nil

Examples of expenditure:	Budget:	Actual:	Number/Size
Research	....	....	
Staff: marketing office	....	....	
Staff: booking and enquiry office	....	....	
Volunteers: custom T-shirts, leaving gifts	....	....	....
Advertising: newspaper / magazine	....	....	....
Advertising: radio	....	....	....
Advertising: posters	....	....	....
Advertising: other: specify	....	....	....
Direction signs	....	....	
Internal signs	....	....	
Printing: tickets	....	....	....
Printing: brochures	....	....	....
Printing: posters	....	....	....
Printing: programmes, site maps	....	....	....
Printing: menus, place cards	....	....	....
Printing: other: specify	....	....	
Uniforms / sashes	....	....	
Badges	....	....	....
Celebrity costs	....	....	
Prizes	....	....	
Complimentary items / give-aways	....	....	
Marketing office hospitality	....	....	
Marketing office travel expenses	....	....	
Display stands	....	....	
Photography	....	....	
Video company	....	....	
Press kit	....	....	
Ticket distribution	....	....	
Postage / mail-out costs	....	....	
Stationery	....	....	
Other items e.g. website	....	....	
Total costs	....	....	

of the target market or 'buyers' for an event can be influenced, or at least informed, of the planned activities.

It is difficult to ascertain the effectiveness of the various methods, but personal contacts are often significantly important to marketing an event and do not show as a cost in a marketing budget, except perhaps as travel or hospitality expenses. In addition to the paid advertising, which an event manager or organizing committee might or might not be able to afford, many events rely significantly on good public and media relations, anything from word of mouth to imaginatively written press releases (see Figure 9.11).

The marketing budget should be carefully prepared and costed. All the items that are needed should be included, how many are required, and their size or type. In addition, for items such as brochures or leaflets, the cost per thousand (if this kind of number is needed) should be compared, to see which type is the most cost-effective. Wherever possible, in the costing process, more than one estimate or cost quote should be obtained (see Figure 9.12).

The marketing schedule

In order for a special event to be marketed properly, not only must the planning and budgeting of the marketing programme have taken place, but a schedule of activities should have been prepared. This schedule is intended to give the organizers an idea of the lead times for various marketing activities, and to plan what needs to be done and when, to get the most benefit from the marketing effort (see Figure 9.13).

In preparing a marketing schedule, it is important to understand that many activities have long lead times. Brochures, for example, may take several weeks: the text has to be written, photographs provided, a draft assembled by the graphic designer or printer, checked for errors, corrected and then checked again before being printed. Similarly, for those particular media that a marketing manager may wish to use, it will be important to check the lead times. National monthly trade magazines might need two to four months notification of an event to get an advertisement in, with editorial. TV and radio shows require up to six weeks notice. Even a website might need several weeks intensive design work, and will itself require follow-up advertising. Local media can work on shorter lead times, but it is best to find out whether their deadlines for stories are a certain day and time of the week. A media kit or press pack can be prepared at an early stage of the activities, and could include various fact sheets about the event, an artist's impressions (or suitable photographs), a media contact list, information about sponsors, beneficiaries and key people involved. However, the first version of the press kit should not include admission prices, as the media might focus too strongly on these at too early a stage in the development process.

Marketing for repeat events and new editions

Up to now, we have tended to stress that many events are one-off, unique activities. In some ways this is true, but all kinds of events are repeated, perhaps annually or biannually, or on some other timescale (e.g. the Olympics

Figure 9.13

Example of a
marketing schedule

Marketing Schedule: Middleburg Garden Festival

5-6 months before opening:

1. Hold meeting to define objectives and to ensure co-ordination of various public relations activities with paid advertising. Establish timetable to match scheduled deadline opening date. Identify target market at a meeting with the organizing committee.
2. Prepare a media kit (information pack, contacts, etc.).
3. Order photographs/artists impressions/logo or design drafts, begin website design.
4. Begin preparation of mailing and media lists.
5. Contact a prospective beneficiaries of the event and start listing VIPs and opinion leaders.
6. Book dates for press conferences at suitable venues (probably off-site to begin with).

4-5 months before opening:

1. Send out initial press releases with suitable pictures to all media (local, regional etc.).
2. Write a "progress bulletin" or newsletter, for agents, media, VIPs and opinion leaders. This can also be used adapted for internal marketing, i.e. to keep site and event staff and volunteers up to date.
3. Begin production of adverts, posters and promotional brochures.
4. Set up enquiry desk and advance ticket office.
5. Test and set up website.
6. Make final plans for the opening ceremony and associated events, including arrangements and invitations for VIPs and other invited guests.

3-4 months before opening:

1. Launch publicity campaign to national media.
2. Send out mailings to all media.
3. Send second progress bulletin.
4. Arrange interviews with local media, also trade media, gardening, design and leisure publications (not at the site, as it will not be ready or well presented).
5. Begin awareness-raising advertising, e.g. posters.

2-3 months before opening:

1. Launch campaign to local and other media with a short lead time, emphasizing the event's contribution to the community, local businesses, etc. Highlight the contribution of volunteers, sponsors and benefactors.
2. Send out a further progress bulletin together with a brochure to the completed mailing lists and to people who have booked advance tickets already.
3. Provide a site model and publicity displays for the enquiry area, or for use in local public places such as libraries and shopping centres.
4. Begin 'behind the scenes' public tours (only if the site is nearly ready).
5. Hold 'hard hat' lunches for invited guests, such as media writers.

1-2 months before opening

1. Send out further progress bulletin, including useful comments from people who have had previews.
2. Undertake a 'mystery guests' enquiry and ticket bookings to test the system. Deal with any problems that arise.
3. Establish final plans for the opening ceremony, send out appropriate invitations.
4. Hold the 'soft opening' (an event where you use staff and their families to test the systems, such as catering, toilets, and parking and queuing arrangements, etc.).

The opening month

1. Final mailings.
2. Hold media orientation visits.
3. Hold opening ceremony.
4. Get pictures of opening ceremony to media, same day.

Post event

1. Send out a further 'progress bulletin', highlighting the success of the opening and especially thanking volunteers, sponsors and beneficiaries.
2. Final media coverage, more photos, success of event, handover ceremony or public date of next event.
3. Thank you letters.

every four years). Even events that happen annually, in the same place and at the same time of year, may not be exact replicas of what has gone on before, perhaps because of a different organizing committee, different participants, different visitors, or any number of changes in the operations and activities taking place. For this reason they are often called 'new editions'. Consequently, these types of events are based on existing knowledge and techniques, but, as with a book, some changes are made each time, perhaps some things removed, or some new things added.

Admittedly, new business often presents a more exciting challenge to event marketers and salespeople than the routine of carefully recording, monitoring and caring for an existing target market. Yet it is this attention to the detail of maintaining, and enhancing, an existing business base that is probably the acid test of a good marketing officer. The development of the existing visitor base into repeat business and also as a lead to further new visitors may be very useful indeed. Careful recording of attendance information about visitors and participants is the first stage in making sure they can be encouraged to return to the next event. It is also important to collect the same information each year, for the sake of consistency and to be able to make accurate comparisons. The basic information that we should be attempting to collect is detailed in the following subsections.

Records of visitor numbers

In assessing total visitor or participant numbers, how many and where from, the 'where from' can be done by sampling surveys or by getting people to fill in some details as part of the booking process – it depends on how big your event is, and what resources you can put into recording. With limited resources, such as volunteer staffing, you have no need to collect details from every single visitor. You will know how many tickets you sold, and of what types. If the event is free, volunteers can still be put on the entrances or gates to give a rough count of people coming in, and if it is in an open area estimates can still be made (see also the Deventer Book Market case study). More detailed information such as place of origin, mode of travel, etc. can be put on a simple questionnaire and attached to the ticket, to be filled in if the visitor wishes and placed in a box near the exit(s). Large numbers of questionnaire replies are not needed to gather this kind of information: if only 100 questionnaires were returned (note the limitations of doing this without a representative control sample that preferably includes some non-attenders to find out why they didn't come), this would still be enough for a modest analysis of the information, and is not too much to collate and write up in a short Visitor Attendance Report. Gathering this information will help you promote the event in the right places next time.

Case Study 25 *Recording of visitor information: Geneva Motor Show*

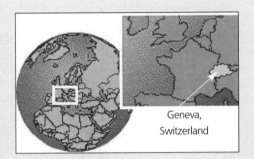

Geneva,
Switzerland

Factbox

- Geneva Motor Show.
- Attracts over 714,000 visitors from 87 different countries.
- 4,700 journalists attended.
- There were 275 stands showing 900 models of cars, covering 90,000 square metres of exhibition space.

The Geneva International Motor Show, has had more than 70 editions, attracts a huge number of exhibitors and visitors to the Palexpo halls in Geneva. The show lasts for 11 days in early March each year and includes not only car exhibits, but equipment and components, events and interactive displays. It is one of a series of motor shows throughout Europe, each country being allowed one International Motor show, as well as domestic shows and dealer exhibitions. The Geneva show in 2000 was of such importance that it was opened by the President of Switzerland together with the President of the Council of State, and other major political figures and celebrities attended the opening ceremony.

The 11-day event takes more than two weeks to set up inside the exhibition hall from the initial layout of where the respective stands will be, through the construction of the stand shells, the delivery of exhibitors' stand equipment, the fitting of power and lighting, the arrival of major exhibits – including the cars, which are covered with

tarpaulins – to the final fitting-out of the stands with furniture and promotional materials ready for the opening day. This sequence of construction can be seen in a series of development pictures on the motor show website.

For marketing purposes, the motor show organization, in conjunction with Palexpo, records and publishes admissions information and also breaks this down into various segments:

Total number of visitors	714,000	
Total number of Swiss visitors	421,000	59%
Total number of external visitors	293,000	41%
Number of countries of visitor origin	87	
Main countries of origin		
France	228,500	32%
Germany	14,250	2%
Italy	14,250	2%
All others	37,750	5%
Total number of visitors in age group 18–54	628,000	88%
Total number of visitors in other age groups	86,000	12%
Total number of male visitors	521,000	73%
Total number of female visitors	193,000	27%

Based on this case:

Identify how the breakdown of visitor information can be useful in marketing terms. Examine a local event (or tourist attraction) in your region for which you can obtain visitor information.

1. How can this information be used for marketing purposes?

2. What kind of details would it be especially useful to know about the visitors at the event, if you had a further edition to prepare for a coming year?

Related websites for those interested in the Geneva International Motor Show: www.salon-auto.ch/ and the Palexpo Halls: www.palexpo.ch

Details of spending and use patterns

How much was spent, and what on? How many people did what, and when? This kind of information helps you find out what aspects were most popular. Your event might have included several different components or activities (the product service mix), and in the next edition you might want to add or remove some of them, or make some of them better, or try out new layouts or locations. To do this you need information on what components of the event people are using and what is popular. This information can be obtained from spot checks and from sampling elements such as queue lengths at given times. More detailed information can be found from ticket sales, and from sales records of catering or other activities. Even where no money changes hands, volunteers can count the number of people using parts of the event, or visitors can be given tokens or ticket strips (carnet strips) to hand in at the various locations, activities or stands as they use them. These can be counted, or just weighed. Gathering this information will help you decide what parts of your event are most popular, and which should be kept or changed next time.

Marketing effectiveness

What parts of the marketing, publicity and public relations effort were successful? It is quite common for people to be asked on a questionnaire, 'How did you find out about us?' You can ask this by getting people to tick boxes on a questionnaire ('Advert in the newspaper; Advert on the radio', etc.), – but, bearing mind what has just been discussed about how people decide and what influences them, it would better to do this by through informal chats to visitors. These can, in fact, be loosely structured by writing down a few short questions and using them as a guide during each chat. Following the chat, write out the responses on a summary sheet (just a list – chat 1, chat 2, etc.). You will be surprised what you learn and, most importantly, this gives people the opportunity to tell you more about what they did and how they found out about you than if you had given them a list (provided you use open-ended questions, such as 'How did you get here?', rather than 'yes/no' questions, 'Did you come by car?'). Gathering this information will help you find out what part of your marketing effort was the most useful, and how you could improve it.

Expectations and satisfaction

What did your visitors expect and were they were happy with their experience, i.e. did your event fulfil their expectations? Like the effectiveness assessment of marketing, checking expectations and satisfactions is probably best done by talking to people. This helps to explore their expectations in a way that would probably not be expressed in a questionnaire. Be careful how you formulate questions. For example, it is very common in a restaurant to be asked, 'Is everything all right?' Remember what we said about asking open-ended questions, as the response to this is almost certainly 'Yes, it's fine'. This is, first, because the question is framed in a yes/no way, and second, because it is socially difficult for people to respond to such a question by saying, 'No. The food is terrible, the service is slow, the carpet is sticky and the toilets smell' (or whatever). Therefore, in exploring whether your visitors are satisfied you need to think carefully about what you will ask them and how, and also what opportunities there are during your event when visitors will be socially comfortable to answer questions. Although we may not use questionnaires during the event itself, it is probably a useful exercise to give people some to take away, or mail some out a day or two later, in order to obtain opinions after the event or after people have had time to reflect. Clearly, the most useful purpose in getting satisfaction information is to help identify strengths and weaknesses and to help grow the potential number of visitors attending by knowing what went well and what didn't.

Summary

Marketing is attractive to many people as an interesting and stimulating activity, one that they enjoy doing. However, as with the other components of events management, from logistics to finance, it requires a high level of skills to undertake it properly. Sound knowledge of the kind of people who will attend an event, whether as participants, visitors or guests, is essential to promoting it and ensuring its success. This knowledge helps the event marketer understand how to raise awareness, advertise, promote, improve an image or maintain the event's impact in the media. Part of the marketing function is also to evaluate how an event is received. Sometimes this is done as an event is progressing, sometimes by feedback at the end. In those cases where there will be a further edition, the knowledge gained from evaluation should enable improvements or changes to be made for the future.

References

Barr, A. (2002) *PR Power: Inside Secrets from the World of Spin*, London, Virgin, pp.21–39.

Harrison, S. (2000) *Public Relations: An Introduction*, London, Business Press, pp.116–39.

Hill, E., O'Sullivan, C. and O'Sullivan, T. (1995) *Creative Arts Marketing*, Oxford, Butterworth Heinemann, pp.26–34.

Kotler, P., Bowen, J. and Makins, J. (1996) *Marketing for Hospitality and Tourism*, London, Prentice Hall, pp.217–36.

McDonald, M. (1995) *Marketing Plans*, Oxford, Butterworth Heinemann, pp.427–35.

Richards, B. (1992) *How to Market Tourist Attractions, Festivals and Special Events*, Harlow, Longman, pp.21–35

Russell, V. and Cotton, V. (1999) 'Marketing Strategies for European Meetings', in *The Meeting Professional*, vol. 19, no 2, www.mpiweb.org/tmp/1999archive/tmp0299/marketing.htm (26 September 2000).

Smyth, H. (1994) *Marketing the City: The Role of Flagship Developments in Urban Regeneration*, London, E&FN Spon, pp.127–61.

Swarbrooke, J. (2002) *The Development and Management of Visitor Attractions*, Oxford, Butterworth Heinemann, 2nd edn, pp.58–68.

Managing the event as a project

Aims

- To provide a framework for managing event projects.

- To discuss the range of risk management, licensing, health and safety, and insurance requirements which are the key to secure operations.

- To provide an overview of the operational activities that take place immediately prior to, and during, an event.

Introduction

The purpose of this chapter is to look at events from the operational viewpoint – how to operate the event as a project (O'Toole and Mikolaitis, 2002; A.T. Kearney, 2002) and how to address some of the complexities (Starr et al., 2003), which, whilst critical, often receive insufficient attention (Westerbeek et al., 2002 and Drivers Jonas, 2002, pp.7–9). In addition, the chapter considers how to make the final preparations, those things that need to be done immediately before an event opens. These should be taken in conjunction with the sections about logistics and about how to run events on the day. The various sections overlap somewhat, depending on how an event is timed and organized. In some cases the preparations will happen all at once in one day, in others the groundwork may take several days and have to be ready well before the public arrives.

The event as a project

There are considerable similarities between the management of projects and of events (Morris, 1994), so much so that many of the techniques developed in the management of large-scale building, logistical or public projects can be used to bring organizational discipline to many kinds of events. Both are unique, time-limited operations. The application of project management techniques to events should therefore provide a vehicle for ensuring the modest success of an event, as opposed to a spectacular failure. Why only a modest success? Well, events management, rather like project management, can be a somewhat thankless task. The outside world does not see the event co-ordinator toiling away for weeks, coping with late nights, wrestling with tricky problems and recalcitrant suppliers to make the event a success, but the first time that the most minor thing goes wrong ('Oh dear, the flowers are red, they should be pink…') the event co-ordinator will get the blame. Reiss (1998), in a usefully chatty book about project management, makes these points very well, and also highlights the opportunities a project manager may have to show how much work is going on behind the scenes.

The management process involves very similar approaches, which the event co-ordinator or organizing committee can seek to use. In setting objectives for an event, these can be tested using the SMART formula:

Specific
Measurable
Achievable
Realistic
Timely

If the objectives are framed or worded badly, or are confusing (rather than specific and precise), then we will have difficulty creating the event from them. The objectives must be measurable, in terms of being able to know whether they are being achieved, or whether progress is being made towards them. This high-lights the need for progress meetings and schedule deadlines. The objectives must be achievable; it must be genuinely possible to put on the event, especially given the limitations of money, staff, management or volunteer expertise that the event co-ordinator might have to contend with. Similarly, the objectives must be realistic, irrespective of whatever flights of fancy (or fantasy) the clients may want you to achieve. Finally, the objectives must be timely, taking into account what can be done in the time available, what the deadlines are and the natural tendency for timescales to slip. We can plan to put on a party in a tent a week from now, but are we being realistic? Is the timing possible? On the computer plan we have prepared it may seem so, but in reality, the weather may be bad, the tenters may take frequent coffee breaks, the ground may be wet, the tent

Figure 10.1

Event and project activities

Event Management Activities

↓

Objectives and getting started

↓

Planning

↓

Organizing and preparing the event

↓

Implementing: running the event

↓

Divestment / legacy

Project Management Activities

↓

Conception

↓

Definition

↓

Production

↓

Operations

↓

Handover or divestments

may be dirty and need scrubbing, the lorry delivering the poles may get stuck in the mud… who would want to be an event co-ordinator?

Having tested the objectives, techniques that can be adapted from project management include:

- The use of work breakdown structures
- Project planning, including identification of critical tasks and external dependencies.
- Gantt charting (related to Critical Path Analysis)
- Risk assessment

These are only a few of the possible techniques that an event organizer can adopt, or easily obtain suitable software to help deal with, and if the event is going to be huge, then hire a project manager and get in all the computer software and gizmos you need.

Work Breakdown Structures

A work breakdown is just what it says it is, the job broken down into its rough component parts. At this stage detail is not needed or expected, as the work breakdown is simply the first stage in looking at what has to be done, identified in its respective component parts by the work that one person or a related team of people can do. It looks rather like an organization chart, in so far as it is hierarchical. It starts at the top, with the event, or major event activity, and flows down the chart to the point where the one person or team has been arrived at.

Project planning techniques

There are various project planning techniques which an event co-ordinator could usefully adopt, including the identification of critical tasks and external dependencies. Once a work breakdown structure has been drawn up, it should be possible to identify those activities that are critical to the event's success. Critical tasks are essentially those functions that must be completed first, in any sequence of activities, for the activity to proceed. This not only helps to concentrate

Figure 10.2

Work breakdown structure for a wedding marquee

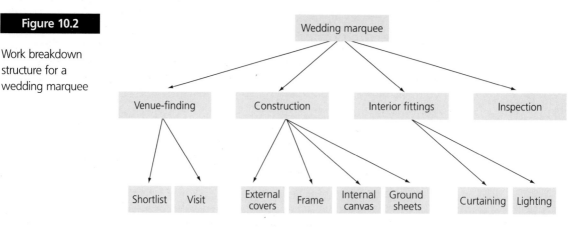

Source: adapted from Nickson and Siddons, 1997.

attention on the jobs within the event that are central to the task, but also provides the framework for setting deadlines for checking progress on event preparations, because the critical tasks must be completed on time for the following activities to be carried out. In the example of the wedding marquee, two critical tasks might be identification of the venue, followed by the construction of the tent. The key aspects of the construction are the setting up of the framework and the fitting of the external covers. Once these things are achieved other activities can take place. For example, once the marquee is weatherproof, the electrician could start installing the lighting at the same time as the tenters are still fitting the internal canvasses and curtaining. These follow-on tasks are called dependencies. External dependencies are those issues that are outside the event co-ordinator's direct control (Starr et al., 2003). Having to hire furniture for an event is an external dependency, as it relies on the furniture hire company turning up with the correct items at the time and place they were ordered for. Without the furniture, there will be no event. Arguably, the more external dependencies a project has, and the more unusual they are, the more risk there is of the project going wrong or failing completely (Heinrich, 1959; Davies and Teasdale, 1994, pp.6–7; Slack et al., 2001, p.624).

It is therefore necessary to turn an initial work breakdown sheet into something that is not only more detailed, but which also shows the exact sequence of activities and how long each will take. This can be done on computer (using software such as Microsoft Project), or, if you had a very small event, can be done by hand using graph paper, but doing it by hand has the limitation that whenever you wish to add something while you are doing the planning, you have to redraw the chart. You need to identify tasks clearly enough so that you know what is going on, but not to over-specify them in such detail that you prevent the free thinking and association needed for creativity. 'Decorate venue' (with due regard to safety) may be a perfectly adequate statement of a task, but 'Put green balloons one metre above the doors' is over-specification.

Gantt charting

There are a range of ways in which task sequences can be shown visually. These include charts that show resource charting, Critical Path Analysis using PERT charts (suitable for the experienced, see Slack et al., 2001, pp.536–39), but the easiest and most applicable kind of chart that event organizers can adopt from the project management sphere is the Gantt chart. This simply shows the various tasks that have to be done in a time-sequence order, so that is easy to see what the various tasks are and, most importantly, how long they should take, when they should be completed and what happens if a task, especially a critical task, is delayed.

Look now at Figure 10.3: this is quite a simple Gantt chart. The filled black boxes indicate the tasks completed so far, the white boxes show those still to be done, so that it is easy to see how preparations are progressing, what is still outstanding and if any problems are emerging. The project started on the 1 May, and the Gantt chart example (see Figure 10.3), gives a snapshot of the work as at the 14 June. Various things were ordered and arranged at the beginning of the process, including the venue, marquee, furniture, and caterers. Only one item is shown as having been ordered during the snapshot period – the flowers, which

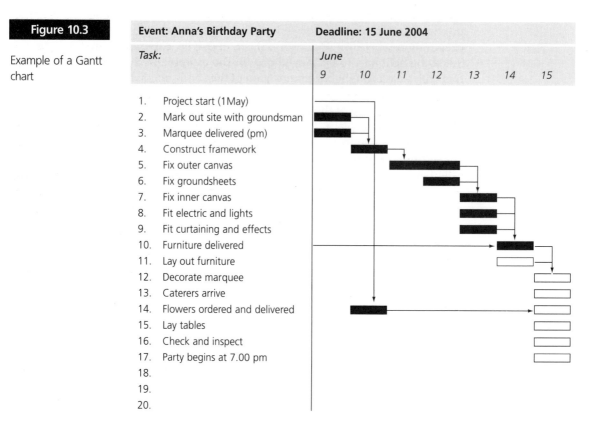

Figure 10.3

Example of a Gantt chart

Event: Anna's Birthday Party		Deadline: 15 June 2004					
Task:	June						
	9	10	11	12	13	14	15

1. Project start (1 May)
2. Mark out site with groundsman
3. Marquee delivered (pm)
4. Construct framework
5. Fix outer canvas
6. Fix groundsheets
7. Fix inner canvas
8. Fit electric and lights
9. Fit curtaining and effects
10. Furniture delivered
11. Lay out furniture
12. Decorate marquee
13. Caterers arrive
14. Flowers ordered and delivered
15. Lay tables
16. Check and inspect
17. Party begins at 7.00 pm
18.
19.
20.

have a shorter lead time than, say, obtaining a marquee. There are some limitations to the Gantt chart. It does not show, in our example, the resources available to do the job or if you have given someone too much work to do in the time available, nor is it really suitable for large projects, as it would be too cumbersome. However, for the modest help it gives to planning events, it can be very useful, not least in that it makes the organizer(s) sit down and think through the steps needed to do the work. In some cases, this planning technique might be best applied backwards, that is to say, starting at the deadline (the end) and working back in order to find out how long doing something will really take. Do not come along and say, 'Hey, we've got three days to get the tent up and sorted, just cram it onto the chart…'. The other important activity that Gantt charting will compel you to do is to find out how long things genuinely take to do. Without this accurate information, the chart will be useless. For example, will it really take two days to get the outer canvas on the marquee? In our example, it does. If you have ordered a marquee, ask the tenters how long it really will take them.

Risk management

Although risk managers might argue that the metrics (size and scope) of risk have not changed, there is, at the time of writing, a heightened sense of concern over risk and this causes problems for event organizers (Hart, 2002; Riley, 2002).

More than ever, the events co-ordinator must address the possibility that something might go wrong at an event; but most risk is minor with little potential impact – although this does need to be managed. Risk assessment is a way of attempting to identify potential risks and taking steps to reduce or mitigate them. It is also the starting point for being able to produce contingency plans and emergency procedures (Tarlow, 2002). Although we will concentrate on risk as a threat to safety, it is important to recognize that the more general approach of risk management (Parry, 2004) is to look at any aspect of a project or activity to identify its risks. In this more general approach, the risk inherent in putting up a marquee is that, as well as the chance it might fall down on top of 200 guests, it might not arrive at all. Perhaps the marquee company went bankrupt and forgot to tell you – so, what contingency is available in the event of that type of risk? (A contact name and number for another marquee company and event insurance.)

Event organizers need to balance offering the best achievable duty of care to visitors and staff with maintaining a sense of proportion. This tension cannot be overstated, and it is critical that you as an organizer wrestle with it early on, or it will prevent you doing your job effectively. The Centre for the Study of Financial Innovation (2002, p.7) reminds us, though, that the risks people look for seem to be driven as much by recent concerns as by any realistic appraisal of coming challenges. The first meeting about risks that an event co-ordinator might hold with an organizing committee might raise a long list of potentially dire consequences for a simple activity (think of the potential dangers of boiling a kettle); but there are established ways of putting such risks into some kind of context and evaluating them. The media can be seen, increasingly, as taking an unpleasant delight in highlighting the downside of issues and exaggerating worst-case

---

Figure 10.4

Various risk categories

- Risks to staff and others, due to confused organization, poor health and safety practice, or the presence of chemicals or other potentially dangerous substances and items.

- Risks in marketing an event, perhaps due to (natural) enthusiasm or optimism about what the event will achieve, therefore the risk of expectations not being fulfilled, but also the risk of the media finding a negative story about an event and making a feature of it.

- Risks in health and safety, especially for the public, and especially at outdoor events that are large and complicated, or involve some inherently risky activity.

- Risks in catering provision, especially for concessions and food stalls, in hygiene and sanitation provision.

- Risks in crowd management, overcrowding, potential crush points, the siting and availability of emergency exits, alcohol provision, noise control and rowdy or violent behaviour.

- Risks in security, particularly at large events or where VIPs are present.

- Risks in transport of items to and from the venue, deliveries and movement at the site of unusual or large items.

Source: adapted from Berlonghi in McDonnell et al., (1999).

scenarios, so that an appropriate response is required (Hall, 2002). The purpose of risk management is, therefore, to help us lead our event through this minefield, by means of a policy of heightened awareness, assessment, evaluation, moderation and recording. Parry (2004), Laybourn (2004), Tarlow (2002), O'Toole and Mikolaitis (2002) and Ridley and Cheney (1999) deal with the detail of these issues.

Since it is critical to begin with a heightened sense of awareness, your planning team should familiarize themselves with issues and approaches emerging from the general debate of risk management. Whilst it might be appropriate to engage a professional consultant, gaining the advice of such experts as the fire brigade, ambulance service, police representatives (or specialists, e.g. for outdoor activities) is a more usual starting point. More formally (Nickson and Siddons, 1997, p.42), interviews can be held with the heads of department to assess risks. It is important that everyone understands the significance of doing this. The outcome of careful risk management might be to save someone's life. You are then likely to be faced with a choice of approach, either fairly conceptual or broadly processual, in deciding the best way forward for your specific event. Those favouring the conceptual approach would argue that flawed thinking is as dangerous as flawed policy, hence you would do well to try and place your critical risks in a table such as Figure 10.5.

The advantages of such an approach are that it is less likely to downplay such unlikely but high-profile risks as a terrorist outrage and that it groups risks by their most likely management response, e.g. transferring the risk to an insurance company or outsourcing its management. The disadvantages are that it requires a fair amount of management focus and still requires decisions as to practical processes. When judging Severity and Probability (as in Figure 10.5), you will find it a lot easier if you use a logarithmic scale, much like the Richter Scale for earthquakes, in which each whole number on the scale represents a tenfold increase in the earthquake's severity. There is a building in a Britain where a plane crash could release 44 times more radioactivity than the Chernobyl disaster (Edwards, 2001); fitting that on the same scale as guests at a dinner receiving a cold meal when it should have been hot will prove tricky, unless you use the Richter Scale approach, in which case you can easily fit all types of potential risk onto a single sheet of paper.

Figure 10.5

Risk analysis
quadrant

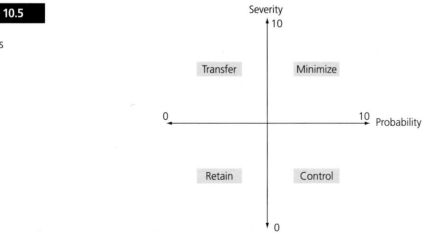

See if you can fit the full range of risks likely to face your event in to the framework in Figure 10.5. For example, did you remember to include fraud? If so, are you sure that it will be as frequent or as severe as you think? Look at the largest risk that you intend to insure: will the insurance company pay as much (or as quickly) as you think? If not, could you still host the event? Which risks are the most difficult to position? Would more information help, or does the Severity / Probability of these risks actually vary over time?

Those preferring a more process-driven approach may well favour the widely used practice of multiplying a risk's probability 'score' with its severity 'score', to derive a ranking for that risk. This seems a sound approach but, for the reasons given already, needs great care if the results are not to become hopelessly flawed. Drivers Jonas (2002, p.23) offers one of the better implementations of this approach, because the worked example addresses 'Time Impact', 'Cost Impact' and requires a 'Mitigation Strategy' – so that you might be able to quantify 'Quality Impact' for your own event and enhance the approach still further.

Having dealt with the criticality of addressing the appropriate scope and detail of the likely risks facing your event, we propose a very simplistic risk management table, in Figure 10.6, to help you address the mechanics of working through a Risk Assessment.

In either case, this process should also be seen as on-going, as anyone who feels they have identified a risk, perhaps whilst some activity is taking place, must be able to flag that risk and have it dealt with immediately. For this reason, all events must have an appointed Safety Officer, who has the power to stop an activity on the spot, or to order the necessary resources to sort it out, and has contact lists for the events team and for the emergency and back-up services.

Figure 10.6

Example of a risk assessment form

Event: Eastern Regional Kite Flying Championships
Location: Low Road Recreation Ground
Date of first assessment: 20th March 2004
Date of this review:

Date of the event: 10th and 11th June 2004
Reviewed by: A. Dangerfield

	Risk Ratings									
	People at risk			A: Worst case outcome			B: Likelihood			Rating
Hazard	Staff	Contractors	Public others	Slight 1	Serious 2	Major 3	Rare 1	Possible 2	Likely 3	AxB
Spectators being hit by cricket ball	✕	✕	✕		✕		✕			2
Cricket player being hit by kite			✕		✕		✕			2
Spectator being hit by kite	✕	✕	✕		✕			✕		4
Overcrowding in event arena	✕	✕	✕	✕			✕			1
Overcrowding in catering tent	✕	✕	✕		✕		✕			2
Members of the public being hit by the fly-away kite in the area			✕		✕		✕			2

In the examples shown in Figure 10.6 and 10.7 (provided courtesy of Tendring District Council, with some details and names amended for publication), the event taking place is a small regional kite-flying championship, which happens to be taking place next to a cricket ground on the same day as a cricket match. Hence, there are some limited risks attached to objects flying through the air. The event does not attract large numbers of spectators, so overcrowding in the arena area of the championship is not thought a major risk. The catering tent is small, and in bad weather could get quite crowded, and with many people in it, as well as quite a lot of catering equipment, in this particular event it has a somewhat higher risk associated with overcrowding than the main arena. Naturally, each event is different, and the impact must be assessed individually.

The risk management of an event takes place in several linked stages: first, the assessment; second, the evaluation, which results in the preparation of the risk moderation form; third, the control measures, which also stem from the risk moderation form, but which may lead either to special preparations before the event, or to special measures during it; finally, a recording activity, particularly important where a further edition might take place, and especially so if other risks were identified during the event itself. These need particularly careful recording and review, as they are often surprisingly important and are learned from experience rather than foresight.

The implication of this last issue is that we cannot foresee everything that might happen at an event. In the end, although we may have taken to every reasonable effort to manage risk, we must always be watchful for something that might still catch us out. It is the tendency of such minor things to trigger a cascade of events that can lead to disaster (Heinrich, 1959; Davies and Teasdale, 1994, pp.6–7).

Figure 10.7

Example of a risk control plan

Event: Eastern Regional Kite Flying Championships

Location: Low Road Recreation Ground   Date of event: 10th and 11th June 2004
Date of first assessment: 20th March 2004   Assessed by: A Dangerfield
Date of this review: ....   Reviewed by: ....

Risk Control Plan

Hazard found	Existing control measures	Additional control measures required	Priority	Person responsible for measure	Complete by:	Action taken	Review date
1	None	Temporary cordon fence installed 20m beyond cricket boundary line.		A. Dangerfield	8/6/04	Fencing instructions sent to T. Sutton and Company	9/6/04
2	None	All kite flying will be sectioned off in areas away from the cricket pitch.		A. Dangerfield & Stewards	10/6/04		
3	None	All kite flying will be sectioned off from the public within a 100m arena		A. Dangerfield & Stewards	10/6/04		
4	None	Stewards and police to take appropriate action		A. Dangerfield, Stewards & police	10/6/04		
5	Catering manager makes people queue outside	None; action adequate		Catering manager			10/6/04
6	None	Stewards to ensure that only competent people fly properly constructed kites		A. Dangerfield & Stewards	10/6/04		

Case Study 26   *Crowd safety: the Moshpit at Roskilde*

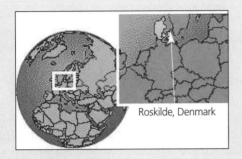

Roskilde, Denmark

Factbox

- Roskilde Music Festival, Roskilde, Denmark.
- Major international rock festival.
- Attracts 90,000 people.
- Features around 170 performers.
- First held in 1971.
- Takes place over four days around seven stages.

One of the pleasures of going to rock gigs and festivals is throwing yourself around the moshpit, the area of the crowd nearest the stage, where the most physical activity is going on, with fans dancing and body-surfing along with the music. In the natural way of things, this area is crowded, and the physicality is part of the attraction of being there. The Roskilde Festival, some 25 km west of Copenhagen, is one of the longest running rock festivals in the European calendar and attracts almost 90,000 people each year.

Approaching midnight on Friday 30 June 2000, after a day of steady rain, the moshpit under the Orange Stage at Roskilde was throbbing with young people enjoying the music of the American rock group, Pearl Jam. There were about 70,000 fans at the festival, a large number of them around the Orange Stage and in particular in the natural crush of the moshpit. As Pearl Jam's set continued it became obvious that the crush was significantly worse than normal, and Pearl Jam's singer, Eddie Vedder, asked the crowd to move back. In the sliding mud, in the overcrowding near the stage, nine fans died of suffocation. Three were from Sweden, one was from Holland, one from Germany, one from Australia and three from Denmark itself.

In the following days, television and newspapers, with a lack of facts and an excess of speculation, alleged that several factors, from faulty sound equipment to drug-taking, people being crushed against the stage or scuffles in the crowd, had caused the accident. None of these has been proved correct. Tests of the equipment that found it to be in perfect working order were barely reported in the media the following week. The Roskilde Festival has a significant reputation for safety, and a measure of this was that first aid staff and police were on the scene immediately, and there were few injuries of any kind beyond those who died. The tragedy also stimulated much moralizing about youth culture, with politicians and public officials calling for all kinds of restrictions on what people do at festivals and events, without first identifying the real reasons for the accident.

For the organizers of the Roskilde Festival, the media reaction came as something of a shock, and is an issue in contingency planning that those members of an events organizing team who have media contacts and who are involved in the public relations activities surrounding events should bear in mind. The festival was especially criticized for continuing after the accident, but the decision to do so was taken in good faith, and to allow festival-goers to keep to their original travel plans, rather than have 90,000 people spill into the street in one massive and unplanned departure.

A useful reference book on crowd safety is the HSE book *Managing Crowds Safely*.

Based on this case:

1. Is the media reaction to disasters normally measured and reasonable, or is it intended to be hysterical and critical?

2. Why should this be the case, and what effects does the lack of a knowledgeable commentary

▶

have, on efforts to identify the genuine reasons for accidents?

3. Does this impact on the ability of those involved and those in authority to react to accidents in a way which will make future events more safe not less?

4. What steps can be taken by organizers to ensure crowd safety at events?

Related websites for the Roskilde Festival, www.roskilde-festival.dk, and overcrowding, www.crowddynamics.com

In assessing the risk at events, our initial judgement of what is involved can be based, at least in part, on existing practice and on an awareness of what constitutes the routine and predictable and what does not. For example, we might consider the level of risk to vary according to the type of event and the activities that will take place:

- 'Low risk' events. Typically, these are indoor events, which, whilst not completely regular or routine, are nearly so, and involve no unusual or specialist activities, and the people involved (both organizers and participants or attendees) are well within their range of experience, and there is already considerable expertise and experience amongst management and staff. Examples might be banquets and dinners, either indoor or in marquees.

- 'Medium risk' events. These might be very large indoor events, in locations that the public might not attend regularly, or that are rather outside their range of experiences (but that a significant number of the attendees, management and staff have experienced in similar circumstances), where the activities are more complicated than normal. Alternatively, where these are outdoor, involving large numbers of people, but with no obvious or perceived dangerous activities. Examples might be large-scale sporting competitions, public shows and street festivals.

- 'High risk' events. These are events involving significantly large numbers of people in activities and locations they are unfamiliar with, or have never been to before, where there is little or no existing knowledge or experience of the event or of the environment amongst management, staff or emergency services, or where there are visible, clear and evident dangers of undertaking the event or participating in it, if the safety features are ignored or are inadequate. Examples might be high speed racing events, large-scale complicated open air events taking place for the first time (hence public and staff unfamiliarity), and small-scale events such as corporate outdoor team-building activities, where the safety rules and the knowledge of experienced staff are the key to safety, but risky for those without experience, expertise or qualifications.

Event managers and co-ordinators should strive to ensure that they not only provide a safe event and a safe environment for all concerned, but also that the systems and emergency procedures are in place in case of an accident or other problem arising. In all events, but especially high risk events, the need for adequate and sufficient staff training, especially of volunteers, is absolutely vital.

Case Study 27 *Emergency service arrangements at events: Clacton Air Show*

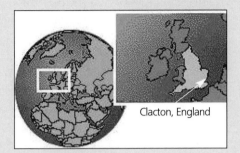

Clacton, England

Factbox

- The event is run by Tendring District Council.
- It consists of two days of air displays, including the Red Arrows RAF display team, parachutists, historic and modern aircraft and aerobatics.
- It attracts 65,000 day trippers.
- Comprehensive risk assessment and procedures.

The small English seaside resort of Clacton-on-Sea hosts a number of annual events intended to attract tourists. These include an annual carnival, a classic vehicle show, a jazz festival, a real ale festival, a sci-fi convention, and its largest annual event, the Clacton Air Show. Such a range helps to stimulate tourism in a resort that relies on its family image, its beaches and its good weather to attract tourist from towns and cities in the east of England and from north London.

The air show is estimated to attract some 65,000 day trippers to the town, in addition to the normal level of tourists. This number is very creditable when compared with some national events, such as the Henley Boating Regatta, which attracts 95,000 people and the Royal Windsor Horse Show which attracts some 80,000 people (source: English Tourist Board). The economic impact of the air show is quite significant. It is a two-day event contributing about €500,000 (an average of €14.50 a visitor)

to the local economy. Visitors to the air show spend money not only at the show ground, but also in local pubs and restaurants, shops and other retail outlets, and at a range of other local facilities and services including the pier, gift shops and other local attractions.

Many of the events that take place in the resort, like the air show, are organized by the local council's Economic Development Department. The tourism section of this department is responsible for three main areas of activity:

- The promotion of the resort and the surrounding area.
- The running of the town's tourist information centre and other information centres in the district.
- The organization and management of a number of larger special events, including the air show.

The air show requires careful organization, especially in terms of risk management, crowd management, emergency services, transport and access, and co-ordination between various public service departments including the coastguard, the fire brigade, the police, the ambulance service and air traffic control. These are crucial, because of the large number of people attending and the potential dangers associated with air displays, aerobatics, parachuting and similar activities. In addition to full risk analysis, the planning phase includes a series of briefings between the public service departments and tourism officer, and other council departments including the Department of Emergency Planning, the Department of Highways and the Environmental Department. This is followed up by briefings to staff and volunteers for the event.

For each air show, a set of emergency service briefing notes is prepared which state the allocation of resources and manpower for various kinds of emergencies. These include back-up plans for dealing with emergencies ranging from an air crash to a bomb alert, or other types of

▶

accident, in order to ensure that the public is as safe as reasonably possible while at the show. This liaison process also includes co-ordination with the council's own staff, who man information points and acts as guides, together with a range of voluntary organizations such as the St John's Ambulance Service, which assists the main emergency services.

Based on this case:

1. Does your local council have a department or unit that deals with tourism in general, and special events in particular, if so, how is it organized and what does it do?

2. What other types of events might require a major input from emergency services?

3. Do even small events require a risk analysis and thought given to emergency procedures?

4. What training should take place to ensure the safety of the public at an event?

Related information for those interested in this case: www.essex-sunshine-coast.org.uk. For event safety guidance, the European code is *The Event Safety Guide*, which can be obtained from: www.hsebooks.co.uk

Source: authors, with grateful thanks to Tendring District Council

Legalities and insurance

The difficulties that organizers of events have faced over insurance cover (Hart, 2002; Riley, 2002) have provided a stark reminder of the need to bear in mind the large number of legalities and similar issues associated with undertaking an event. These include licensing, health, safety, and insurance requirements, which are the key to secure operations. Practice about how these are dealt with varies considerably across the European Union countries, making it difficult to generalize. However, permits and licences are generally dealt with at a local level (town, city or district), although a few may be dealt with at regional or provincial

Figure 10.8

Permits, licences and legalities

Permit	Suggested place of enquiry
Alcohol	Licensing Justices/Local Council Licensing Committee
Bingo, lottery or gaming	Local Council Licensing Department/Licensing Justices
Fireworks	Fire Brigade
Food handling	Local Council Environmental Health Department
Marches and parades	Police/Local Council Highways and Transport Department
Music	Copyright Owners/Broadcast Authority
Occupancy (maximum numbers)	Fire Brigade/Local Council Licensing Department
Parking	Local Council Highways and Transport Department/Police
Parks (use)	Local Council Parks Department/Park Owners
Public Assembly/ Entertainment	Local Council Licensing Department
Sea or beach use	Coastguard/Local Authority Tourism Department
Signs and banners	County Council Highways and Transport Department
Street closure	Local Council Highways and Transport Department/Police
VAT	Department of Customs and Excise

level, within a framework of national and European Union legislation. It will be necessary for events organizers to check locally to identify what legal requirements prevail for aspects such as staffing, permits, licences and other regulatory issues (UK: Croners, 2000). Figure 10.8 provides some possibilities, but is by no means definitive.

The applications procedures for these vary from country to country, so that local documentation should be checked for whom to apply to for permits, and what kinds of permits are needed (licences for the sale of alcohol are obvious, but even the placing of a waste skip on a public road may need the permission of the local authority). In addition to permits and licences, requirements for insurance need sufficient time to be investigated with a reputable insurance broker, or with insurance companies specializing in the events field. Insurance, however, does have some commonality of approach, and various insurance companies have experience of dealing with cross-European events. Normal events insurance would cover items such as: cancellation; venue operator's bankruptcy; non-appearance of celebrities; failure to vacate the venue; damage to property or premises; legal liabilities; damage to equipment and public liabilities.

Case Study 28 *Insuring international events: I-tech, Maastricht*

Maastricht,
Netherlands

Factbox

- I-tech International Armaments Fair.
- International exhibition for the arms industry.
- Various serious security risks.
- Threat of terrorism.
- Threat of direct action by peace groups.
- Not a popular concept with the public.

Events activities range from the inherently safe to the rather dangerous. Certainly in terms of public perceptions, you might feel safer at a family dinner party than you would be as a participant in the Annual International Parascending Competition, even though you could get run

over by a bus the moment you left the dinner party, but might not so much as receive a bruise whilst parascending. But the nature of risk, and why an event might run or be cancelled, could be more complicated. Suppose you were the organizers of the I-tech International Armaments Fair, what risks might you want your event to be insured against?

The I-tech international armaments exhibition is an annual opportunity for defence buyers and sellers to get together, just as any other industry might showcase its products, at a major international trade show. This trade fair originally took place in Dusseldorf, Germany, but became the focus of action by the German peace movement, to the extent that shots were fired during heated protests and the exhibition organizers cancelled the event.

The event was insured against cancellation, and as an immediate consequence it was moved to Maastricht in the Netherlands. Maastricht has a major exhibition and congress centre, opened in 1988, which has a capacity of 17,000 sq m in three interlinked exhibition halls, and 24 conference rooms, the largest of which

▶

can accommodate up to 350 people. The centre has extensive facilities, including a 500-seat restaurant, a business centre, bank, hairdresser, pub and two hotels, the Golden Tulip with 180 rooms and the Hotel Tulip Inn with 103 rooms.

The insurance arrangements for the event are:

- Public liability cover up to €5 million
- Employer's liability cover for staff, including casual and volunteer staff
- Cover for equipment loss or damage
- Cancellation or abandonment cover (including severe adverse weather conditions).

For this particular event the cover included 'financial cause insurance' (e.g. exhibitor going broke) and insurance for damage to the venue. It is also possible to cover for the non-appearance of key speakers or entertainers, and failure to leave the venue at the prescribed time (e.g. snow blocks the venue). Exclusions for event insurance typically include small items damage (up to the first €400); damage to ground/grass surface; mechanical fairground rides; bungee-jumping (this may require very specialized insurance).

Based on this case:

1. Why are the risks for this particular event unusual?

2. If you were the organizer of a less sensitive event, such as a public carnival or festival, what might the most risky activities be, and would these be considered high, medium or low risk?

3. Is this classification of risk linked in any way to the nature of the insurance provision for events?

4. What activities might constitute high risk for participants and spectators?

5. If you have identified a need for insurance of your event, have you allowed for the cost of it in your budgets?

For those interested in the Maastricht Exhibition and Congress Centre: www.mecc.nl, and for those requiring more information on events insurance: www.expo-sure.com.

Source: with grateful thanks to Albert Kemp of Insurex Expo-sure.

Apart from permits and insurance, various kinds of contracts will be needed if the event provides entertainers, musicians, pyrotechnologists (fireworks showmen), guest speakers or celebrities, in order to ensure the arrangements are correctly made. Contracting of this kind needs to be undertaken carefully, bearing in mind that bookings for specialists have to be made long in advance, together with some kinds of payments in advance, and arrangements in the event of cancellation of either party to the contract. Where such a contract is likely to be used, some legal advice should be taken, especially if the contract is out of the ordinary or non-standard in some way.

Systems set-up and ticketing

When setting up an event, it is very easy to become deeply involved in the weight of effort and detail needed to get it off the ground, and for public events, the effort and the excitement of promoting it. A word of warning, then, in the form of a definition of marketing by Gerry Draper (in Lickorish and Jenkins, 1995, p.136). The marketing activity, according to Draper, is 'ascertaining customer needs, tailoring the product as closely as possible to meet those needs, persuading the customer to satisfy his needs [sic], and, finally, ensuring the product is easily accessible when the customer wishes to purchase it'. The organizer of special events should take careful note of the last point. If there is a common failing in events organization, it is often at the beginning of the delivery stage, and that delivery stage starts with enquiries and the issue of tickets.

For all its modern complexity, the final piece of the events jigsaw, the buying, that is, the purchase of tickets, still depends on one element – the visitor picking up the phone and wanting a ticket, or walking in and paying for it. It is true that 'picking up the phone' may mean faxing you, emailing you, using the Internet, or sending someone along with a wad of cash on the bus, but it is still down to someone showing an interest in the event, and that display of interest has to be responded to efficiently and effectively.

Setting up a system to deal with enquiries and sell tickets might be as simple as putting your phone number on the posters for the village fête and getting the barman to sell them from the village pub. In all probability, though, for those events for which the public can buy tickets, you need to give some careful thought to making it easy for them. Do not exclude part of your potential target market by making it difficult, or impossible, for them to get the tickets or make the booking they want to. Ideally, you should have as many ways of selling tickets and as many outlets (besides the central enquiry and ticket office) as you can imaginatively think of and can reasonably service (Pick and Anderton, 1996). That is to say, you have to be able to supply outlets with tickets, to monitor what is being sold, and to react to increased sales at any one point by being able to increase the allocation, if that is reasonable given the number of people you can admit (or have seats for, within the capacity of the venue). A central computer at your main office, with a software programme such as 'Ticket Pro', should be able to cope with these demands easily, and perhaps also, if a system has been set up, to report daily sales.

In setting up your advance ticket sales, there is no reason not to use various methods and channels. If your main method is from your own central ticket office, then think about how the weight of demand can be reduced if you have other sales channels, such as selling tickets on-line. On the other hand, you might decide you have a big event to prepare and only modest expertise, in which case the activity could be contracted to a ticketing agency, which will earn a small commission from each ticket they sell, but relieve you of the whole activity. Finally, you might have an event where the number of tickets is strictly limited for genuine reasons, and in such a case, one central office, with carefully considered limitations, might have to be your solution.

Figure 10.9 Ticket design: information to include on a ticket	• Name of the event. • Date and start time. • Sequential number. • Price and type of ticket. • Conditions or disclaimers. • Site map (if applicable). • Contact phone number(s). • Security imprint (if applicable). • Colour coding (if applicable), especially for wristband-type 'tickets'.

Case Study 29 *Event on-line booking systems: ECOC, Rimini*

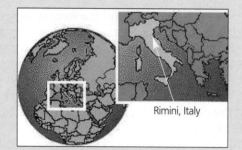

Rimini, Italy

Factbox

- ECOC 2003, Rimini.
- International conference dealing with optical communications.
- Around 1,000 delegates from up to 40 countries.
- Has a four-day programme including workshops, seminars, technical sessions, a welcome reception, a banquet and local tours.

The process of booking for events varies considerably depending on the type of event and the target market. On-line booking systems are a feature of certain types of events, especially in the organizational category, where large numbers of people in the target market have access to the Internet. The annual European Conference on Optical Communication (ECOC) is an international event taking place in a different European country every year. The conference deals with optical communications, and one of the organizing bodies is the Institute of Electrical and Electronic Engineers (IEEE).

The conference has an international reputation and includes an intensive programme of sessions over the four-day period. Delegates include not only industrialists and professionals in the industry, but also academics and students. The event is organized in such a way that delegates can attend the whole four days and as many sessions as they are interested in, or select particular activities. Delegates wishing to

participate have to register (book) prior to the event. This is normal for this kind of event, and registration can be made in a number of ways:

- Booking by phone, post or fax to the organizers themselves
- Booking by phone, post or fax to an organizing agency or professional conference organizer (PCO)
- Booking by email or Internet.

In the case of this particular event, potential delegates are informed that the preferred method of booking is on-line (provided by Adria Congrex), and they are encouraged do this in preference to any other method. Clearly, as this is a conference, not a public event, there is no booking on the day at the entrance, as final numbers are needed for room lay-outs, meal ordering, etc. beforehand. This approach to booking has the advantage of administrative efficiency, since all bookings go to one central location where they can be co-ordinated and confirmed on-line, allowing organizers to check the status of bookings in real time, on a common system, without, say, having to check through and count individual correspondence. The system has the further advantage of saving staff time, as the potential delegate fills in requirements on a standard on-line form.

Nevertheless, whilst useful for some types of events, this approach is not suitable to all. It could not be used on its own for sporting events, as many people will make a decision about attending shortly before the event and will buy a ticket on the gate. So, too, with many voluntary and charitable events, public open events and so on, where the equipment and systems do not exist to deal with this kind of on-line activity, nor might the potential target market have access to on-line systems or even be computer literate. For these reasons, event organizers must think carefully about the ticketing and booking systems they wish to set up in relation to their target markets, and to the usual

▶

way in which those target markets might buy a ticket or pay the entrance fee for an event.

Based on this case:

1. Why is on-line booking very suitable for organizational events of this type?
2. Why might such systems not be suitable for, perhaps, a public garden show?

3. What systems must be set up to support the booking process, by way of recording, dealing with enquiries, controlling total numbers, monitoring demand and gathering market research data about attendees?

Related websites for those interested in the ECOC and the IEEE: www.ecoc.it and www.ieee.org

Taking tickets 'on the door' also requires a little forethought. The most important issue is whether your 'door' will be able to cope with the demand. If only 20 people turn up, no problem. But what if 2,000 come? What do we know about selling tickets 'on the door'? What we do know, from research done in cinemas (which have to have quite good 'on the door' systems) is that the average time taken to process a ticket request from a member of the public is about 20 seconds. A little simple maths shows that 2,000 members of the public waiting at your (narrow) gate for tickets for your evening extravaganza would progress at three a minute, totalling almost 670 minutes – eleven hours. You need more gates, more ticket sellers, and more people to deal with the odd enquiries that block up the system.

It should be remembered that tickets not only act as evidence of payment or permission to enter an event, but are also a means of security. Tickets should be checked as visitors arrive; to ensure that they are properly directed to their seat; to ensure that the ticket itself is genuine; perhaps to exchange the ticket for some other evidence of entry or means of obtaining services, such as wristbands (different colours of which may represent entitlement to entry or use of, say, VIP or media areas). Collecting tickets is also a means of confirming the number of people who actually attended and can be used to check attendance against revenue.

Operational activities

The big day is almost upon us, we have done as much planning as was needed, we have organized all the various people, parts, organizations, supplies and equipment that we planned for, it's six in the morning and time to throw ourselves out of bed with enthusiasm and get the tea or coffee on. This is not a joke. You are going to be awfully busy on the big day, and you might have little or no chance to eat and drink; if that happens you become dehydrated and your blood sugar levels fall, you become poor at decision making, and you won't notice problems quickly enough. So make the time, have a decent breakfast or other meal before the event and drink a lot during it. It will help to ensure you are competent. And while you're having your breakfast, check the weather report and local travel news.

Correspondence and schedules check

To help prioritize your activities, check for any last minute changes, notes left for you, correspondence, phone messages or emails. Once you've done this, re-read your planned schedule for the set-up and make any amendments or notes. Carry a notebook around with you, as people have a habit of mentioning things as you go round that you may need to deal with. It will be a busy day, and you will forget otherwise. Whenever you sit down to rehydrate (have a drink), check your notebook. As the event co-ordinator or floor manager, you would normally expect the arrival of other staff, volunteers and helpers early on the day, or, in the case of large events, possibly before (particularly if staging, rehearsals or complex setting-up is required). A check can then be made of arrangements between co-ordinator and staff to deal with any final requests or changes to the booked details. Experienced clients can be expected to phone or call in, up to a week beforehand or the day before, in order to make general checks. This is to be encouraged, as is a 'pre-con' meeting between the venue, yourself and the other organizers to iron out any last minute problems.

The organizer's office

In order to reduce stress on organizers, helpers, staff and visitors, ensure that there is a central point of enquiry for an event. An organizer's office should be provided whenever an event is going to be large, long-running or VIP in nature. Where possible, offices should be in a convenient location (preferably not a hotel bedroom) and can be anything from a portacabin to a desk in the parkkeeper's potting shed. As a minimum, everyone should know where it is, and it should be supplied with

Figure 10.10

Pre-operations on the day

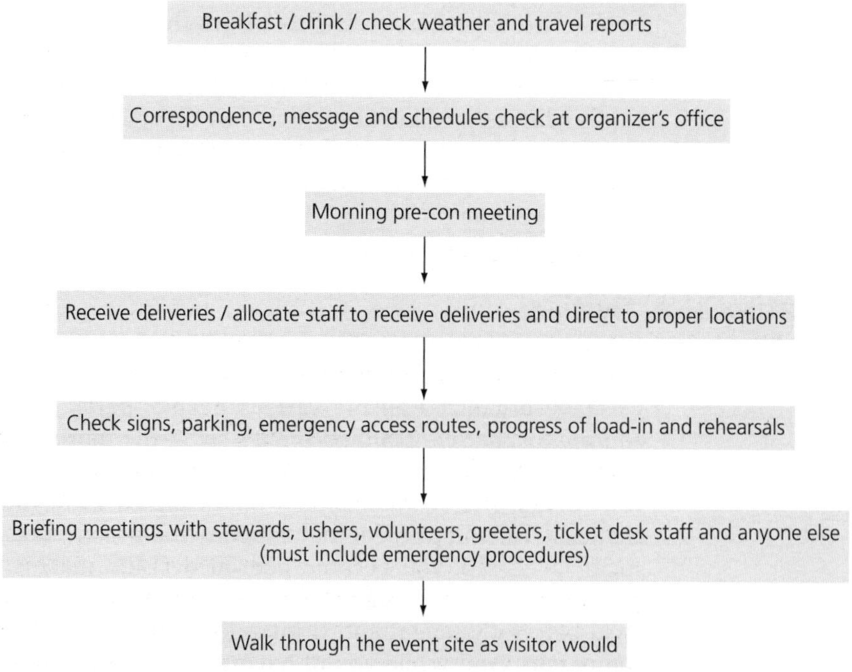

Breakfast / drink / check weather and travel reports

↓

Correspondence, message and schedules check at organizer's office

↓

Morning pre-con meeting

↓

Receive deliveries / allocate staff to receive deliveries and direct to proper locations

↓

Check signs, parking, emergency access routes, progress of load-in and rehearsals

↓

Briefing meetings with stewards, ushers, volunteers, greeters, ticket desk staff and anyone else (must include emergency procedures)

↓

Walk through the event site as visitor would

(continued in Chapter 11, Figure 11.11)

a land-line phone and, preferably, a fax machine. Without it, the venue itself (in the case of a hotel or public hall) will become the clearing house for any activity relating to the event, or people will simply stop and ask the first person they find. Before the event, the arrival of the staging, lighting and PA equipment, suppliers and speakers with queries, the sponsor's chief executive wanting somewhere for a 'quiet meeting' will have to be dealt with. Providing a room is not a matter of politeness, but of good planning. Without this, staff can be inundated with enquiries that they may not be able to deal with directly, or find the organizer in time to deal with them. If you, as an event organizer, are out and about around the venue, arrange for a mobile phone or 'walkie-talkie' radio, and if it stops ringing, that's because it's broken, not because no-one wants you. Make sure you go back to the office at some specified times to check that things are going satisfactorily and to deal with anything that can't follow you around.

Receival of supplies

Various items will be delivered as preparations progress, and make sure these are carefully checked against the purchase orders by the designated person. One of the difficulties faced by events organizers is that an event is at the end of a supply chain which is very time-specific. To illustrate this, if you had 300 best porcelain plates delivered to a hotel as new stock, and they were the wrong size, the wrong colour or the wrong design, the hotel could send them back and continue to operate using its older, existing plates. However, because events are unique and one-off, perhaps limited to a few hours of high-pitched activity, and 300 best porcelain plates are delivered that are the wrong size, what do you do? First, you don't send them back, as they might be the only ones you can get in time, and you can't serve 300 chicken dinners on the tablecloth. You accept them, writing on the delivery note that they do not comply with the purchase order number and you then phone the supplier to see if they can get you the right ones in time. Be careful to set up a controlled delivery acceptance system. It might have to be a volunteer helper standing next to the main gate with a list, whose job is to check what is coming in, sign for it and direct it to the place where it needs to go, but better this than having to chase around every time a surprise in a lorry turns up.

Transport and parking

With some major events, particularly international ones, there may be a need to make suitable arrangements to transport participants to and around the event, to deal with baggage, and to make arrangements for materials and equipment both in advance and afterwards. Various companies specialize in ground handling, that is, the movement of transport, baggage and goods. Related to this are activities such as venue/terminal and venue/hotel transfers. In the case of venue/terminal and venue/hotel transfers the nature of transport varies, depending on distance and ease of finding the venue. Participants and visitors may be able to walk; there may be public transport laid on; or taxi services may be appropriate and may be provided formally or informally. There are many events, in all categories, where transport and transfer of people is significant. At the top end of the scale would be the provision of chauffeur-driven executive cars to deal with VIPs and dignitaries, but coaches may also be hired, and typically range from 18 to 52 seats, including luxury vehicles with on-board toilets, drinks, video facilities and host/hostess guides. Coach hire of this kind is particularly useful for both executive travel and transfers of large numbers of people to remote venues. On the other hand, for many kinds of events, people will simply arrive on foot, use their own car or come by public transport. Adequate and convenient car parking arrangements will need to be made, including arrangements for mobility-impaired visitors, for which close liaison with the local authority and the police, who have a role in traffic flow and control, will be necessary in advance. You may also need to provide volunteer or staff car park stewards on the day.

Load-in

The most likely item to arrive after the organizer at a major event is large staging (some may take several days to construct and this should be foreseen in the scheduling and booking of the venue). A ground plan should be made by the co-ordinator, and a copy left with the venue to enable work to proceed if the organizer is not yet present or has been held up. A stage set will often be followed by the technical equipment, lighting, sound rig, etc. a part of the set-up that is sometimes referred to as 'Load in or Bump-in'. Doing this properly, with stage and layout plans and with the area clearly marked out (having been carefully measured for the original plans) should help ensure that getting a set and its technical equipment up and running is done quickly and efficiently, in time to be tested or used for rehearsal.

At this point, once all the equipment is in place, cleaning can be done, message boards put up, together with signing and other support activities, such as the layout of arrangements for visitors arrival. It is important that the event is properly signed, and signs are needed for two main purposes:

- information
- emergencies.

Information signs deal with aspects like normal entry and exits, the location of services and activities, where to queue from, and how to do particular things. Emergency signs deal with emergency procedures, emergency exits and escape routes, how to operate emergency equipment and how to call for help. The design of these two types of sign must be distinctly different. In general, emergency signs of various kinds can be obtained from specialist suppliers, from office or workplace suppliers or from suppliers listed in the phone book. Most indoor venues will be already properly signed for emergencies, as this is a legal requirement. This can be checked during the risk assessment process. For events that are in an unusual venue, or are outside, careful thought needs to be given to emergency signposting. As part of the planning stage, a ground plan of the site should have been drawn up, including the layout of emergency exits, access for emergency vehicles such as ambulances or fire engines, and plans for emergency routes. These can then be signposted and roped off, with stewards allocated to keep them clear during the event.

The design of the information signs depends on what sort of event you have. If this is going to be a large-scale professional event, then you can employ a professional sign-making company. If this is a modest volunteer event, then the design of the signs depends on your skill with a computer. You will not even need any fancy software. Keep your design simple so the signs can be seen from a distance, and if you draft them up on A4 paper using the largest font you can fit on it, you can always get them enlarged and laminated at a print shop to A3 so they are easier to see from a distance. They do need to be all the same design and font. This is not just a matter of how professional your signs will look, but that visitors should be able to recognize information or emergency signs from the mass of background material they will encounter when visiting your event.

Security and the media

Certain types of event will involve security issues. For VIP or political events a security check may take place at some point prior to the start of the event, usually between set-up and public arrival (in these cases, the set-up will have to be completed at least a day before the event). Police or Interior Ministry security (in England called the 'Home Office') may want to physically check the venue site and may well use sniffer dogs and metal detectors to do so. In some cases, visitors or the audience may be required to pass through metal detectors of the kind found at airports, with specialist security staff on duty, video surveillance and security checks of staff. At this level it is also likely that staff may be required to hold special passes, although it is common for all staff to be badged in some way, not only as a courtesy to delegates, guests and visitors, but for routine security. Advice on security can be sought from the local police for smaller events, and from security companies, some of whom specialize in security at events such as rock festivals. Security is a serious matter, but a note of caution – do not make a big performance out of it. Making security into a major issue can be counter-productive to people's sense of feeling secure. If security is too obvious people will wonder why it is there, possibly leading to them feeling more fearful, not less. Second, remember media reactions: if your marketing department organizes a press call, or gets a TV crew to your event, the media will almost naturally look for the bad news. You will watch the TV later to see what great pictures of your event are shown across the national network, to find that the TV presenter stood in front of the largest security guard on the entire site (usually holding an enormous dog on a leash), made one positive comment about your event and then talked on national TV for five minutes about the heavy security and a non-existent 'terrorist threat'.

This tendency to latch on to the smallest whisper of bad news can give your marketing and public relations team nightmares. Reporter: 'Did the ceremony go well?' Your press officer: 'Yes, we had an excellent day, with 30,000 people attending, although there was a bit of an argument between two blokes in the catering tent over a cream bun.' Later, the paper has the headline: 'Public brawl ruins opening ceremony'. In case you think this cannot really happen in real life, the headline from the opening ceremony of the Welsh Highland Railway on 7 August 2000 was: 'Tractor protest mars Welsh Highland opening' (Johnson, 2000). During the culmination of a ten-year, €5 million effort by volunteers, a farmer left his tractor across the track and 'the police were called'. This is rural Wales: when someone leaves a tractor on your railway and you have to ring the police, the nearest policeman is probably 20 km away, but the impression given in the media is of a major incident. Nevertheless, appropriate care should be taken of the media, and proper facilities provided for them. This might include their own media centre, tent, etc, equipped with its own power (for broadcasts) and phone lines, fax lines and computer workstation(s), as well as adequate and sufficient refreshment (but not alcoholic, because they will write about how extravagant the hospitality was on public money).

Rehearsal and briefings

A rehearsal may take place for the technical facilities, particularly of the sound and presentation systems for many kinds of events. Whilst a rehearsal may be a purely technical activity for certain types of high profile organizational events, product launches or public relations events, it is possible that it may be of the 'full dress' kind, including practice by actors, musicians, entertainers or other artists, including timing arrangements, acoustics, and so on. Ushers, if required, can be briefed at this point, together with any meeters/greeters the organizer may have arranged.

Briefings (see Figure 10.11) for casual and specialist staff should include elementary issues such what the event is for, who is coming and the opening and closing times, also details such as the location of toilets, cloakrooms, organizers office, refreshment areas, check-in areas and what to do with the VIPs (such as direct them to a VIP hospitality room), how to assist mobility-impaired visitors into the event, and what action is required in an emergency, including the nature of the alarm system, emergency exits, assembly points, location of the medical centre if there is one, or how to get a first aider quickly if there is not. All staff at the event must be given a copy of the site map, information sheet, emergency contact list and emergency procedures. The site map and information page should be one sheet of A4, the emergency contact list and procedures should be on another sheet of A4. Any more than this, and staff will not read it. Clarity is essential.

Welcome visitors

The entrance areas or visitor reception area should be ready for use prior to the start time; even in the case of a small informal event, this amounts to no more than a table with programmes for people to pick up as they arrive. At large events, for convenience of organization, the layout of the arrival area might be alphabetical or use several entrances. It may also be necessary to provide greeters or an information desk, or both, as minor queries from incoming arrivals can slow down the entry process. Queries can be dealt with by the greeter moving along the queues.

Figure 10.11	
Pre-event briefing meeting for all staff (or done in departments by departmental leaders)	**Agenda (Give out staff briefing and emergency sheets)** 1. The purpose of the event, type of visitors, likely numbers 2. Opening and closedown times, the programmes, facilities and services 3. Parking and access, facilities for the mobility impaired 4. Who you report to and arrangements for staff refreshment 5. Emergency contacts, systems and procedures, checking that emergency, routes and exits are clear 6. Who to direct the media to 7. Questions and answers

The greeters have the additional function of helping to direct visitors; whilst signage is necessary and important, people arriving in unfamiliar locations will look first for someone to ask, and only secondly for (inanimate) directions. Toilets should also be located near the entrance areas: the first request, especially if your event attracts the public, and particularly families, will be for the toilets.

Where it would help, packs, site maps, entry badges and tickets (such as refreshment tickets) and programmes should be laid out in boxes to ensure the arrival process goes quickly. It is preferable that in this layout process all items (programme, site map, badges, tickets and pack) are put into large envelopes or 'goody bags' and stacked (for those events or occasions where the visitor is going to receive a pack). Not only does this increase the speed of entry, but it saves a great deal of stretching across a vast array of material spread on a table. Any urgent messages can be displayed on a board at the arrival point, or even mounted on stage screens during refreshment breaks. It is preferable to have your most experienced staff available at the entrances, as first impressions count, and an impression of confusion given by inexperienced staff at the doors will reflect badly on the event as a whole. In planning the arrival areas, thought should also be given to providing power, and phone points for tills (both for enquiries and if automated transactions are to take place), and to the way in which the tills will be supervised, supplied with cash and change, emptied and the income recorded and banked.

If the event is a conference or VIP invitation-only event, a list of delegates or guests expected, plus badges (for conferences) or some suitable small gift (for invited events, such as corsages or chocolates), should have been made up prior to the event. (Where security is an issue, guests must be politely required to wear their badges, although normally most guests are happy to do so; at informal events, or where there is no security issue, not everyone may wish to wear a badge and should not be compelled to if they are unwilling.) But it is important that guests are checked against the guest list, as this will provide accurate final numbers of the people attending and can be passed on to catering staff for any last minute amendments to seating or refreshment arrangements This also acts as a key security check, which should not be overlooked in case of gatecrashers. In addition, it is also common at conference-type check-ins to issue information packs, including agendas; working papers; delegate lists and a little information about the venue for delegates to take away with them. This latter should be provided by the venue marketing department to the client, if the organizer is making up their own packs to ensure that a selling opportunity for the venue is not missed. For this kind of event, co-ordinators would be supported by check-in staff, normally every one to 50 delegates, either provided by the organization itself or by the venue, to ensure delegates find the right conference and do not get mixed up with any other activities taking place (Seekings, 1999). Normally, the co-ordinator would be on hand at least half an hour before the published start time to deal with supervising the arrival area.

Summary

We have attempted to provide an overview of some of the more serious issues regarding the project management of events, including risk management and key aspects of insurance, as well as of legal, health, safety and licensing requirements, or at least where to look for further information about them. The HSE book, *The Event Safety Guide*, is especially recommended when dealing with health and safety issues. We have also sought to provide an overview of the operational activities that take place immediately prior to, and during, an event, noting that efficient preparation and due thought to operational issues will reduce the risk of something going wrong. The set-up process should not be seen as separate from the activities of running the event on the day, as this is often a continuous process, and the reader should also look at the chapter 11, under 'Running the event on the day', for more information.

References

A.T. Kearney (2002) *The Main Event: Best Practices for Managing Mega-sports Events*, Chicago, A.T. Kearney (http://www.atkearney.com/main.taf?p=5,3,1,49) (15 April 2003).

CSFI (2002) 'Banana Skins 2002: a CSFI Survey of Risks Facing Banks', London, Centre for the Study of Financial Innovation (http://www.pwcglobal.com/images/gx/eng/fs/bcm/bananaskins02.pdf) (15 April 2003).

Croners (2000) *Croners Hospitality Management*, Kingston upon Thames, Croner CCH Group.

Davies, N.V. and Teasdale, P. (1994) *The Costs to the British Economy of Work Accidents and Work-related Ill Health*, Sheffield, HSE Books.

Drivers Jonas (2002) *Stadia Development Handbook*, London, Drivers Jonas (http://www.driversjonas.com/djsport/?doc=1606) (15 April 2003).

Edwards, R. (2001) 'The Nightmare Scenario: what would happen if a passenger jet ploughed into a nuclear plant ?', *New Scientist*, 13 October, pp.10–12.

Hall, C.M. (2002) 'Travel Safety, Terrorism and the Media: The Significance of the Issue-Attention Cycle', *Current Issues in Tourism*, vol. 5, no 5, pp.458–66.

Hart, S. (2002) 'Gambling on the threat of terrorism', *Sunday Telegraph*, 8 September.

Health and Safety Executive (1999) *The Event Safety Guide*, Sudbury, HSE Books, pp.3–20.

Health and Safety Executive (2000) *Managing Crowds Safely*, Sudbury, HSE Books.

Heinrich, H.W. (1959) *Industrial Accident Prevention: A Safety Management Approach*, 4th edn, New York, McGraw-Hill.

Johnson, P. (2000) 'Tractor protest mars Welsh Highland opening', in *Steam Railway*, no 248, 18 August, p.16.

Laybourn, P. (2004) 'Risk and decision making in Event Management', in Yeoman, I. et al., *Festival and Events Management*, Oxford, Elsevier, pp.286–307.

Lickorish, L. and Jenkins, K. (1995) *An Introduction to Tourism*, Oxford, Butterworth Heinemann, p.136.

McDonnell, I., Allen, J. and O'Toole, W. (1999) *Festival and Special Event Management*, Milton (Queensland), Jacaranda Wiley, pp.198–99.

Nickson, D. and Siddons, S. (1997) *Managing Projects*, Oxford, Butterworth Heinemann, pp.17–18.

O'Toole, W. and Mikolaitis, P. (2002) *Corporate Event Project Management*, Chichester, Wiley.

Parry, B. (2004) 'Risk Management', in MacMahon-Beattie, U. and Yeoman, I. (eds) (2004) *Sport & Leisure Operations Management: A Textbook for Courses and Modules*, London, Thomson Learning.

Pick, J. and Anderton, M. (1996) *Arts Administration*, London, E&FN Spon, pp.103–6.

Reiss, G. (1998) *Project Management Demystified*, London, E&FN Spon, 2nd Ed., pp.1–4.

Ridley, J. and Cheney, J. (1999) *Risk Management*, Oxford, Butterworth Heinemann, pp.1–22.

Riley, A. (2002) 'Hidden peril of the lone terrorist', *Times* 'Law supplement', 10 September, p.5.

Seekings, D. (1999) *How to Organize Effective Conferences and Meetings*, London, Kogan Page, pp.320–41.

Slack, N., Harland, C., Harrison, A., Johnston, R. and Chambers, S. (2001) *Operations Management*, London, Pitman, 3rd edn.

Starr, R., Newfrock, J. and Delurey, M. (2003) 'Enterprise Resilience: Managing Risk in the Networked Economy', *Strategy & Business*, Spring (http://www.strategy-business.com/press/article/?art=30100980&pg=0) (15 April 2003).

Tarlow, P.E. (2002) *Event Risk Management and Safety*, Chichester, Wiley.

Westerbeek, H.M., Turner, P. and Ingerson, L. (2002) 'Key success factors in bidding for hallmark sporting events', *International Marketing Review*, vol. 19, no 3, pp.303–22.

11 The organization manager and the team: during the event

> ## Aims
>
> - To identify the kinds of organizations found at events.
>
> - To explore organizational effectiveness.
>
> - To discuss recruitment issues for paid, voluntary and permanent staff.
>
> - To consider issues about event management 'on the day'.

Introduction

The organization and staffing of special events vary considerably. Personal events, for example, often involve friends and family and volunteers. Organizational events may employ events management companies or professional events organizers. Both paid and volunteer helpers are common at a large number of events, notably those involving community activities, sports, and so on. Professional organization is common, but expensive for some kinds of event. As a typical example, weddings could be undertaken entirely by volunteer help, or entirely by professional help, or by a mixture of both – it may simply depend on the budget. The event organizer must be aware, though, that this is not the only criterion: the issue is partly one of knowing what volunteer help can accomplish, or when to bring in professionals for reasons of size, safety, standards or other reasons.

As with many other labour-intensive service industries, the events business has a considerable need for staff. This is satisfied by on-the-job training and by the recruitment of staff from outside, whether direct from the labour pool or by recruiting from colleges and universities. Unlike other service industries, however, there are only a limited number of events-specific courses in the current academic world, which means that the events business has to rely very heavily on adapting its staff from other sources, such as the hospitality or tourism industries, and from courses in these fields, as well as from marketing, business and leisure programmes.

For all the considerable effort that goes into preparing an event, running it on the day can still prove a challenge. The co-ordination of a wide range of disparate and even unusual activities, facilities and services can be overwhelming. Events management has to be effective, and events managers must be good communicators and good delegators in situations that may be constantly changing. The importance of preparation is that it reduces the variability and uncertainty of what is taking place during the event, and allows the event co-ordinator to concentrate on those matters that require immediate or constant attention.

Organization

One of the themes that has emerged in the preceding chapters is the diversity of events. The organizational issues mirror this diversity. It is extremely unlikely that any two events would have exactly the same organizational structure or staffing. This said, there are some similarities, and we would expect core services to be organized in broadly similar ways. There is a probability that event organizational structures would include five main functions: visitor services operations, support services operations, marketing, administration and finance. These five functions can be further sub-divided depending on the nature and size of the event, but a survey of the organization charts of a number of events would probably show that all five functions would probably be present in some form.

The organizational structure for an event forms the framework around which the various activities and services operate. It has been previously noted that events provide a mix of products and services, for example: ceremony and celebration; food and drink services; presentation and technical services; support and ancillary services. These activities will probably come under an operations department, which might itself be subdivided into visitor services and support operations (as in Figure 11.1, the former for parts of the event that have public contact, the latter for those that do not). In addition to the operations department which will be specific to any given public event, the organizational structure will typically have a marketing department whose role may be to cover sales activities, and perhaps enquiries and ticketing, depending on the type of operation. There is also likely to be an accounts and control function, to deal

Figure 11.1

Simplified events
organization
structure

both with outgoing and incoming invoices and financial business, and which may also include a purchasing role, particularly in larger events. Underpinning the support activities will be an administration department, covering not only general administration but also personnel issues, recruitment and induction, payment of wages, etc.

In this kind of organizational structure, the key members of staff, or key managers, might be the only paid staff at the event, and the actual staff doing the work might otherwise be volunteers. Similarly, if the event is being run by a club or society, the key staff might simply be the members of that organization's normal committee. Committees are extremely common in events. In consequence, in many events organizations it is common to find a core body of officers, managers or co-ordinators who have the job of organizing the activities and of supervising either volunteers or paid casual and part time staff. This body is the skeleton and framework of the organization and is sometimes called a cadre.

The organizational structure for an event may simply consist of the cadre and their helpers. At a small village flower show, the total number of people organizing and helping to organize and run the event might be fewer than 20, with only six of them being the cadre, or key organizers, perhaps because they form the village horticultural club's regular committee. On the other hand, the organizational structure of an event may become enormously complex, with a mixture of key organizers, volunteer helpers, paid full-time, part-time and casual staff, and the organization might also include some outsourced activities such as catering or concessions, resulting in something that is well suited to the event taking place, but which would be regarded as extremely odd if it were a conventional organization.

The organizational structure (example in Figure 11.2) may appear very conventional. This is because there is a need, in an organization where unfamiliar people are working together, to know exactly who is in charge. There must be no ambiguity over the safety of the public and the efficiency of the organization (which, having been created to run an event, may be a relatively short-lived entity).

Figure 11.2

Visitor services department at the Middleburg Music Festival

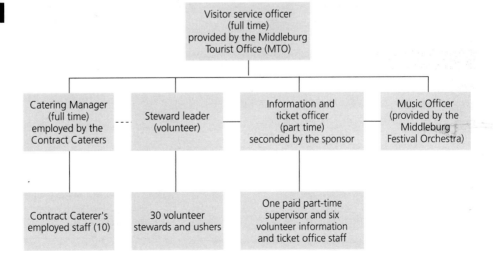

The lines of communication, in events organizations, not only pass up and down the hierarchy but also run from side to side. This is essential to ensure that information gets passed around the organization quickly, and does not get bogged down by having to be transferred up to line managers and back down again. For example, if there is a change in the music programme, the Music Officer needs to tell the Visitor Services Officer, but also needs to be able to speak directly to the information and ticket office without waiting for other managers or officers to turn up – staff who might be part-time or only at the venue at certain times. The one person who is slightly detached in this example system is the Catering Officer, whose own organization tends to be self-contained.

In this type of organization, we can also see a mix between paid and volunteer staff, and that staff might originate from a number of sources. Suppose a festival is being organized by a city tourist department, rather than by a voluntary committee; in this case the cadre may be provided by members of that tourist department (see Deventer Book Market, case study 31). Other members of staff might come from other organizations involved in the festival, including performers, contractors, sponsors or volunteers.

Case Study 30 *Volunteers at the Mainz Carnival*

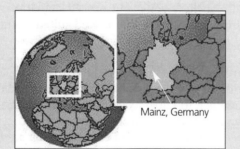

Mainz, Germany

Factbox

- Mainz Carnival.
- Known as 'The Fifth Season of the Year'.
- Comprises Saturday Youth Carnival, Sunday Carnival Guards Parade, Rose Monday Carnival Procession and three days of costume balls.
- Admission ticket, with grandstand seats, a costume ball and a carnival show: €70.

Volunteer support co-ordinated by a central carnival office is a key feature of the three-day Mainz Carnival. Local people are intensively involved in the carnival preparations, which take many months and include special preparations by a large number of carnival clubs, made up of volunteer members who wish to contribute in some way to the success of the event. The carnival has a long history associated with the traditional German festival of 'Fastnacht', which takes place on Shrove Tuesday. In the Mainz Carnival, there are three days of celebrations from Saturday to the Monday before Lent (called Rose Monday).

The Mainz Carnival is organized by a carnival office (secretariat), the Mainzer Carnivals Verein. It co-ordinates the efforts of official bodies, professional organizations and the many volunteer carnival clubs. The carnival office has a small permanent staff, which is increased for the carnival itself by the addition of volunteers and additional casual staff, who have many years' experience of running the event. Carnival organization officially begins in the previous October, to allow enough time for the complex work of providing the intensive three-day celebration in March. In practice, however, preparations and planning are more or less continuous throughout the year for such a large-scale activity.

The carnival organization is a combination of effort by public, voluntary and private sector

▶

bodies. Local government involvement helps provide tourist promotion and logistics support, whereas the private sector provides local business help with funding, sponsorship, displays and other support for the voluntary organizations involved. The voluntary element, from the carnival clubs, together with many other local clubs, societies and recreational organizations, makes up a very significant part of the carnival effort. The clubs range from sporting to theatrical clubs, from music clubs to historical re-enactment societies, and they provide marchers in the procession, floats, displays and tableaux, and ensure that the carnival is loud and colourful. A very wide range of activities takes place in addition to the major carnival processions, including carnival shows with stands and displays, and costumed and masked balls, where participants,

guests and visitors dress up, are wined and dined, and enjoy dancing and other social activities.

Based on this case:

1. What role do the various voluntary organizations play in making the carnival a success?
2. What is the function of the carnival secretariat?
3. How does the existence of carnival clubs improve the standard of the carnival and the range of activities being put on?
4. Compare this organization with your own local carnival or annual festival: how do they differ?

Related website for those interested in visiting the Mainz Carnival: www.mainz.de

Source: Information kindly provided by Touristik Centrale Mainz

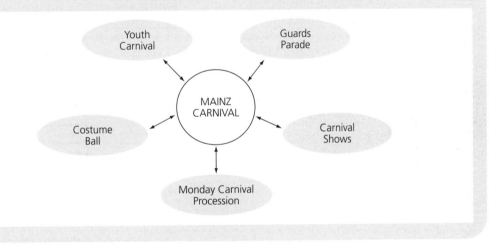

Organizational effectiveness

The culture of an organization is thought to impact on an organization's efficiency and ability to do its job. However, most research into culture has centred on permanent organizations. The modest research undertaken on short-life organizations, such as that quoted by Mullins et al. (1993), suggests that culture may be of only secondary importance to identifying, transmitting and delivering 'the main objective', which Mullins (wrongly) supposes is the 'generation of profit for stakeholders'. In the events business, there may be some types of events whose purpose is indeed to make a profit, but we should be careful not to generalize about profit. Perhaps it could more legitimately be said that events are about creating wealth: wealth of experiences; wealth in socialization;

wealth in community spirit; but 'profit' is too limited a concept. In our analysis of events so far, we have repeatedly made the point that it is the purpose of only certain types of events to make a profit. For the family and friends organizing a wedding the objective is not to make a profit, but to celebrate the wedding; for the athletics club running its annual sporting competition, the primary objective is not to make a profit, but to showcase the best performers in the sport, to encourage supporters and athletes and to test these athletes in competition, and if a little money is taken on the gate, well and good, but this is secondary to the sport.

The issue for event managers, then, is about how to organize an effective event, possibly with a disparate range of people, whose reasons for being there may be social rather than commercial, and who will work towards an objective over a relatively short period of time without too much concern about the style of the organization they are working with. Additionally, although an event may be undertaken by a professional organization, the nature of many events is still largely informal and social. Events are significant social activities; they are often communal and good natured, and this is reflected in their culture.

The typology of events in chapter 1 noted the difference in the scale of organizational complexity and levels of uncertainty. In organizational development terms, the simpler an event, the fewer contributing organizations and individuals. Consequently, the development of the organization's culture may be faster, and may also impact more quickly on its effectiveness. It is rather easy to assume that because an events organization might be made up of happy volunteers who want to contribute their skills and enthusiasm, the event will be a runaway success. Richards (1992) makes the eloquent point that while volunteers 'can be the backbone' of an organization, they may also have their limitations: an initial

Figure 11.3

The culture of an
event organization

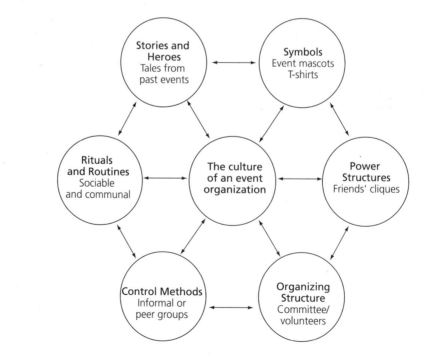

Source: adapted from Johnson and Scholes, 2002.

rush of enthusiasm may fade away, or they may have volunteered for reasons completely unrelated to the needs of the event (hence the requirement for a selection procedure, even for volunteers), or they may also be diverted from their task by other enthusiasms. For this reason, careful thought is needed about how to make the best use of volunteers, but also how to reward those whose efforts are genuine and will add considerably to the event.

Volunteers are people who choose to contribute their time, skills, effort and experience, without pay, to benefit a cause, or the community in which they live. As such, their motives for volunteering are personal and possibly social, as by volunteering they may be involved in hobbies they enjoy, or be undertaking a role that enables them to meet new people, or to spend time with friends, or that might provide satisfaction or self-esteem. It might also enable them to exercise their skills, or to remain active if they are retired. These motives must be taken into account when volunteer labour is being used. In creating an effective volunteer organization or team, it will naturally help to know what their reasons are for being there, and what they hope to get out of it.

The creation and development of teams in short-life organizations and their effectiveness in situations that may be unusual or new to them can vary. The classic approach to team building is that teams go through a number of processes before they become effective, for example, the 'forming, norming, storming and performing' scenario, bearing in mind that not all teams reach the performing stage. However, this approach presupposes that there is sufficient time to organize teams and for them to socialize through the process. In the case of special events, this method and approach to team building may not be appropriate or suitable. There may simply not be sufficient time to team build, in which case a partici-pative style of management will be needed by the team leader. Additionally, since many events are reliant on volunteer staff, the timescale for organizing them and socializing them into the culture of the event organization may be very short indeed. In this case, the effectiveness of the organization may not rely on group

Figure 11.4

Framework for an event organization's performance

Source: adapted from Mullins, 1995.

development at all, but on a wide range of factors, some of which may ultimately be beyond the control of the organizing group (see Figure 11.4).

The event we have worked so hard to organize may not be a success. It may be a failure for any number of reasons, internal or external: success is sometimes elusive, for all our market research, for all the effort put in to producing something that we hope will be excellent. In the end, the public might not actually buy tickets, and the reasons for this might be beyond the control of the event organizers. However, let us assume that everything is going very well. We have a packed programme, enthusiastic and knowledgeable volunteers, advance sales of tickets have taken off and what we need to do is keep up the momentum. With volunteer staff, our effectiveness depends on good leadership, clear objectives, thorough communication and adequate support for the volunteers from the event organization. They should be given proper encouragement and praise for their efforts, be carefully listened to for their ideas and comments (and these should be acted on), be given flexibility in how they can perform a task, if they require it, they should be in relatively small teams so that they can socialize and enjoy themselves, and be given suitable rewards. The emphasis with volunteer staff is that they have volunteered because they are committed and interested, but they are unpaid, and this lack of pay should be offset by careful thought about the support and rewards they get for doing the task. Support may be anything from providing proper meals for volunteers and their own dedicated facilities, to proper induction and basic training. Rewards can be anything from special uniforms, badges, custom-made sweatshirts or small gifts when they leave, to holding social events and parties, or giving celebrations and prizes for the volunteers at significant points in the event, rather than just a farewell party at the end, in order to recognize their efforts. It is also important that volunteers are mentioned in the internal and external marketing of the event, in newsletters and press releases, and that, following the close-down of the event, careful efforts are made to thank volunteers in writing. It may also be necessary to provide some financial support in the form of the payment of travel or other subsistence expenses, or the provision of travel passes when an event is so large that it has its own transport arrangements.

Staffing: professional or volunteer management?

If you were the client for an event, perhaps a company wanting a product launch, or a celebrity wishing to hold a charity benefit, then there is a reasonable degree of certainty that you would wish to employ a professional organization to provide it. The events industry has not only management companies, but also production companies, as well as individual professional organizers and consultants, who can put your event on. You simply employ one of these, set up a project brief and pay them a given fee to get on with it. In fact, some companies employ or retain an events management operator, perhaps on a contractual basis. In this type of relationship, events operators may be invited to tender for the business, based on a brief of what is required, in much the same way that marketing agencies can tender for promotional programmes for client companies. Event Management Companies (EMCs) and organizers can be found in the phone book or on the Net, may be stand-alone operations or ones that have developed out of a related service provider, such as a caterer (some being divisions of catering companies). Others have grown out of production companies or are part of hotel or venue booking agencies. EMCs tend to be involved where the organizers have a requirement for major or high profile events, specialist dinners, celebrity parties, high profile charity fund-raising events, or where an event demands specialist design, innovation, or a major media impact.

Looking at an event, the organizing body, client or buyer may simply say: 'Our event requires a professional paid organization, let's get some quotations in and watch some presentations, then we will choose an organizer and pay them to get on with it'. However, the diversity of events is such that this is only one way of doing it. The alternative is that the organizers, clients or buyers do it themselves. This is extremely common and takes two forms. First, where the organizing body employs a full-time person or even has a department to under-take events organization. This is especially the case for trade activities, such as conference organization and fund-raising efforts amongst companies, associations and charities. It is also the type of structure found in public sector organizations such as town and city council tourism, leisure or economic development departments. These departments often have the task of providing events to support council aims, such as to increase tourism, community inclusion, eco-nomic expansion, etc. Second, where the activity is directly run, but not part of a separate department within the client's organization, it might be that whoever wants an event in an organization just gets on and does it themselves or in a group; this is often the case for conferences, staff parties, birthdays, and so on.

Probably by far the most common type of events organization is none of these, but is the committee of volunteers. The committee might be in the position where it runs special events as part of its role. Alternatively, a special committee may be set up just to deal with a given event (we could even interpret the organ-ization of a wedding by the respective families as a type of volunteer committee).

Figure 11.5	

Example job advert for an events co-ordinator

> **CREATIVITY**
> *Event Co-ordinator*
>
> We are a leading provider of corporate hospitality and event management services, working for a range of high profile companies in Europe. Our activities include sport, the arts, corporate incentives and conferences. We are seeking an experienced event co-ordinator with the following qualities:
>
> - At least two years event management experience
> - The ability to create imaginative programmes to meet specific briefs and budgets
> - Must be confident, self-reliant and mature. Own vehicle essential, knowledge of French or a second language useful.
>
> Salary €30,000 plus attractive benefits package
>
> *For further information contact Trudi van Heater, Creativity Ltd, 150 Festival Park Road, Middleburg, SG1 3PP or phone us on +44 (0)1786 123456. Closing date 1st March 2004.*

Source: adapted from an advert in the *Guardian*.

But what if you have to start completely from scratch? You have a brief to organize an event, on your own. Most people, at this point will pick up the phone and ring their friends to ask who could lend a hand. Instinctively, you probably do two things:

- Think about who you know has the ability to help.
- Think about who you know might like to help.

In setting up something slightly more formal than a few friends putting together a dinner party, much the same approach can be considered, if in a rather more formalized way. You need to know some basic details about the event you are planning, but essentially you need to consider what talents or skills you will need and who might have them. Some people are good organizers, some are good communicators, some are good with their hands, some with figures, computers, or design. But it's not as simple as this. You will be putting together a team of volunteers, which means you will not necessarily get exactly the skills and talents you think you need, and you will most likely have a disparate group of people who want to be involved and who are enthusiastic, but who might have to undertake tasks they have never done before (although this can be one of the pleasures of volunteering). In short, you may simply have to attach the most suitable people to the various tasks you have identified, by intuition.

On the other hand, you might look around your team and think, 'Now what?' First, this is a special event and you have a tight timescale; it might have to be enough that you have some helpers; and you will probably be thankful just they have turned up. Also, for short-life organizations, there is little time for group development, so that you may wish to get this group of individuals to choose their own roles, to ensure that they are doing something they like, or know a

Figure 11.6

A committee of volunteers

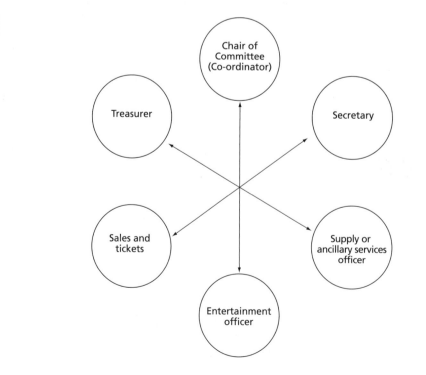

little about, and will put their best efforts into. But a couple of things should be borne in mind: individuals are just that: one person's best effort will be completely different from the next person's best effort, and taken together with their abilities and experience you may get completely different results from two people doing the same job. Bearing in mind the limitations or opportunities in the skills and talents that people have, in addition to letting them identify the jobs they might most like, you can divide up ancillary tasks amongst them to cover those things for which there might not be no direct expertise in the group. In this way you should be able to deal with gaps in your group's knowledge and talents, set against your original list of what needs to be done. After all, lots of people will probably be able to say, 'I can help out in the catering tent...' but you may not get anyone who says, 'I'm an expert at health and safety'.

A voluntary committee (or any committee) can vary considerably in the number of people involved in it, what they do, what their titles are, and so on, but it will probably form the basic organization structure for many types of events (see Figure 11.6). It is important that the leader of the committee is the best person who can be found for the job. This will mean they have enough time to undertake the role, that they should have some previous experience of committee work and some knowledge of organizing events. The implication of this is that the person who sets up the committee to run an event might not be the one who becomes the chair of it.

Factors influencing the number and type of staff

With the framework of the event organization up and running, the next stage is for the respective officers or heads of department to identify how many staff they need, and of what type. This process is often based on experience, either of previous events or of members of the committee. Alternatively, a list of tasks can be drawn up (or the work breakdown structure used) and the number of staff estimated. This will result in the basic outline of a staff plan, which can then be developed and costed into a staffing budget. Various factors will affect the number of staff each department needs to run the event (see Figure 11.7).

Figure 11.7	
Factors influencing the number of staff required	• The size of the event, numbers attending, likely demand
	• The balance between types of staff: paid, full time, part time, casual, volunteer
	• The layout and components of the event
	• The method by which the services are provided
	• What functions are carried out 'in-house' or contracted out
	• The demand patterns and scheduling of staff, number of staff per activity
	• The expertise required for the event

The size of the event

This is a simple enough place to start. How big is this event going to be? Can you put it on with a few friends and relatives, or will it need thousands? (The 2000 Olympic Games is said to have required over 40,000 staff, a very large proportion being volunteers.) Do you know what the likely demand will be? (How many people will come?) Have you done any market research? Is your event limited by the capacity of your venue? If the site capacity is 300 people, or has licensing only for 300, then that is the maximum number of people you need to staff for. (See also chapter 8 on logistics, especially for catering staff numbers.)

The balance between staffing types

There are variations between what your staff can achieve, given their expertise, ability, knowledge and experience. Full-time paid staff may have all these things in abundance, and one full time staff member may be able to achieve what would normally take two volunteers to do. (But this does not allow for enthusiasm: a volunteer is working at your event because he or she wants to be there and they may well work harder than a full-time member of staff who doesn't want to be there! This is a variable.) Perhaps you may have a choice about how the event will be staffed. Within the limits of your budget, you might decide you can afford three full-time staff to cover a particular task, say the information office. But that might mean – allowing for days off – that you might only be able to cover the Information Office with one person on a shift most of the time: if, for example, it is open 9 am to 9 pm and you know it will get busy in the afternoons, you have a range of choices:

- You can run it with the full-time staff, knowing that the one on duty in the afternoon will be swamped.

- You could use one member of full-time staff as supervisor and trainer, and have six volunteers to do the work, and use the money you save for another task.

- You could have three full-time equivalents (this may mean six half-time staff), which might give you more flexibility to cover the tasks.

- You might not be able to get any full-time staff, and you might finish up using a range of part-time, agency, casual or volunteer staff in various roles, to get the job done.

These alternatives depend largely on the circumstances you find yourself in. Full-time staff are not very common at the operational level of events, because running one event over a couple of days can hardly be described as full-time. Full-time staff are found mostly in festival cadres, or in those companies, such as contract caterers, which have large numbers of events to put on, and staff, especially at a management or co-ordinator level, travel from one to another setting them up, running them and closing them down, then going on to the next one. In some companies, casual staff are taken on for a season, and can then be moved from event to event within a given geographical area. This saves time and money on training, and requires less overall effort on local recruitment (Cole, 1997).

The location of activities and concentration of staff at key points

The location of the activities at an event can have a number of impacts on staffing, as the wider the area that has to be covered, the more the staff who may be needed, and the more difficult communication with them may become. Ideally, for their own safety and peace of mind, staff should not be alone in locations isolated from the main centre of activity without the means to communicate with it. The range of activities at an event is a major factor in staffing. In general, the more going on, and the wider the range of services, facilities or components of an event, the larger the number of staff needed. In terms of physical layout, some events can be designed with ease of staffing in mind. It might be possible to concentrate all the services and activities on one central location, where the various staff, being multiskilled, can do whatever needs doing. These 'service cores' tend to be centralized, so that fewer staff can operate and supervize a larger number of activities. Concentration of design also reduces transit times for staff moving from one part of the venue to another, and has the benefit of concentrating utility and store provision in one location (see Figure 11.8).

The method of provision

This is chiefly an issue of the provision of services such as catering or retail, where there are opportunities to provide the service 'in-house' (i.e. with your own staff or volunteers), as against contracting the activity to a specialist company. There are advantages and disadvantages of doing either, but in staffing terms, getting in a contractor will have the effect of relieving the organizers of having to bother about covering that particular task with their own staff. Related to this is the issue of quality. The contractor may have highly trained and expert staff and be able to provide something better than you could, within your limited resources. On the other hand, contracting sometimes leads to a loss of control and problems in the maintenance of quality.

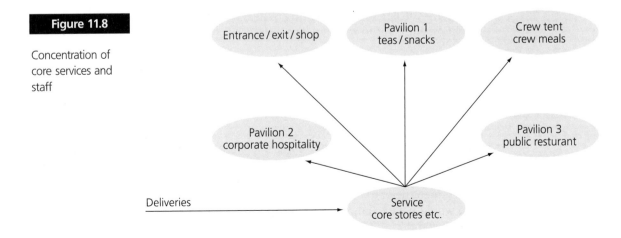

Figure 11.8

Concentration of core services and staff

The demand for, and scheduling of, staff

Demand is a baseline determinant of staffing. At any event, there will be a fixed level of staff below which it is not possible to fall (for example, one administrator may be required to be on duty at any time between 8.30 am and 6.00 pm five days a week to deal with even a low level of business – visitors, general paperwork, enquiries by phone, fax, email, etc.). The one administrator may be able to deal with greater demand only up to a certain level. Quite simply, as demand increases, so too will staffing. The issue is often about how to schedule the staff to deal with peaks and dips in demand. For this, it will be essential to be aware of when the event is going to be busy and when it is not, and at those peak demand periods, which parts of the event will be most busy and need most staffing. Suppose the peak arrival time at our village fête is between 10 am and 11 am, clearly we would need extra staff at the entrance, selling tickets. The peak period in the catering tent might be between 1 pm and 2 pm, so that spare staff could be transferred from the entrance to the catering tent. The peak period in the arena might be between 3 pm and 4 pm, with visitors buying items at stalls and playing games, so spare staff could then be transferred there. This is a simple example, but illustrates the point that we need to give some thought to what parts of an event are busy and when, and how we can deploy our staff to cope.

The control of the cost of staffing is also a major concern. Rosters are produced by management to schedule staff, yet cost control is as much dependent on effective forecasts of demand and careful rostering as it is on the sheer number of staff. A comparison of two managers compiling a roster for the same event, the same demand forecast and the same staff could still produce a significant variance in cost due to the ability of each to complete an appropriate roster effectively. More efficient rostering could, perhaps, reduce the number of staff needed and is thus also a factor in staffing, although possibly not a major one (Medlik, 2001).

Paid staff might not be a concern. Even a relatively large-scale event can be accomplished by capable volunteers, provided it is both relatively simple in format and requires no major technical expertise. If we consider a play as an example, almost all the aspects of putting on a play, from preparing the stage sets to designing the costumes, could be done by experienced volunteers, but elements such as lighting or electrical systems would need expert volunteers. The concept of an expert volunteer might seem a little odd, but is perfectly common – the person volunteering to deal with the lighting of the play might be a lighting engineer in real life, or a retired one, or do it as a committed hobby.

The expertise required

This brings us to probably the most important issue for an events organizer – what kind of expertise is available for the planned event?

The various tasks identified earlier should be developed into a series of job descriptions to help the matching process (an example job description form is given in Figure 11.9). The labour pool must be considered carefully at this stage: what staff are available, what are they capable of, what is their expertise, what things might need to be done for which either training is needed, or professional help would have to be paid for? Even seemingly simple choices can have serious staffing complications, both in terms of staffing numbers and knowledge. This is

Figure 11.9

Job description form

Job Title _____

Department _____

Base location area _____

Needed from _____

Hours of work _____

Department leader _____

Event co-ordinator _____

To _____

Work pattern _____

Duties and responsibilities

_____

_____

_____

Essential skills, talents or qualifications required

_____

_____

_____

_____

Induction and training to be given

Event background and tour	❏	Date _____	Given ❏
Health, safety and fire	❏	Date _____	Given ❏
Food hygiene	❏	Date _____	Given ❏
Hosting skills	❏	Date _____	Given ❏
Manual handling and lifting	❏	Date _____	Given ❏

Specific task training (state) _____

Date _____   Given ❏

Rewards and benefits (pay/expenses/transport/parking permit/meals/uniform/items in kind)

_____

_____

Any other comments

_____

_____

Copies: 1 to personnel file; 1 to department leader's file; 1 to member of staff involved

often highlighted by catering issues, where an organizer might choose a dish that he/she particularly likes, only to find it not only completely unsuitable for, say, a wedding reception in a marquee, but also almost unproduceable for the numbers involved. Organizers have been known, for example, to put Crêpe Suzette on a function menu because they saw it once in a restaurant and liked it only to find, on the day of the reception for 400 people, that only one member of the catering staff had ever prepared it before and had no chance whatsoever of producing more than 20 an hour. This is one reason why many function caterers will test dishes in advance for a customer who requests something unusual. Food is only one example of the problem of expertise. An events organizer is best advised to list the expert knowledge of regular staff, or to ask his/her team of volunteers what they can do, what they have experience of, what their normal job is and what their hobbies are. Such a list will help identify where the staffing expertise lies, and where it does not.

Staffing is, therefore, as much an issue of identifying what expertise exists as having large numbers of people to do things, unless, of course, the event actually requires large numbers of people to do very simple tasks – but these still have to be organized in some way.

Finding staff

Recruiting paid staff

The recruitment of paid staff can be done in a relatively conventional way, through advertising in newspapers, or in events trade magazines, and marketing, tourism, leisure and hospitality magazines are common sources of staff for events. Paid staff can also be found through employment and staffing agencies, some of which specialize in various types of personnel, and these can be identified from the phone book. For large-scale events more than one agency may be needed, and it is common for contracts to be signed to ensure that both parties know what is required. The quality of agency staff varies. Some staff work for an agency regularly and are both experienced and flexible, while others may attend your event as their first-ever job for the agency. Sources of potential paid staff include colleges and universities, where students are not only looking for a job on graduation, but may also be seeking part-time work whilst they are studying, to help their income. Paid staff can also be sought through the Internet (newspapers often duplicate job adverts on their websites) and via industry contacts. Many companies which operate in the events business, especially those in hospitality and catering, retain staff records for events and activities put on in a particular location. This enables them to use people whom they have previously employed for repeat events, especially casual and part-time staff, as lists are kept by geographical area, so that if a particular venue is used frequently for different events, there is an existing pool of staff that can be called on.

Getting staff may not always be easy for events companies. There are areas (towns and cities) where the local labour market is stretched – that is, most people have jobs – there is low unemployment, and finding part-time or casual staff can be extremely difficult. In such cases, staff may have to be transported to the event from some distance away, adding to the labour cost.

Recruiting volunteers

This can be done informally, by asking around friends, colleagues, acquaintances and relatives. This might well yield a range of helpers. However, it will be useful to explore what skills or talents they have, so that where a conventional application form for a job might explore a person's background or job roles, an application form for volunteers should contain a 'talent and skills' section that will be significant in identifying what a volunteer can bring to your organization and event. This could include previous experiences of events: hobbies and pastimes; experience of groups, formal or informal, as a member or as part of a committee; whether they have even visited similar events, so that they know what one could be like (even if not how to run it); what the main elements of their normal work or daily roles are; what they did before they retired (if appropriate), and, most important of all, what they would be most interested in doing for the event, as a volunteer.

This means that as event organizers we have to look at the event to identify the range of jobs and tasks that need to be done, and seek to match our available volunteers to them. This matching is part of the selection process, and not all those who apply (even volunteers) are necessarily needed or suitable, so that some may have to be refused.

There are various sources of volunteer staff. First, volunteers immediately associated with an event or an event organization as part of their job or hobby.

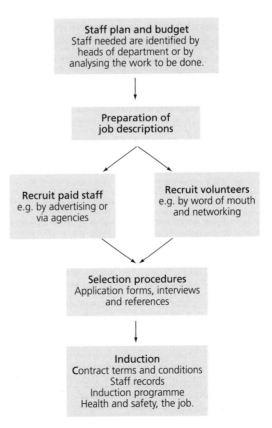

Figure 11.10

Staffing an event

This type of volunteer may be a member of a society or a friend, relative or acquaintance of someone involved in that club or society. For example, an annual town flower show may be run by the Horticultural Club. In order to put on the event, members of the club will participate, members of its committee will organize friends, and relatives of members may join in to help produce the show. Second, some events require large numbers of volunteers, for which this type of informal personal networking approach may not be sufficient. In this case, a member of the organizing committee will have to be responsible for getting volunteer labour, or the task may even have to be given to a recruitment agency. In either case we would have to seek to attract volunteers by advertising in the local media, by making presentations to other interested voluntary bodies, by networking (word of mouth), or by organizing recruitment drives (i.e. preparing a comprehensive plan about how many people you need, how you will attract them, what sort of network you might need to do so, etc.).

Finally, we have assumed up to this point that volunteers are individuals, but a large-scale event might involve not only the key organizing body, but also a range of voluntary bodies that wish to participate. This is the case with carnivals and festivals, where a central co-ordinating body may well be the focus for the activities of a wide range of participants, from commercial organizations to voluntary bodies, charitable organizations, and so on, and the success of staffing the event depends on the co-operation between them.

Recruiting permanent staff

In order to achieve sufficiently high standards of service and management of events it is necessary to employ people with adequate skills and to provide additional training. Even if individual events are short-lived, events management companies, production companies and caterers require permanent staff, as they are dealing with an entire business composed of events of all kinds, in venues and sites within their geographical area. Historically, the acquisition of suitable staff for events management has been achieved by two main methods:

- The employment of staff with a good basic education to be trained by the organization and developed as a skilled member of staff and/or as a manager.
- The employment of staff with an appropriate vocational and educational background in the field or a related field.

The first method, effectively on-the-job training, is the most prevalent for operational staff. Staff, and managers, have been developed in-house by experience or by the company providing some form of basic training. In the case of relatively unskilled jobs, such as steward leaders or stage crew, these have usually been based on recruiting a person with satisfactory potential and good handling skills, who can learn the job by experience through working with other existing staff. This method is sometimes backed up by short-course training, in addition to fundamental activities such as induction and fire training. On this basis, it is still possible for a member of staff to work their way up through an organization to supervisory or management level by experience over time.

The second method, based on vocational education, provides not only operational staff but also supervisors and managers. Larger organizations recruit from colleges or universities that run appropriate courses, and then tend to add their own programme or training course to develop managers with a specific knowledge of their company. Yet it must be noted that there are limited event industry-specific further or higher education courses around Europe, although this is beginning to change quite rapidly. In order to recruit, say, a junior event co-ordinator, the most likely educational background would be vocational courses in the hospitality and catering field, in leisure and recreation, or in some business studies courses where the programme contains events management as a subject or module. These range from courses at the operations level to undergraduate courses at degree level. At degree level some colleges and universities do include event management modules, or, in a very few cases, events management pathways to their degrees, and there are some postgraduate programmes too. Other potential sources of vocationally educated people are the travel and tourism fields; sales and marketing, and business administration. Typically, people employed from these areas, particularly the hospitality field, will have a good background knowledge of business generally and some awareness of events as an activity, but will still need specific training, for two reasons:

- Every organization is different.
- Every job is different.

Even using graduates from those colleges and universities where the degree programme contains a specific events element, an events company will need to tailor the graduates it has employed to their particular organization and role. Nevertheless, there is a good level of co-operation between educational establishments and events companies and bodies. These links range from industry co-operation with assignment work and field visits, up to providing year-long paid placements for undergraduate students. By this method, the events industry not only influences the curriculum content of courses, but also effectively provides 'seed corn' for future employment amongst those students with an interest. A number of the companies providing year placements may well employ some of the placement students ('interns') once the latter have completed their course. This system is particularly well established between events venues and the larger hotel schools. It is mutually beneficial and often seen as a model of good practice for other industries.

In addition to the above, the ebb and flow of employment in general provides a large number of staff and managers within the events business: people moving jobs from one location to another; people moving into events management from related fields (e.g. hotels, tourism, retail, catering, business travel); people newly employed in their first job; and staff being transferred around the larger, more diverse organizations that may include several divisions as well as types of events. All these methods contribute to the supply of potential staff. Some are better trained than others, but in all cases there is a good business argument for organizations to have a well-trained, well-motivated and well-managed staff (Swarbrooke, 2002). This also is the reason why many organizations have a definite staff development policy, progression routes and comprehensive staff training programmes, some of which are targeted at quality issues such as programmes like 'Investors in People', which are intended to achieve not only high levels of staff training and good service for visitors, but also to achieve public recognition in general.

Running the event on the day

For all the considerable effort that goes into planning an event, running it on the day can still prove a challenge. The co-ordination of a wide range of disparate and even unusual activities, facilities and services can be overwhelming. Events management has to be effective, and events managers must be good communicators and good delegators in situations that may be constantly changing. The importance of having done the planning for this, is that it reduces the variability and uncertainty of what is taking place, and allows the event co-ordinator to concentrate on those things that require immediate or constant attention. Some elements are essential, on the day of the event, for the event co-ordinator: drink enough so you don't dehydrate; eat enough to keep your blood sugar levels up, otherwise your decision-making and problem-solving abilities will decline; wear the most comfortable pair of shoes you've got; and keep a change of clothes somewhere convenient, because you never know if some fool is going to spill a load of stuff all over you.

The nature of the event business is such that each occasion is unique, and a production line approach can rarely be adopted. The activities undertaken to provide one event effectively may not necessarily accomplish the next quite so effectively, although there are clearly common features. Thus the recurrence of routine tends to be in the framework – in the approach, organization and management, rather than in the implementation or the operation. On a simple level, the same ordering system can be used almost universally for all events; but the number of people, the timing, the amount of supplies and requirements will be unique for each event. It is this uniqueness that systems and staff must be sufficiently flexible to cope with. Systems and staff are intended to work hand in hand. In general, to reduce costs, especially labour costs, if an operation can be systematized or automated, it should be, but this supposes a more or less standard product. Nevertheless, many event-related activities, such as food production, can be systematized; whether this is cookery according to standard recipes or whether is the buying in of a standard dish from a supplier.

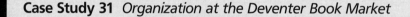

Case Study 31 *Organization at the Deventer Book Market*

Deventer,
Netherlands

Factbox

- Deventer Boekenmarkt.
- Attracts some 120,000 visitors.
- 850 stalls with more than 6 km of shelves.
- Has become the biggest book fair in Europe.
- Associated activities include music, street theatre and an evening poetry festival in the gardens of the Bouwkunde Theatre.

The fine old eastern Dutch city of Deventer, in the province of Overijssel, famous for its history as a member of the Hanseatic League (an association of mediaeval trading cities in Northern Europe), holds a number of events each year. These include the annual Book Market; the Christmas Dickens Festival; the international street-theatre festival: Deventer on Stilts; and 'Op Den Berghe' (a popular mediaeval festival). The Book Market, held each year on the first Sunday in August, attracts not only the general public, but also booksellers and antiquarians from throughout the Netherlands and other parts of Europe.

The Deventer Book Market is organized by the events bureau of the Deventer Tourism Department (Vereniging voor Vreemdelingenverkeer: VVV). The department has the equivalent of some 12-and-a-half staff (some full-time and some part-time) who cover five departments. The organization and running of events is funded from a range of sources, including Deventer City Council; local business members of the organization, such as catering, retail and market trade businesses; sponsoring organizations; and through admission charges and related income, such as the sale of programmes, city maps, etc.

For the running of the event, an operating group of 5–6 key people, including the Director of the Bureau and his assistant, plus, at most, a further 15–20 helpers, will be on the ground during the Book Market to co-ordinate activities. This is deliberately not a large number, in order to prevent confusion. It also ensures that the Director can maintain informal contacts with participants, visitors, local businesses and officials to ensure the smooth running of the event. This process is, in effect, management by walking around; contact is maintained by mobile phones and the Director is seen to be there.

The Book Market attracts between 90,000 and 120,000 people each year. This varies according to the weather and other incidental factors (e.g. alternative events). The measurement of attendance is done by comparison of data from sales outlets (e.g. comparing the event days' sales of ice cream against a normal day's sales), also from information supplied by the railway company (Nederlandse Spoorwegen, which is able to report the difference in ticket sales to Deventer for the Sunday of the Book Market as against a normal summer Sunday). Knowing the number of people who travel to the market by rail, as a proportion of the total number, allows the total number to be estimated. However, the number of visitors is not always promoted in press releases, as the attendance clearly varies, and also the amount visitors spend. In one year there might be more visitors who spend less, and the next, fewer visitors who spend more – there is considerable variation, even though averages can be given, such as an average spend for day trippers of about €25 a day. (This helps prevent negative press coverage.)

The Book Market and the other major festivals, Dickens, Deventer on Stilts, Op Den Berghe and a smaller comedy festival, are key to the strategy that the events bureau operates. This strategy has a number of central objectives:

- To stimulate cultural tourism in Deventer and its nearby region of Overijssel.
- To generate added value for tourists to Deventer.
- To improve the marketing and the image of the city.
- To generate positive publicity in order to attract tourists.
- To highlight the strengths of historic Deventer and stimulate return visits.
- To make the city livelier.
- To improve the living and working environment.
- To encourage residents to be involved in the art and culture of the city.
- To encourage people to use the city for recreation and culture.

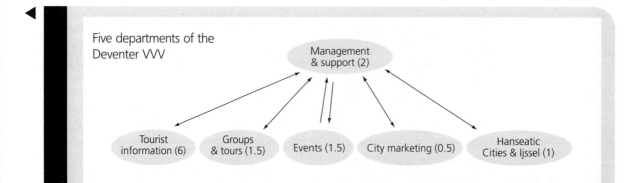

Five departments of the Deventer VVV

Management & support (2)

Tourist information (6) — Groups & tours (1.5) — Events (1.5) — City marketing (0.5) — Hanseatic Cities & Ijssel (1)

Based on this case:

1. How is the organization of the Book Market undertaken?

2. In what way do the festivals in Deventer satisfy the strategic objectives of the VVV?

3. What reasons, including the weather, might there be for variations in visitor numbers and average spend at an event?

4. How might the media react to changes in published visitor numbers when headlining their stories, and would the view taken by the media make the strategic objectives difficult to fulfil?

5. Identify a festival or event in your district and consider how that event fits in with the style, environment, history or surroundings of the place.

Related website for those interested in Deventer: www.deventer.nl

Source: kindly provided by Mr Hein te Riele, Director, Deventer VVV

The maintenance of standards in non-routine service activities is a significant concern of management in the events business. The non-routine and non-systematized nature of anything from site layout to variances in individual audience requirements needs to be accommodated by allowing flexibility of operations, whilst maintaining adequate supervision and control (Lovelock, 1994). Simple managerial control may be exercised by detailed supervision and the use of checklists; by techniques such as 'management by exception', or by improving the quality of staff and staff training to the level at which quality control can largely be placed in the hands of the staff themselves. This can be difficult in short-life organizations at events, because there is limited time for training staff and limited time to get to know what abilities they have.

Perhaps the most common management technique used by events co-ordinators is 'management by wandering around'. Draw up a checklist of things you need to keep an eye on and give yourself a route to go round, preferably covering your main department leaders and those places you regard as 'pinch points' – where things are likeliest to go wrong, or be busiest, or need support at crucial times. A regular events co-ordinator will know this from previous experience, but for the beginner, the best advice is to follow through what your potential visitors will do, including driving into the visitors car park when you arrive and entering the site or venue through the same entrance that they will. In this way you will find out in time if locations are signposted badly, if the area is not clean enough, and so on. Do a walk through of all the things a visitor will do, including the toilets. Test the things a visitor will ask for, for example, have a coffee in the catering tent – don't just get a coffee and walk out, take it and sit where the visitors will sit, because by doing so you will find unexpected aspects that can make or break people's experience of your event (see Figure 11.11).

Above all, communicate actively and frequently as you do your rounds. It is important that you delegate wherever you can, so that your regular staff learn to handle and solve problems for themselves; step in if you have to, but remember, you are the last resort, and you should not be trying to sort out minor problems when your staff could do so on their own. In fact, as a manager, if you have to do tasks that your people should be capable of, then you have failed: you have failed to educate them in their abilities and remits, you have failed to give them the resources and confidence to do their job.

Organization and briefing of staff, stewards and volunteers

In running an event on the day, you cannot handle everything yourself, and will have a number of helpers, whether professional or volunteer. Your event needs to have a structure of organization, in effect a chain of command, in order to operate properly, as noted earlier in this chapter. On the day of the event you will have to rely on your heads of department and their management skills, as well as your own. For many events, however, you may have a large number of staff who are present only for the event itself, and possibly the most significant

Figure 11.11

Activities on the day (continued from chapter 10, Figure 10.10)

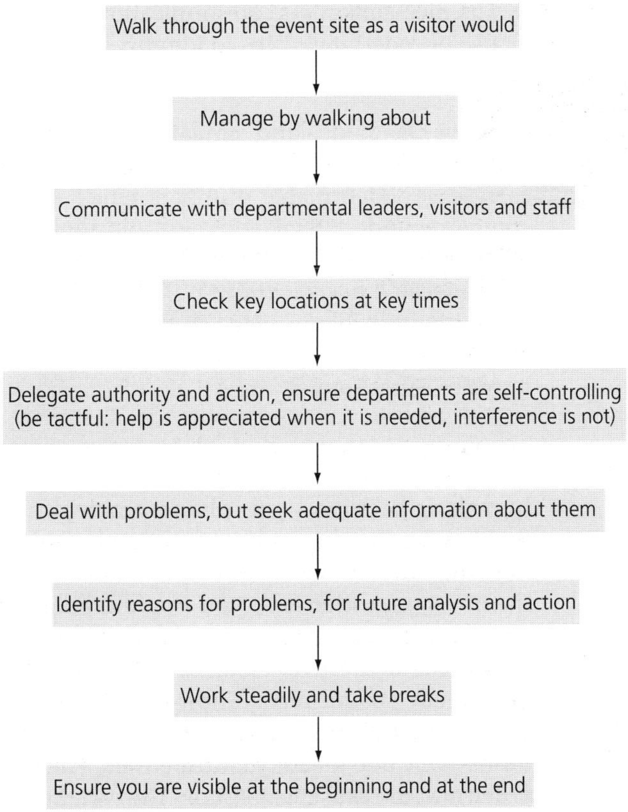

Walk through the event site as a visitor would

↓

Manage by walking about

↓

Communicate with departmental leaders, visitors and staff

↓

Check key locations at key times

↓

Delegate authority and action, ensure departments are self-controlling (be tactful: help is appreciated when it is needed, interference is not)

↓

Deal with problems, but seek adequate information about them

↓

Identify reasons for problems, for future analysis and action

↓

Work steadily and take breaks

↓

Ensure you are visible at the beginning and at the end

of these will be the Stewards Department. In order for the stewards and guides to work effectively, they must be properly briefed. This may be done prior to the event, or as part of a comprehensive induction or training session for all staff (records of which must be kept). In the case of a small event it could be done on the day. The briefing session would normally cover a number of key issues:

- Responsibilities for health and safety of visitors and participants, and the reporting mechanism for urgent problems, how to get help and the sequence of call-up of managers in an emergency.
- A tour of the layout of the site, highlighting emergency exits, assembly points, toilets, catering and other facilities, access for disabled visitors and for emergency vehicles or staff.
- Issues in crowd management; the operation, opening and closing of exits; ensuring that emergency exits are open throughout the event.
- How to direct and help the public, audience or participants and the need for a calm and courteous approach to all involved.
- How to recognize and act on signs of crowd or individual distress; how to deal with overcrowding by dispersal or by the opening of further exits or entrances to overflow space.
- What action to take in the event of an accumulation of rubbish or fire risk; action to take if a fire is found; how to raise the alarm; how to respond to a small fire or small emergency.
- The mechanism for communication between stewards and managers; the use of coded messages to identify types of emergencies and planned responses to them.

Stewards, guides and similar members of staff should be easy to identify by means of colourful or 'high-visibility' jackets, tabards or sashes. These may also carry easily identifiable numbers which should be clearly visible. No steward should be under 18 years of age, and there must be no consumption of alcohol or other substances while the steward is on duty, nor should any of them leave their allocated posts without permission or relief (HSE, 1999). The Chief Steward should have a rota in place so that no one spends too long a period doing the same repetitive job, and to ensure that stewards are adequately provided for in terms of refreshment.

Problem-solving

In making decisions and solving problems, it is vital to be aware of the factors that have led to the problem and to be able to take the correct action. It may be that you have to take action first and ask questions later, but it is essential to ask the questions, otherwise you might fail again: by failing to identify the source and origin of a problem correctly, it will re-occur, and you may not be able to get yourself and the event out of it the next time. A good decision is therefore dependent on the recognition of the right problem. Bear in mind the media reaction to disasters. At the Roskilde Music Festival, the media claimed that nine deaths were due to faulty loudspeakers. The loudspeakers were in perfect working order, and the cause was simply the weight of numbers of people at the front. In the 2000 Concorde airliner disaster in Paris, the media at first claimed that the catastrophic engine fire was caused by a faulty repair done hastily before the plane took off. The engines were working perfectly, and the disaster was caused by a small piece of metal on the runway that lead to a series of improbable but explosive failures in the undercarriage, the wing, the fuel tanks and then the engines.

In your efforts to solve problems and make decisions, keep a notebook in your pocket and take a minute to write the problem down, as well as what you did to sort it out. For those events where you are running a new edition or a repeat of an event you have run before, make sure you took the time to look at last year's feedback notes and any questionnaires that were given out. In this way you can help avoid problems happening again, or concentrate resources in places where you think they might recur. Work steadily through the event, take breaks when you can, sit down when you can and take drinks when you can. It is important that you pace yourself.

Summary

The organization and staffing of an event, its co-ordination and management, are all factors integral to its success, and it is arguable that for certain kinds of events as much can be achieved with talented amateurs and enthusiastic volunteers as with professional paid staff. However, there is a place for both professional and volunteer staff in the events business. Events are varied and diverse, and their organization and staffing reflect this.

References

Cole, G.A. (1997) *Personnel Management*, London, Letts, pp.110–21.
HSE (1999) *The Event Safety Guide*, Sudbury, Health and Safety Executive Books, pp.51–53.
Johnson G. and Scholes, K. (2002) *Exploring Corporate Strategy*, London, Prentice Hall, 6th edn, pp.74–75.
Lovelock, C.H. (1994) *Product Plus*, New York, McGraw-Hill, pp.160–90.
Medlik, S. (2001) *The Business of Hotels*, Oxford, Butterworth Heinemann, 4th edn, pp.71–93.
Mullins, L.J. (1995) *Hospitality Management – A Human Resources Approach*, London, Pitman, pp.52–85.
Mullins, L.J., Meudell, K. and Scott, H. (1993) 'Developing culture in short-life organizations', in *International Journal of Contemporary Hospitality Management*, vol. 5, no 4, pp.15–19.
Swarbrooke, J. (2002) *The Development and Management of Visitor Attractions*, Oxford, Butterworth Heinemann, 2nd edn, pp.226–42.

Close-down, evaluation and legacies

Aims

- To discuss the issues involved in closing down an event.

- To consider the activities relating to the evaluation of an event.

- To consider post-event use of sites, divestment and legacies.

Introduction

It's three o'clock in the morning, your guests have just gone, having eaten you out of house and home, told assorted improbable stories and drunk all your best port. You are both happy that the dinner party went well, and exhausted. Best to shut the door on the dining room and leave the washing up until tomorrow. Of course, if it's three in the morning and you are the co-ordinator at a major event venue where the guests have just gone, you might still have a whole night's work ahead of you. The close-down of an event should be approached in much the same way as it is set up, and remember the lesson often quoted in the mountain climbing world: most accidents don't happen on the way up, but on the way down. At the end of a long event, you and your staff will be tired, many will want to get cleared up and go home, but it is important to be able to handle the close-down and to clear up properly, and carefully.

Once the whole operation is closed down and handed back, there is still some administration to be done. This can be anything from filing to sorting out the accounts, paying the bills, or collecting questionnaires. The final administrative details need to be completed, and the event – especially if it is to happen again in the future – should be properly evaluated to see what can be learned from it and what could be done better next time, not only from the visitors point of view, but also from your own organizational point of view; it is valuable to look back and assess the outcome.

For some events there will be no next time. The purpose may have been strictly limited to a one-time-only activity, although in some of these cases, especially where the objective was economic or social in origin, there may be various legacies, some intended, some perhaps unintended. The significance of such legacies may have been carefully planned – this is particularly the case for regeneration events. Often, however, it is physical regeneration that is planned, and social regeneration comes as a surprise.

Close-down

There are several elements to closing down an event. Besides clearing out the venue and closing the doors, there will be a range of administrative tasks to tie up. These will include the completion of the accounts, payment of final bills to contractors, and final marketing activities such as closure press releases and providing information about future plans. There will also be various personnel completions, in particular the final payments to all staff, the bringing up to date of staff records for future reference, together with the need to do some evaluation of the event (see Figure 12.1).

The most obvious close-down activities are the physical ones: the big clear-up once the doors have closed and the last visitors have gone. This should be approached in much the same way as the set-up. A work breakdown schedule can be created, based in part on the activities leading up to the opening, but in reverse. Understanding that there is a sequence of close-down is significant, otherwise people will make inappropriate attempts to get their gear out before it is safe to do so. In the same way that it is important for everyone to know how to set up, it is also essential for them to know how to break down. This information can be handed out in a summary sheet to staff during the event, and in a close-down briefing given over a meal immediately following the public's departure; otherwise you will be overrun with tired and frustrated people wanting to throw their stuff in a truck, without knowing that the truck doesn't arrive for another hour.

As a general rule, the clear-up operation moves from small items to large ones. You cannot get the stage down until you have cleared the equipment and the furniture. You cannot clear these items until you have cleared at least some of the litter, and collected and stored small valuable items. Staff should be properly briefed on this process, and control maintained till the very end, for reasons of safety and also of security of goods and equipment. Some tasks can be done in parallel (at the same time), providing there are enough staff to do them, and the various departmental leaders should continue to supervise these activities. Items of stock to be re-used, such as catering stock, linen, consumables and small equipment should be returned to a central storage place prior to collection, and returned to the stores, or to the supplier, or to your contractor's central depot.

Figure 12.1

Final phase of event activities

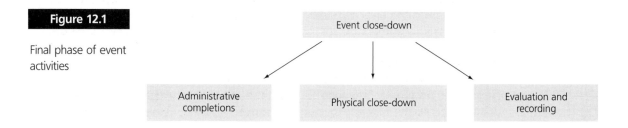

Exit routes for goods, equipment and materials should ideally be separate from public exit routes, which might still be busy whilst the event is being closed down. Congestion is often a problem, particularly at large-scale outdoor events. The removal of utilities will also need to be carefully considered in terms of what goes last. Remember you will still have people on site clearing up, so don't cut off the power or remove all the toilets straightaway; see what can be removed first and what can wait till last. In many sites, there will be some permanent supplies and utilities, but it can be surprising how many do not have them, and this needs to be taken into account.

Case Study 32 *Clearing up: World Golf Championships*

Valderrama, Spain

Factbox

- World Golf Championships, Valderrama.
- Three-day event involving 62 international players.
- Large crowds to watch the golf.
- Top prize of about €1 million.
- Won in 2000 by Mike Weir.
- Event sponsored by American Express.

Clearing an events site can be a major task. It can involve anything from the removal of large amounts of litter, debris and other general waste, to having to restore lawns, gardens and other natural features. Many events are run in locations that are sensitive to use by large numbers of people, and care has to be taken that crowds do not damage the area and its surroundings. This is particularly the case for open-air events.

The arrangements for major golf tournaments require particular care. Crowds of up to 100,000 people are often possible, putting huge strain on the resources at golf courses. For major tournaments, stands have to be built, facilities provided for the media, including locations for broadcasts and media centres for journalists and other reporters. Additional facilities and power have to be provided, to cover catering and refreshments, first aid, toilets, retailing, and so on. Thoughtful crowd control at Valderrama is absolutely essential, in order to prevent accidental damage from large numbers of people to the course itself, to the fairways and greens. As a consequence, most facilities, including parking, tend to be kept away from the main course, and walking routes for the crowd to watch the golf play are carefully set up, roped off and controlled by stewards. The international course at Valderrama is extremely well kept and is known for its ecological approach. This being the case, areas of the course are kept isolated from the public, because of the presence of wildlife and rare plants.

The process of clearing up after a championship is quite intensive (see diagram):

Although the clear-up period is relatively short, as the site is more or less clear of its extra structures and equipment within a week, the repair to the areas used by large numbers of visitors, especially if there is damage to the ground as a result of heavy public use, takes the greenkeepers and groundsmen a great deal of time. Where the green areas have to be re-sown, the new grass may take up to six months to properly grow again, for example.

▶

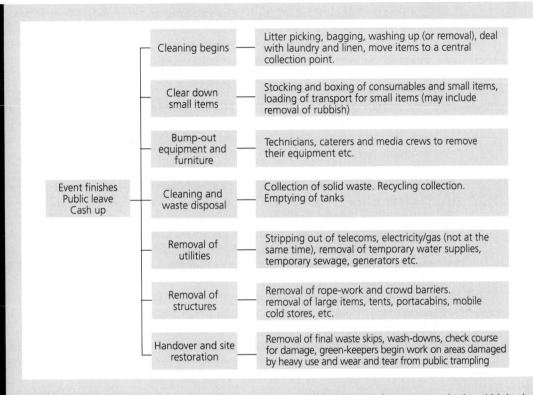

Based on this case:

1. What are the effects, on a site, of having large numbers of the public present?

2. Because site damage is mainly caused accidentally, or because of the mass of people, how could you attempt to mitigate the effects of large crowds on open-air sites (think also of Glastonbury)?

3. How can you plan the close-down of a site, and in what order should items be removed?

Related website for those interested in Valderrama Golf Club: www.valderrama.com

Be sufficiently prepared for the clear-up operation: consider not only the tasks, but also the number of people and equipment you will need to do the job. Many such operations are held up because of shortage of even the most basic equipment, such as brushes, mops and buckets, cleaning materials and refuse sacks. Have these kinds of things stored, and ready for collection at a specified time by department leaders, so that you can get the work done speedily.

Much of the equipment, materials and resources you may have used for your event will be recoverable for re-use. Ensure that you have an efficient and careful storekeeper to collect this material, record what has been returned, take stock and calculate any losses. Careful storekeeping and the ability to redeploy equipment, resources and other materials may save a great deal of money and possibly effort next time, especially for those things that are often overlooked at the planning stage, such as electrical extension leads, special signs and small administrative equipment. Experienced administrators will prepare 'ready boxes' of basic office needs such as tape, scissors, staplers, glue, Blu-Tack, Velcro fixings, pens, etc., from the returned materials so that a box can be taken out of stores and used easily, at the next event, without wasting time chasing round for a box of staples or a washable marker pen. Many contracting organizations take the same approach. Contract caterers will collect, wash, stock-take, then re-count and box items, such as crockery or cutlery (for example into batches of ten) ready for their next use.

If there is an element of organization that is neglected by venues and organizers, it is the close-down. Some effort should be made to ensure that all went well. Co-ordinators should be around to speak to visitors and VIPs on departure to obtain verbal feedback and pick up comments. Comments need noting as part of a quality control cycle, and can be recorded as part of the 'event history' to be referred to next time round. Even relatively simple issues such as the speakers preferring lapel microphones, or the need to have some spare umbrellas in the central office, whilst not being perceived as very serious, are significant to that event and one less worry at the next edition. In addition, particular care should be take to record contact information about participants, exhibitors, presenters, stand providers and so on, in order to make the job of contacting people easier for a new edition (see Figure 12.2).

Allen (2000) makes the point that it is essential to thank all those involved, in particular key staff, in writing, 'as you never know who you might need again'. In any case, it is both good manners and a courtesy. In particular, thanks to volunteers and members of the community for their efforts are important, and this is also a matter of good relationship marketing for future events. On the subject of relationship marketing, if you are going to repeat this event, did you put the next date on the tickets or in the programmes? You want people to return, so start by helping the process along. Again, various people may be interested in your event organization or the venue, and whilst they would not normally step out of their way to obtain information, can be asked for their business card or address as they leave and information can be despatched to them. A sales opportunity is a sales opportunity, and personal contact is far more effective than advertising.

The final administrative issues about event close-down are those regarding contract acquittal, dealing with outstanding bills and completing the accounts. Contract acquittal is not only a matter of making final payments to contractors and suppliers, but also of deciding, for the future, whether a supplier has done a good job. Key to our own success as event organizers is the ability to have the materials and supplies required, delivered in the way in which they were ordered, on time and correctly. A good relationship with contractors and suppliers is therefore vital, and one of the functions of contract acquittal is to identify those companies that will be retained for the future, and those that may have to be changed.

Preparation of the final accounts for the event will be a matter for the treasurer, financial officer, or our own accountants. These accounts will tell us how the event went financially, and where an event has run in the public domain (i.e. one that is not commercially private) the accounts will need to be published as part of a final report to the client body, which might be government, local councils, or other funding or sponsoring bodies. In any case, a copy of the accounts should be included in our event history file for future reference and as an aid to planning any new edition.

Figure 12.2

Event history:
contact record form

Name of contact _____   Name of organization_____

Address _____   Phone number_____

_____   Mobile_____

_____   Date made_____/_____/_____

_____

Type of activity _____

Exhibition stand / stall / concession / entertainment / catering / retail / information / event support /

emergency service / other (specify)_____

_____

Space required

Length _____ m Width _____ m   Height _____ m

Power required

Type _____ voltage   Number of sockets _____ m

_____

Shell scheme

Name on information board _____

Shell required: yes ❑   no ❑

Furniture: Chairs _____ m   Tables _____ (size) _____   Other _____ m

Linen: Tablecloths _____ (size) Colour _____

_____

Notes, history, remarks and special requirements

_____

_____

_____

_____

_____

Evaluation

A short period after the close-down of the event, certainly within a month, there should be a meeting of the various interested parties (organizers, clients, sponsors, etc.) to evaluate the event. The evaluation should use all the various sources of information available (see Figure 12.3) and should consider not only the visitor's perception of the event, but also that of the organizers, because lessons may need to be learned from all points of view (Bowdin et al., 2001). The potential sources of information are quite extensive. However, it should be noted that many events, especially smaller ones, record and keep very little information indeed, sometimes only the number of people who bought tickets and what the various departments took or sold. This limitation is partly due to a lack of expertise at recording, partly to the effort needed to collect useful information, and partly due, for events management and similar companies, to the need to get going with the next event, consequently there is little time to either collect information or review what has been collected. However, care in evaluation is an aid to future planning and should not be overlooked.

One of the limitations of evaluation is the inability to make use of the process. Most events organizations will have a meeting to review major events, but the process may end there. 'We had the meeting, and we'll look at the minutes of it next year when we start planning the next edition...' (an intention that is then forgotten). The purpose of evaluation is for managers to learn how an event went and to be able to improve on it for the future. This 'improvement' can be looked at in several ways. Firstly, there might be activities that went well but could be strengthened further; second, there are activities that went well in such a way that they are best left untouched; third, there are those activities that went badly and that need sorting out. These issues have to be evaluated, and even where only a modest amount of information is collected, perhaps by formal means (e.g. questionnaires), there might be a lot of underused information sources (see Figure 12.4).

There are quite a large number of sources of information, even for a small event where no formal research has been done. However, where the information is unstructured, we must be careful about its use, otherwise the analysis of it could be based on little other than someone's opinion, which may be more or less worthless, without support. There are probably two key evaluation issues:

Figure 12.3	*Quantitative information*	*Qualitative information*
Types of information for evaluation of events	Visitor and participant data, sales	Visitor perceptions
	Target market – visitor profiles	Questionnaires returned, exit surveys
	Attendance statistics, target market information	Recorded (structured) chats or interviews
	Financial reports and accounts	Staff and volunteer feedback
	Financial balance sheet	Management notes and commentary
	Economic impact analysis	Social impact analysis
	General statistical information	Social benefits balance sheet

- Did the event meet its objectives?
- What can be improved for the next edition, if there is one?

A review of the event objectives, in light of the information available, needs to be done, not only for the satisfaction of the event co-ordinator, but also to enable stakeholders to be reassured about the event's effectiveness, and also, if stakeholders such as councils, sponsors and clients put money into the event, that the money was well spent. This is the reason for the publication of final reports and accounts, particularly for big public events.

The usefulness of some formal or structured research and observation at events becomes most obvious when looking at what might need to be done for future editions. The identification and solving of problems can only be carried out properly if there is enough information to ascertain the real cause of a problem. It is no good saying: 'We had a brawl in the beer tent, when the beer ran out and the vicar got hit over the head with a two-metre plastic banana...' We need to know the causal origin. If the apparent cause was the beer running out, why was this? Was it under-ordering, or high demand, or did the beer delivery get stuck in the mud? Without adequate information we cannot deal with this problem and prevent it happening again. Related to this is the question of how to allocate resources and time to solving problems. What were the major problems, were they serious and did they constitute critical failures in the eyes of our visitors?

In general, knowing what is best or worst about an event will help to increase satisfaction levels and reduce dissatisfaction – a process that may also help identify persistent problem areas that need time and effort to solve. By collecting and collating the 'problem area' information you can then rank the problems in order of priority or seriousness, 'Most serious to least serious' or 'Most frequently stated to least frequently stated', and then, having set out this list of priorities, you can attack and sort out the most serious problems, so that in the next event edition, they will not re-occur or will at least be less of an inconvenience for your visitors, and you will have improved the visitor's experience of your event. Once a particular problem has been identified, it is best to give the task of sorting it out

Figure 12.4

Sources of information for evaluation

to one person who has the authority and the means to do so, or to a small sub-group of the organizing committee, than to have the problem discussed endlessly in big committees and not get solved.

In any list of problems, the ones that cause the most difficulty should be dealt with first, and to do this we need to be able to measure the impact of a problem. When we are looking informally at our list of problems, it might simply be down to a 'gut feeling' about which would be the best to solve, because, given limited management time and expertise, not every problem on a list can be dealt with (although some of the lesser problems could perhaps be given to junior staff or volunteer helpers, as this might result in more creative solutions than professionals might provide). On the other hand, we might be running a major event again next year, and the effort put into evaluative problem-solving might be well worth the effort (O'Neill et al., 1999), hence the need for some kind of measurement.

This type of approach is used in various industries. For example, British railway companies use a system known as Golden Asset Identification. Delays to trains are analysed by cause, and the total delay to trains caused by physical assets is measured in minutes. This is then costed, so that the total cost of an asset failure or specific problem is known. Problems are then ranked by severity, and the cost of solving them is compared with the cost of delays. By this method it has been found that very large delays (and costs) can sometimes be solved at very small cost indeed. Suppose that a set of points (track turn-outs) near a major station has been identified as the cause of regular delays – perhaps 20,000 minutes of delays to trains up and down the line. The cost is €10 a minute (less than the real cost, but a convenient figure to use). The total cost of the problem is €200,000 a year. The track engineers say that the wrong grease is being used to keep the points moving, because someone decided to buy cheap grease that was €20 a can less expensive than the proper grease. In this case the cost of solving a €200,000 problem is €20 a year, as one can of grease lasts a year. For those who think this is a fictitious problem, the set of points is just south of Purley in south London.

How can event managers use this approach? It might be felt that an event is more of a personal service activity than a railway, events being less dependent on physical assets, but it is a useful place to start. Here is a sample visitor satisfaction report from our good friend, the Middleburg Music Festival.

In this example (Figure 12.5) there is a problem with parking. It might be a problem for several reasons: not enough space, not enough access, everyone leaves at once creating a queue, and so on. In short, the problem may be quite complicated

Figure 12.5	
Visitor satisfaction at the Middleburg Music Festival	**VISITOR SATISFACTION ANALYSIS** *Problems identified from structured chats and post-event questionnaires returned.* Total attendance this year: 6,400 visitors Most frequently stated problems (sample of 138 responses):

Parking (exit congestion)	48%
Parking (general congestion)	27%
Catering	26%
Seating too far away from the stage	10%
Printed programme poor quality	7%
Not enough for kids to do	4%
Etc, etc.	

to solve and need several approaches. In order to solve it, we need more inform-ation from other sources, not just the visitor survey. In regard to the car park, there are two other sources of information. The first comes in the form of the 'mystery guest' reports (see Figure 12.6). The festival organizers employed six people from the local university (three lecturers and three students) to visit the festival as customers and prepare a structured report about their individual experiences.

In this example, the mystery guest report was corroborated from a second source, the Head Car Park Steward: 'Yes, the car park was a mess to get out of, you took your life in your hands when you pulled out onto the main road. We set up signs saying "concealed entrance slow down", but they didn't look official enough so many drivers on the main road ignored them.'

The problem is an obvious one, and has a safety issue, so action is essential, without a need to measure it. But the reader may wish to give some thought to how this kind of problem could be measured. The solution, in this example, may include better liaison with the road authority and the police to have a temporary speed restriction applied to the main road, have official signs put up and have the bushes cut back. Internally, we need to look at the car park layout, to re-sign and re-line the car park, to make the traffic flow simpler. It may also help to take some of the weight of cars away from the car park by providing a 'park and ride' bus to another car park, or a bus to the city centre or rail station; it might mean better signposting of the exits or staggering the finishing of different parts of the events to reduce the rush for the gates. The solutions that get the most management attention should be those that will have most impact on the problem, and then moving down the list of solutions to those that have respectively less, but still positive, effects. In the above example, we have supposed it has been identified only at the end, but monitoring should be going on during events, and where it takes place over more than one day, some urgent changes could be made once the event closes for the day, or overnight, or even during the event.

The costs of some problems and service failures may be hidden, perhaps because they deal with visitor satisfaction and enjoyment, or are not terribly obvious in some way. These costs might involve a hidden loss of revenue; the distraction of event managers from key activities whilst solving problems; time taken in dealing with complaints because the service was inadequate; and so on. Consequently, the issue related to identifying the problems is to be able to identify satisfaction with events. In simple terms, people might have enjoyed the event, despite the problems they encountered, or alternatively, these irritations might have spoilt their experience altogether. We can make an event look pretty, have fancy marketing, have standardized management systems, provide smart

Figure 12.6	Question 2

Mystery guest report (extract)

Were access and parking arrangements adequate?

No, I found a great deal of difficulty getting out of the car park. First there was a huge queue as the car park was not properly marked out, so cars were not flowing in the right directions, but crossing over each other before they could get to the exit. The exit was bad to see out of because of overgrown bushes on the roadside, and it was amazing there were no accidents because of the speed of people coming down the main road and then being surprised by the festival visitors trying to pull out of the car park.

uniforms, but if the event itself is no good, and our guests have not enjoyed themselves, all these mechanisms will have not enhanced guests' impressions of the event or guests' experience of it. You can go to see a play in a clean and well-kept theatre, with polite and efficient box office staff, prompt service at the bar during the interval and in company of good friends, but the play might still have been lousy. This is also true of events. What, then, affects people's impressions?

There is a view that visitors' impressions of an event are influenced by two sets of judgements (Love and Crompton, in O'Neill et al., 1999), based on aspects of an event that satisfy them, and aspects that dissatisfy them. Things that work as satisfiers are the ambience, excitement, social involvement, relaxation and other positive emotional states, together with some service elements. Things that work as dissatisfiers tend to be physical and basic service features, such as the parking, the toilets, availability of information, queues, etc. In analysing satisfaction levels using this approach, a formal method of research is needed, based on both questionnaires about the service quality features of an event as well as observations by trained observers. This kind of research could be done by a market research agency, but should result in the analysis of visitors' perceptions of the event and identification of those factors that were satisfiers, and were thus critical to its success; and those that were dissatisfiers and thus critical failure points. These results could also be put into graphical form to illustrate the levels of satisfaction that visitors experienced (see Figure 12.7).

It is important to recognize the limitations of what can be achieved in evaluating events. We are never going to achieve complete and total satisfaction. There will be, in the human nature of events, many factors that impinge on people's perception, even though we might go to considerable lengths to identify and deal with the critical incidents.

Figure 12.7

Visitor experience chart

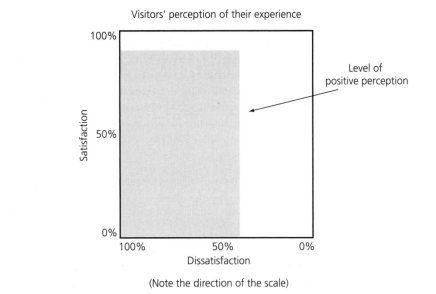

(Note the direction of the scale)

Divestment and legacies

Many events are repeat editions, others are not. Some events are designed for a single 'one-time-only' purpose (such as garden festivals, whose purpose may be regeneration); some do not normally recur in the same place twice (such as the Olympic Games), even though they may leave substantial legacies in terms of buildings and facilities; some events leave only social legacies.

If the event has been a one-off, with regeneration or re-use in mind as objectives for the site, the divestment needs to be planned into the process at the beginning. There will be a target date for the handover to the site's new owners or managers, and the site must be given over in the condition that the original objectives intended, or that the plans specified (unless this is done properly, financial or other penalties may be incurred in order to put things right). It will be essential to hand over not just the site, but also the knowledge that goes with it, about its nature, utilities, environment, problems and limitations. Consequently, a handover may not simply be a case of saying, 'Here are the keys' and leaping into your Ferrari.

There should be a period of overlap between the event organization closing down and departing, and the redevelopment organization, agency or new owners starting work. In some cases this may even mean the continuance of certain jobs or roles between the two organizations, perhaps for posts such as site manager or marketing officer. This will improve the transfer of important information between the organizations concerned. Copies of important documentation will also be handed over, including copies of the final reports and the events history file (in case parts of the event occur again or certain suppliers need to be contacted). In some cases a formal handover ceremony may take place, with the media being present, to stress the change in the site's circumstances.

The type of post-event use of an event site, where regeneration or re-use has been planned, may vary, as may the kind of organization taking over the site. In the case of the series of garden festivals held in the UK in the early 1990s, most sites were handed over to local development agencies (public sector bodies), whose task it was to re-use the sites to create employment and other positive development outcomes, as well as to retain part of the site as public open space parkland or nature reserve. For more recent development of event sites, such as the Millennium Dome site and parts of the Hanover 2000 site, development companies were allowed to purchase these with various projects in mind. In the case of the Dome, perhaps to create a casino (the latest, in 2004, of a long line of unfulfilled proposals); in the case of parts of the Hanover site to create residential housing (an aspect that was planned for the parts of the Hanover site at the beginning and as a method of re-use of exhibitors' accommodation).

Re-use varies according to what facilities were provided for the event. In the case of the 2002 Commonwealth Games in Manchester, the re-use has been primarily in sporting and leisure facilities. In the case of the Hanover site the objectives stressed ecological sustainability; thus the Expo was intended to make use of existing exhibition facilities rather than to create new ones. Consequently, the re-use objectives at Hanover were considerably more modest than for any previous Expo, such as that in Seville in 1992. For smaller-scale events, re-use may not actually imply any new use or a transfer of ownership. Where an event recurs year after year in new editions, the site may simply have to be restored to its normal condition, e.g., as parkland, or as a public venue of some kind. The effort in these cases is mainly one of restoration and maintenance, rather than any form of rebuilding.

Case Study 33 *Event legacies: 2002 Commonwealth Games, Manchester*

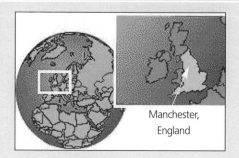

Manchester, England

Factbox

- Commonwealth Games, Manchester.
- Television and sponsorship revenue exceeds €30m, claimed as a record for a UK sport event.
- 5,650 athletes and team officials, from 72 nations, across 17 sports; 15,000 volunteers.
- 1,100 technical officials and 4,500 accredited media.
- 5,000 new permanent jobs, derived from the Games, were forecast.

First held in Hamilton, Canada, during 1930, as the 'British Empire Games', this four-yearly event welcomes athletes from around the British Commonwealth. The run-up to the XVII Games were overshadowed by concerns as to whether the event could find a place in the crowded athletics calendar and media stories of government money 'bailing out' another flawed event. Manchester had prepared well, though, and the local community took an active interest – it was quickly hailed as the most important multi-sport event Britain had seen since the 1948 Olympics.

An intention to provide a lasting legacy from the Games, for Manchester and the Northwest of England, had been an explicit objective from the bidding stage, which had three themes:

- Ensuring the whole region benefited from hosting the Games.
- Ensuring that disadvantaged communities were, and felt, involved.
- Ensuring that businesses in the region benefited from the activity generated by the Games and its potential spin-offs.

To this end, the 'Commonwealth Games Opportunity and Legacy Partnership' was established in 1999, bringing together such key agencies as the North West Arts Board and Sport England North West.

Following the XVII Games, some €103 million was quickly committed to Sportcity, in addition to the Games being a catalyst for a number of major physical improvements; including Piccadilly Plaza and Gardens, and the Ancoats Urban Village – plus a number of other developments across the region, including the €24.75 million investment of the Economic and Social Legacy programme. The regeneration of East Manchester was a key objective of Manchester City Council and of the development of Sportcity. With the City of Manchester Stadium – now converted to the new home of Manchester City football club – as its centrepiece, it was seen as critical to the area's regeneration strategy.

The volunteer programme was also seen as a great success and workshops were held to both confirm accreditation for this experience and to encourage individuals to build upon it; helping to provide a pool of volunteers for the region to draw upon – including the 10,500 non-successful applicants which boosted the

▶

Post Games Volunteer Project to some 22,000 people.

The Games benefited from being able to use legacy venues from previous initiatives and event bids, such as the Manchester Evening News Arena (Europe's largest multi-purpose indoor entertainment and sports arena) and the Manchester Velodrome (developed as a joint venture between the English Sports Council, Manchester City Council and the British Cycling Federation). It remains to be seen whether the event will help to restore England's image as a venue for top-flight events; having suffered from the debacles of the Millennium Dome, Wembley Stadium and the Picket's Lock athletics stadium shambles, this reputation must be restored if future bids to hold the Olympic Games and World Cup in England are to be treated seriously.

Based on this case:

1. What was more important, the Games or the legacy?

2. What was critical to Manchester leveraging a region-wide legacy from the event?

3. What was critical to leveraging a nation-wide legacy?

4. Are legacies something which every event can provide?

5. How has Manchester benefited from the legacies of previous bids and events?

6. Do repeat editions of an event leave legacies?

7. If so, of what kind?

Related website for those interested in the Commonwealth Games: http://www.common-wealthgames.com/ and 'Manchester 2002: Post Games Report – Volume 1': http://www.thecgf.com/games/volume1.pdf

Source: authors, 2004.

The legacies of many kinds of events may not be conceived in physical terms. Although much regeneration activity is regarded as physical and economic, to make a derelict or previously damaged area into something useable and better may be beyond the scope of many events. The impacts of an event whose aims are not targeted at re-use are probably much more limited and social. They may be intended to improve the image of an area, or to sustain tourism by increasing awareness of a destination (Hall, 1997), or they may simply be to enhance social integration and improve the confidence of a community in itself. These social aims may be more than worthwhile, and may have more positive outcomes for a community than any physical legacies. It depends on what the event objectives were.

Summary

Event close-down is one of those aspects of management that receives insufficient attention, as the temptation is to get cleared up and finished as soon as possible. But this can be a recipe for disaster, or at least for accidents. The large number of people who are milling round, moving heavy items or trying to get out of the venue in a hurry, has to be overseen and modest control achieved. Once close-down is over, and the event team has had time to sit back and reflect, the opportunity should be taken to evaluate and to learn for the future. For repeat events, this process is both necessary and important to running a better event, or one at least as good, in the future. For one-off events, there are still lessons that the team can learn for its own benefit, and the evaluation process might also have to feed into some closing report or event history file, so that information should be collected and analysed to help wrap up loose ends. Finally, events leave a legacy. This may be in personal memories or friendly social contacts made at the event, or it may be in some item handed over – anything from a park bench, bought from the modest surplus of the village fête, to the donation for an honourable or charitable cause, to the grand arena built to regenerate a city. It may be transient or long-lasting. Either way, some thought should be given the setting of objectives at the beginning, to the legacy.

References

Allen, J. (2000) *Event Planning*, Etobicoke (Ontario), Wiley, pp.235–38.

Bowdin, G., Allen, J., O'Toole, W. and McDonnell, I. (2001) *Events Management*, Oxford, Butterworth Heinemann, pp.270–86.

Hall, C.M. (1997) *Hallmark Tourist Events: Impacts, Management and Planning*, London, Belhaven, pp.164–75.

Kotas, R. and Jayawardena, C. (1994) *Profitable Food and Beverage Management*, Sevenoaks, Hodder and Stoughton, pp.215–20.

Nickson, D. and Siddons, S. (1997) *Managing Projects*, Oxford, Butterworth Heinemann, pp.120–22.

O'Neill, M., Getz, D. and Carlsen, J. (1999) 'Evaluation of Service Quality at Events', in *Managing Service Quality*, MCB University Press, vol. 9, no 3, pp.158–66.

Smyth, H. (1994) *Marketing the City*, London, E&FN Spon, pp.237–58.

Watt, D.C. (1998) *Event Management in Leisure and Tourism*, Harlow, Longman, pp.5, 13–21, 75–77.

Glossary

Assembly
A large group of people gathered together, convention style, for deliberation, legislation, worship, lobbying or some political activity.

Attendees
A group of people attending an event, for a range of purposes, from watching the event take place, to actively participating in some or all of the event's activities.

Audience
The group of people engaged in watching an event or (usually) passively participating in some aspect of the event activities.

Blag
To attempt to get into an event by gate-crashing, or get tickets under false pretences.

Bowser
A tanker designed to stand by at events to provide fresh water or other liquids.

Break-even
The point at which an event's costs equal the revenue received for it.

Break-out session
Where small groups formed of the delegates of a larger event work together, usually in separate areas or rooms, breaking out from the main event.

Break-down
That part of the close-down activities of an event after load-out, when the final jobs of site clearance and dismantling of infrastructure are taking place.

Brief
A document or specification prepared by a client that states the requirements for an event, which is used either as the basis for an EMC or PEO to tender for, or as a basis for the design of the event itself, or both

Bump-in (also, **load-in**)
The arrival of equipment, stage crew, staging, materials, sound and lighting rigs and other various items of event set-up.

Bump-out (also, **load-out**)
As bump-in, but leaving.

Capacity
The maximum number of people who can be accommodated at a venue.

Cash bar
A bar set up during a function where the guests or delegates, rather than the host, pay for drinks individually.

Cherry picker
A lorry with an extendable arm and platform on the end, used for reaching high places.

Client
The person or organization purchasing or specifying an event.

Chill-out room
An place set aside for attendees (usually at events such as gigs) to cool off and relax in quieter surroundings than the main arena or stage area of an event.

Concurrent sessions
When sessions of a meeting are held at the same time in different rooms, usually allowing delegates to choose which to attend.

Conference
A meeting whose purpose is the interchange of ideas.

Convention
A conference gathering of greater importance, size and formality;

perhaps with more than 300 people in attendance.

Corporate hospitality (or 'corporate entertaining') involves inviting groups of people, usually clients of a company or high profile organization, to public events.

Critical path
The key time-limited route through a number of time-critical activities in the planning of an event.

Critical Success Factors
Those issues that are key to the success of an event, as laid down by its objectives, and that are criteria by which its success can be judged or measured.

Critical tasks
Those tasks or jobs that must be completed in a sequence, before any other, or all other tasks, can be done.

Cut-off date
The designated date on which an organizer must release reserved but unconfirmed space, or confirm a booking by payment.

Day delegate rate
Is the price quoted by conference venues for providing one delegate with meeting facilities and refreshments, such as morning coffee, lunch and afternoon tea, normally for a single 9.00 am to 5.00 pm session.

Delegates
The main term used to describe people who attend conferences, seminars, workshops and similar events.

Delegate day
This is a measure of the number of people attending a conference each day. Thus, ten people attending a conference for one day is ten delegate days.

Dumper truck
A truck used at building sites for moving heavy stuff around, such as sand or gravel, usually painted yellow.

EMC
Event Management Company.

Event co-ordinator (see also **PEO**)
The individual who manages an event on behalf of a client.

Event organizer
The individual, or organization, who promotes and manages an event.

External dependencies
A task performed by an person or organization outside the direct control of the event organizer, perhaps by a contractor or supplier

'External' events
An event arranged by an organization, particularly in the corporate market, to disseminate information to external audiences (e.g. to wholesalers, distributors, dealers, consumers, the press).

Final Exit
The termination of an escape route from an event site in the case of an emergency, giving exit to a place of safety or dispersal to an open space (e.g., in case of fire).

Gantt chart
A project planning chart that resembles a horizontal bar diagram.

Gig
A concert of rock, pop, house, or other popular musical style.

Guaranteed number
The minimum number of guests at an event, for which the host has paid or will pay, irrespective of the actual number attending.

Gully emptier
A tanker lorry designed to suck drainage out of gullies or drains or to clear septic tanks.

Head count
The actual number of people attending a function or event.

Incentive
An event designed to be a perk or reward for staff in an organization. Although some incentives have a serious element, the principal purpose is to motivate, encourage or reward. Incentives are often for salespeople (and may include their partners).

'Internal' events
These are events where attendance is confined to personnel inside the organization, such as the sales force, workforce, departments and groups, and to people attending internal – as

opposed to external – training courses, (thus 'in-house' or 'in-company').

Jam session
A practice or friendly session before a set.

Letter of agreement
A document that confirms all the requirements, services and costs that have been agreed between the organizer and the venue. In effect, a contract.

Load-in (also **bump-in**)
The arrival of equipment, stage crew, staging, materials, sound and lighting rigs and other various items of event set-up.

Load-out (also **bump-out**)
As load-in, but leaving.

Logistics
The discipline of planning and organizing the flow of goods, equipment and people to their point of use.

Means of escape
A structured way of providing a safe route for people to travel from any point in a building or site, to a place of safety, without assistance (such as a marked corridor, or pathway enclosed by rope).

Moshpit
The place at the front of a gig audience where the liveliest activity takes place.

Occupant capacity
The maximum number of people who can safely be accommodated at a venue.

PEO (see also **Events co-ordinator**)
Professional Event Organizer.

PERT
Programme Evaluation and Review Technique. A project management planning technique for plotting work to be done in a given timescale, generally in a computer programme.

Participant
A person attending an event who is actively taking part in it, or in some activity related to it.

'Pear-shaped'
Description of something which goes wrong or turns into a shambles.

Pit
The place immediately in front of a stage, that provides a gap between the audience and the performers.

Pre-con
A meeting between the organizers, the co-ordinator or floor manager, and other key team leaders to confirm details just prior to the event.

Production schedule
The scheme of work to be done, in time order, to ensure an event is set up properly.

Product launch
A 'show' to introduce an audience, such as the media, to a new product or service. It may also be aimed at an organization's internal management and staff, sales force or external dealers and customers.

Public event
An event attended by members of the general public.

Road show
When the same event is staged in several different geographical locations.

Seminar
Describes small gatherings similar to the break-out sessions, where a group, but not the whole plenary, will discuss an issue.

Set
The performance given by one individual or group at a concert or gig.

Set-up time
The time needed to arrange, or rearrange after a previous function, the necessary facilities for the next event.

Show
A full sequence of sets, or more simply, the event itself, (in terms of musical, artistic or similar activities).

Skip
A large waste or rubbish container that is moved by lorry.

Special event
The phenomenon arising from non-routine occasions that have leisure, cultural, personal or organizational objectives set apart from the normal

activity of daily life, and whose purpose is to enlighten, celebrate, entertain or challenge the experience of a group of people.

Syndicate

See break-out session

Trade show

A gathering for a trade or competitive exhibition, often with accompanying social events, a conference or workshops and entertainment, which is probably not open to the general public.

VIP

Very Important Person.

Work Breakdown Structure

A schedule of the various jobs that have to be done to complete an event.

Workshop

A small gathering of people to discuss a specific topic, exchange ideas or solve a particular problem.

Organizations in the events industry

EUROPE

Association for Conferences and Events
    International
Riverside House
High Street
Huntingdon
Cambridgeshire
PE18 6SG
England
Tel 00 44 1480 457595
Fax 00 44 1480 412863
www.martex.co.uk/ace

Association of Festival Organizers
PO Box 296
Matlock
Derbyshire
DE4 3KU
England
Tel 00 44 1629 827014
Fax 00 44 1629 827014
www.afouk.org

Association of National Tourist Offices
37 Peter Avenue
London
NW10 2DD
England
Tel 00 44 20 8459 4052
www.antor.com

Corporate Event Association
Ferdene House
Windsor Walk
Weybridge
Surrey
KT13 9AP
England
Tel 00 44 1932 831441
Fax 00 44 1932 831442
www.cha-online.co.uk

European Arenas Association
Jacob Obrechtstraat 67
1071 KJ Amsterdam
The Netherlands
Tel 00 31 65 32 30457
Fax 00 31 20 47 03166
www.eaaoffice.org

European Association of Exhibition
    Organizers
XM Europe
PO Box 168
3454 ZK De Meern
The Netherlands
Tel 00 31 30 662 1838
Fax 00 31 30 666 3336
www.xmeurope.com

European Association of Event Centres
EVVC Geschaftsstelle
Hotel Frankfurt Airport
Mörfelder Str. 113
D-65451 Kelsterbach
Germany
Tel 00 49 61 07 987790
Fax 00 49 61 07 987799
www.evvc.org

European Federation of Conference
    Towns
BP 182, B 1040 Brussels
Belgium
Tel 00 32 2 732 6954
Fax 00 32 2 735 4840
www.efct.com

European Festivals Association
Chateau de Coppet
Case Postale 26
CH-1296 Coppet
Switzerland
Tel 00 41 22 776 8673
Fax 00 41 22 776 4275
www.euro-festival.net

European Outdoor Events Association
7 Hamilton Way
Wallington
Surrey
SM6 9NJ
England
00 44 20 8669 8121
00 44 20 8647 1128
www.eoea.org

European Sponsorship Association
ESA Secretariat
Farm Cottage
14 Water Lane
Cobham
Surrey
KT11 2PB
England
Tel 00 44 1932 866875
Fax 00 44 1932 866875
www.sponsorship.org

Incentive Travel and Meetings Association
26–28 Station Road
Redhill
Surrey
RH1 1PD
England
Tel 00 44 1737 779928
Fax 00 44 1737 779749
www.itma-online.org

International Association of Conference
  Interpreters
10 Avenue de Secheron
CH – 1202 Geneva
Switzerland
Tel 00 41 22 908 1540
Fax 00 41 22 732 4151
www.aiic.net

International Association of Congress
  Centres
AIPC Secretariat Office
55 Rue de l'Amazone
1060 Brussels
Belgium
Tel 00 32 2 534 5953
Fax 00 32 2 534 6338
www.aipc.org

International Festival and Events
  Association – Europe
PO Box 270
2000 AG Haarlem
The Netherlands
Tel 00 31 23 534 8482
Fax 00 31 23 551 9170
www.ifeaeurope.com

Meeting Professionals International
46a Avenue John F Kennedy
L-1855 Luxembourg
Grand Duchy of Luxembourg
Tel 00 352 2687 6141
Fax 00 352 2687 6343
www.mpiweb.org

Production Services Association
1301 Stratford Road
Hall Green
Birmingham
B28 9HH
England
Tel 00 44 121 693 7127
Fax 00 44 121 693 7100
www.psa.org.uk

Society of Event Organizers
29a Market Square
Biggleswade
Bedfordshire
SG18 8AQ
England
Tel 00 44 1767 316255
Fax 00 44 1767 316430
www.seoevent.co.uk

Union des Foires Internationales
35bis, rue Jouffroy d'Abbans
F-75017 Paris
France
Tel 00 33 1 42 67 99 12
Fax 00 33 1 42 27 19 29
www.ufinet.org

NORTH AMERICA

Association of Destination Management
  Executives
3041 Quebec Street, Suite 4050
Denver
CO 80207
USA
Tel 00 1303 394 3905
Fax 00 1303 394 3450
www.adme.org

Canadian Association of Exposition
  Management
6900 Airport Road, Suite 239A, Box 82
Mississauga
Ontario, L4V 1E8
Tel 00 1905 678 9377
Fax 00 1905 678 9578
www.caem.ca

International Association of Assembly
  Managers
635 Fritz Drive
Coppell
TX 75019
USA
Tel 00 1972 906 7441
Fax 00 1972 906 7418
www.iaam.org

International Association of Convention
  and Visitor Bureaus
2025 M Street, NW, Suite 500
Washington
DC 20036
USA
Tel 00 1202 296 7888
Fax 00 1202 296 7889
www.iacvb.org

International Association of Fairs and
  Expositions
PO Box 985
Springfield
MO 65801
USA
Tel 00 1800 516 0313
Fax 00 1417 862 0156
www.fairsandexpos.com.org

International Festival and Events
  Association
World Headquarters
2601 Eastover Terrace
Boise
IO 83706
USA
Tel 00 1208 433 0950
Fax 00 1208 433 9812
www.ifea.com

International Special Events Society
401 North Michigan Avenue
Chicago
IL 60611-4267
USA
Tel 00 1 312 321 6853
Fax 00 1312 673 6953
www.ises.com

ASIA–PACIFIC

Asian Association of Convention and
  Visitor Bureaus
AACVB Secretariat
c/o Macau Government Tourist Office
2/F Tourist Activities and Conference
  Centre
Rua Luis Gonzaga Gomes
Macau
Tel 00 853 7984 156
Fax 00 853 703 213
www.aacvb.org

Asia Pacific Exhibition and Convention
  Council
APECC Secretariat
PO Box 1871
Toowong
QLD 4066
Australia
Tel 00 61 73 870 4777
Fax 00 1 73 870 4666
www.apecc.org

International Special Events Society
  Australia
PO Box 1375
Maroubra
NSW 2033
Australia
Tel 00 612 9344 4755
Fax 00 612 9344 4755
www.ises.org.au

South Pacific Tourism Organization
Level 3, FNPF Place 343-359
Victoria Parade PO Box 13119
Suva
Fiji Islands
Tel 00 679 330 4177
Fax 00 679 330 1995
www.tcsp.com

**Other organizations and associations can be identified by searching the links pages of
www.worldofevents.net**

Index

advertising *see* marketing

aims *see* objectives

ambience

    atmosphere 16, 139, 141

        see case 23, 139

    elements of 16

    event components 30

amenities and cleaning 138

audio-visual support

    backdrops and staging 134

    lighting 136

    production companies 41

    production schedule 135

    sound and communications 137

    technical facilities 134

Berlin Film Festival 28

break-even analysis 103, 104

briefings

    close-down 215

    emergency 211

    health and safety, in case 27 175

    pre-event and rehearsals 186

    pre-event 211

budgetary authority 110

budgeting

    break-even *see* case 20 105

    break-even point 103, 104

    budget breakdown 102

    cash flow 99

    comparisons 104

    costs 108

    creating a budget 100–7

    detailed budget 108–10

    differential pricing 101

    general budget form 107

    income from sources other than tickets 112, 114

    income from tickets 101

    marketing 156

    mistakes 100

    petty cash 110

    preliminary outline budget 102

buying process 151

cancellations insurance 177

capacity 103, 122

car parking *see* parking

catchment 146

categories and typologies 4–6

catering

    central services 127

    companies 44

    components of a theme dinner 141

    considerations 131

    flow in cafeterias 129

    food and drink service 128

    logistics 127

    party planners 44

    seating plans 130

    service experience 142

    set-up considerations 133

ceremony 10, 15

ceremonies

    at historic Olympic Games 7

    component element map 141

Coronation of Elizabeth I 10
Millennium Dome Opening 88
Peace of Aix-la-Chapelle 11
production schedules for 135
Roman Wedding 8
Scottish Parliament 85
setting the night-watch, Ripon 15
Welsh Highland Railway opening 185
characteristics of events 13–18
charitable activities 35
Clacton Air Show 175
cleaning 138, 215
close-down 215–20
    see case 32 216
committees 47, 65, 66, 198
Commonwealth Games, Manchester 226
communications
    contact lists 137
    organizational 186, 211
    ring 138
community implications see case 12 52
community implications of events 50
companies and their roles 40–46
comparative budgets 104
complexity of events 23
components of events 30, 155
concept screening 70
contract listing 137
control
    at events 181, 208
    budgetary 91, 110
co-ordination 208
Coronation of Elizabeth I 10
correspondence see event office management
costs see budgeting
creating the ambience 139
critical paths 78
crowd safety
    briefing of staff to identify 212
    emergency service planning see case 27 175
    overcrowding see case 26 173

risk management 168–76
staggering the finish 223
cultural events see case 3 4, 10

definitions 3
deliveries see supplies
demand
    and operational planning 87–91
    determinants 25
    planning see case 19 88
    potentials 32
    structure of 32
determinants and motivations 25–32, 149
development of tourist destinations 53
development implications see case 15 60
developmental implications of events 59–61
Deventer Book Market 208
distribution channels 40
divestment and legacies 225–27
donkeys
    at Roman weddings 8
    sexual prowess of 9
drinks service 133

Ecclesbourne Valley Railway Dinner 105
ECOC, Rimini 180
economic implications 54–56
    and scope of events (figure) 23
    see case 13 55
elements of tourism 54
emergency provisions
    at events see case 27 175
    briefings see case 27 175
    categories 174
    communications 138
    contact list 137
    risk control plan 172
    signs 184
environmental search 72, 84
environment search see case 18 85
equipment see supplies

estimating market size *see* case 6 24

European Grands Prix 21

evaluation of events 220–25

evaluation *see* questionnaires

event

    as a project 164–68

    budget 107

    catering companies 44

    component mix 30

    feasibility 68–69

    funding 113

    history form 219

    management

        as a career 45

        before the event 181

        companies 40

        on the day 208

        organizational issues 190

        staffing requirements 202

    office management

        at close-down 218

        communications 137

        committee set-up 198

        correspondence 182

        ready boxes 217

        thanking people 218

        the office 182

        visitor arrival 186

    screening 70

events

    as projects 164

    close-down 218

    organizations – private sector 39

    organizations – public sector 36

    screening 70

        see case 17 73

    screening form 75

exhibition contractors 46

expectations

    experience chart 224

    of the event 152

    satisfaction afterwards 220, 222

    service experience 142

expertise 202

facilities

    amenities 138

    car parking 183

    catering 128

    layout of services 201

    supplies, transport, distribution 126

    technical 134

    toilets 138

    visitor arrival 186

failures and problems

    a bad day in the catering tent 142

    Concorde disaster 213

    cost risks 92

    in equipment receival 183

    management by wandering around 210

    problem-solving 213

    problem-solving at evaluation 222

    risk management 168

    Roskilde overcrowding 173

    screening to reduce failures 70

    Stone of Scone political failure 57

    the Crêpe Suzette problem 204

    the 'salt pot' syndrome 132

    ticketing at Millennium Dome 89

feasibility 68

feedback 220

festivals and carnivals

    Berlin Film 28

    Deventer Book Market 208

    Glastonbury 139

    Mainz Carnival 192

    North Sea Jazz 31

    Notting Hill 52

    Roskilde Music 173

    Salzburg International Music 67

    St John Oporto 125

    Welsh Garden 60

financial

    break-even *see* case 20 105

    break-even point 103, 104

    breakdown (failure) costs 92

    breakdown costs *see* case 19 89

    budget breakdown 102

    budgeting 96, 100

    cashflow 99

    close-down 217

    comparisons 104

    costs 108

    detailed budget summary 109

    differential pricing 101

    funding types 112

    general budget form 107

    income from sources other than tickets 112

    income from tickets 101

    management 97

    marketing budget 156

    mistakes 100

    objectives 97

    petty cash 110

    planning 91–92, 97

    preliminary outline budget 102

    screen 76

    sources of revenue 109, 112

    sponsorship and public funding 114

    ticket pricing 100

    value-added tax (VAT) 103

final phase 215

finding ideas 68–70

finding the venue 121–23

fixed timescale 17

food and drink *see* catering

frameworks 3

French Grand Prix, Nevers 55

funding income 112

    grants 117

    public 114

    sponsorship 114

    tickets 100

Games and sporting events

    Commonwealth 226

    European Grands Prix 21

    French Grand Prix 55

    Lake Vyrnwy Marathon 148

    Olympic 7

    Tour de France 114

    World Golf, Valderrama 216

Gantt charting 167

Geneva International Motor Show 161

generating ideas 70

getting organized 65–67

Glastonbury Festival 139

ground-plan

    briefing tour 212

    service core and staffing 201

    service cores at Glastonbury 139

    site and load in 184

health and safety *see* safety

historical contexts and precedents 6–13

human resources 196, 199, 204

I-tech Fair, Maastricht 177

implications of events 50

income

    from other sources 112

    from sponsorship 115

    from tickets 100

influencing the market *see* motivation

information

    environmental search 72

    for event planning 87

    for final evaluation 220

    gathering 71, 84

    provision for visitors 179, 186

infrastructure of the business 36

Inntel Conference and Events Agency 42

insurance

    and legalities 176

    issues *see* case 28 177

intangibility 15
International Festivals and Events Association
    37

job advert 197
job description 203

key dates *see* lead times

labour-intensiveness 17
Lake Vyrnwy Marathon 148
law *see* legalities and insurance
layout of the event
    method of provision 201
    mix of components 16, 141
    staffing as a layout issue 201
lead times
    critical path analysis 167
    critical paths 78
    marketing 93, 158, 159
    operational planning 78
    production schedule 135
    supplies, authority to order 110
    ticketing *see* case 19 89
    venue-booking 91
legacies
    development *see* case 33 226
    developmental 61
    divestment and 225
    in objectives 77
    political 59
    social and community 50
legalities and insurance 176–78
leisure events *see* case 1 7
licences 176
    see case 23 140
lighting 136
load-in 184
load-out
    close-down 215
    see case 32 217

logistics
    amenities and cleaning 138
    backdrops and staging 134
    catering 127
    communications 138
    concentration of staff 201
    Gantt charting 167
    lighting 136
    load-in 166, 183
    load-out 215
    overview 124–38
    production schedule 135
    purchase orders 111
    sequence 127, 166
    sound 137
    supplies ordering 111
    supplies receival 126, 183
    technical facilities 134
    technical services 46
    transport and distribution 126

Mainz carnival clubs 192
management
    before the event 181
    by wandering around (MBWA) 210
    companies 40
    financial 97
    MBWA *see* case 31 209
    on the day 208
    organization 190
    process diagram 124
    project 165
    risk 171
    staffing requirements 202
market segmentation
marketing
    budget 156
    budget form 157
    catchment 147
        see case 24 148
    component mix 30, 155

determinants for participation 150

distribution channels 40

effectiveness 162

elements of the marketing plan 154

expectations and satisfaction 142, 152, 162

expenditure 156

feedback 142, 162, 220

for a new event 155–58

for repeat events 158–63

influencing the market 149

lead times 93

mystery guest reports 223

plan 153–55

planning 92–94

public relations 156

questionnaires and surveys 71,162, 220

schedule 93, 158, 159

screen 71

target market 149, 155

media

and security 185

attitudes to risk 169

habits of target markets 149

in marketing schedule 158

in timing press releases 78

Millennium Dome Opening Night 88

Moshpit at Roskilde 173

motivation of volunteers 195

motivations for attendance 26, 149

see case 7 28

see case 8 31

multimedia companies 46

mystery guests 223

North Sea Jazz Festival 31

Notting Hill Carnival 52

objectives

and financial planning 97–100

determination of 84–87

examples 77, 98

in marketing plan 155

of events *see* case 31 209

review of event proposals 77

Olympic Games 7

on-line booking systems 180

operational

activities 181–87

briefings 211

close-down 218

close-down, in case 32 216

correspondence 182

legalities 177

legalities, in case 23 139

on the day 208

on the day, in case 31 208

organizational issues 190

organizer's office 182

planning 87

pre-ops 182

receival of supplies 127

ticket system 179

operations screen 72

opportunity cost 56

organization

change over time *see* case 16 67

culture 194

on the day 208

see case 31 208

overview 190–93

performance 195

organizational effectiveness 193–96

organizational events *see* case 4 12

organizational structures 66, 190

organizations

involved in events 39

private sector 39

public sector 36

voluntary 47

other sources of income 112–14

outline budget 102

paid staff
 job adverts 197
 job description 203
 recruitment of 204
Paris Exposition 12
parking
 arrangements 183
 locations *see* case 32 216
 problems 32, 222
party planners 44
perishability 14
permanent staff 206
permits *see* legalities
personal contact 16
personal events *see* case 2 8
petty cash vouchers 111
philanthropy
 as a source of funding 118
 in the events business 35
 in social implications of events 50
 in voluntary activities 47
physical setting of an event 16, 141
pilot questionnaires 71
planning
 activities 82
 amenities and cleaning 138
 budgets 100
 catering 127
 communications 138
 concentration of staff 20
 demand 87
 event components 30
 financial 91
 Gantt charting 167
 load-in 166, 183
 load-out 215
 marketing 93
 operational 87
 process 82–84
 production schedule 135
 purchase orders 111

reflection time 94
 supplies ordering 111
 supplies receival 126, 183
 the event component mix 30
political implications of events 57–59
political implications *see* case 14 57
political stakeholders 58
pre-event planner 79
preliminary budget form 102
private sector 38
 see case 10 42
 see case 11 45
problem-solving 213, 222
production companies 41
production schedules
 marketing 93
 operational/logistics 135
professional bodies 233–36
professional events organizers 44
programmes
 print deadlines for 94
 readiness on arrival 187
 timing the day's programme 135
progressing the idea 76–78
project management
 activities 165
 Gantt charting 167
 overview 164
 planning techniques 166
 work breakdown 166
public relations *see* marketing
public sector 36
 see case 9 37
publicity *see* advertising
purchase order form 111

questionnaires
 evaluation and sampling 142,162, 220
 pilot 71

records
  administrative close-down 218
  communication contact list 137
  evaluation 220
  event history contact form 219
  expectations and satisfaction 162
  marketing effectiveness 162
  spending and use patterns 110, 162
  visitor information 22
    see case 25 161
  visitor numbers 160
recruitment
  of paid staff 206
  of permanent staff 206
  of volunteers 205
registration
  of delegates or visitors 187
rehearsal 186
revenue *see* income
risk management
  analysis 170
  assessment form 171
  categories 169
  control plan 172
  crowd safety 173
  overview 168–76
ritual and ceremony 15
Roman wedding 8
Roskilde Music Festival 173
running the event on the day 208–13

safety
  briefings 186, 211
  contact list 137
  crowd safety 173, 212
  emergency services briefings *see* case 27 175
  overcrowding 212
    see case 26 173
  risk management 169
  signs 184
  telephones 138

Saint John's Festival, Oporto 125
Salzburg International Festival 67
satisfaction *see* expectations
schedules
  checking 182
  marketing 93, 158, 159
  operational planning 78
  production 135
  ticketing *see* case 19 89
scope of events *see* case 5 21
scope of the event business 20
scope of the market 23
Scottish Parliament re-opening 85
screening process 70
security
  at Glastonbury Festival 140
  at Millennium Dome 89
  badges 187
  blaggers 152
  checking guest list 187
  media and 185
  over-emphasis 185
  wristbands 181
Sheffield Student Games 56
size and scope of the events business 20–24
SMART 165
social implications of events 50–54
sound 137
special events definition 3
sponsorship 114–18
sponsorship agreements 116
sponsorship at events *see* case 21 115
staff, at events
  briefings 212
  catering 132
  centralization with core services 201
  factors affecting staffing 199
  finding staff 204–8
  organization of 211
  overview 189
  paid staff 204

permanent staff 206
recruitment 204
volunteers 205
staffing factors
balance between types 200
demand for and scheduling of 202
expertise required 202
location and activities 201
overview 199–204
professional or volunteer management 196–99
size of the event 200
stakeholders 58
see case 18 86
stewards 211
Stone of Scone 57
structure
of demand 32–33
of events services 36–40
management 47, 65, 196
supplies
authority to buy 110
distribution on site 201
ordering 111
receival 127, 128, 183
systems 126, 201
systems set-up and ticketing 178–81

target market
at North Sea Jazz Festival 31
catchment 146, 147
decision-making process 153
influencing 149–53
key questions about 146
overview 145–49
structure of demand in 32
with event component mix 31
technical facilities *see* logistics
telephones 138
thanks 218
tickets
agencies 178

design 179
on-line bookings *see* case 29 180
operations 179, 187
pricing 100
pricing mistakes 100
printing lead time 94
problems *see* case 19 89
records of visitor numbers 22
security purpose of 181
systems 179
time taken to issue 181
timing *see* lead times
toilets
cleaning 138
ordering 111
removal 216
sex in 138
vomit on the way to 138
toolkits
for events 82
volunteers 82
Tour de France 114
tourism 54
training
briefings at induction 186
catering 131
emergency 175, 211
on the job 206
pre-event briefings 212
transport and parking 183
typologies 5

UK wedding market 24
uniqueness 14
University College, Cork Hockey Club 73
use patterns 162

VAT 103
venue-finding
checklist 122
inspection visits 123

overview 121

visitor

decision-making process 153

expectations 152

experience chart 224

satisfaction 142, 152

services department 191

welcome 186

visitor numbers

assessment of *see* case 31 209

records of 160

spending and use patterns 110, 162

voluntary bodies 47

volunteers

at carnivals

see case 22 125

see case 30 193

briefing of 186, 212

committees 65, 198

expertise 74, 198, 202

limitations 194

motivation 195

recruitment 205

rewards 196

toolkits 82

welcome visitors 186

Welsh Garden Festival, Ebbw Vale 60

who spends what 110–12

work breakdown structures 166

World Golf Championships, Valderrama
216